D1557574

Bacchanalian Sentiments

BACCHANALIAN SENTIMENTS

musical experiences

and

political counterpoints

in trinidad

Kevin K. Birth

duke university press 🐾 Durham and London 2008

© 2008 Duke University Press
All rights reserved
Printed in the United States of
America on acid-free paper ∞
Designed by Jennifer Hill
Typeset in Chaparral Pro by
Keystone Typesetting, Inc.

Library of Congress Cataloging-
in-Publication Data appear on the
last printed page of this book.

to margie

contents

preface

A while back I was very saddened to hear of the death of my friend and fellow parandero, Naz. He died too young. He was a quiet man who spoke loudly with his virtuosity on the guitar. In many ways, his skill and involvement with the genres of chutney, soca, and parang is what motivated me to write a book that explores the resonances between these genres rather than to follow the more traditional path of focusing on a single musical tradition.

Musically, Trinidadian musicians and their audiences go sonically where scholars rarely tread. We remain mired in an effort to generate knowledge that will endure. Music's ontology is quite different from that of a scholarly book. The sounds come and go, and they linger in memory. My memories of Trinidadian music are forever fixed not only to sound, but also to a variety of sensations at particular moments. Paradoxically, if there is anything transcendent I try to capture about Trinidadian music, it is the episodic quality of its experience.

To do so, I struggled with a variety of theoretical perspectives to frame the ethnography—this is not the book it was when I first thought I had finished it. As I struggled with the ethnographic representation, I felt a disconnect between theoretical models I had inherited as a social scientist and what I recorded and remembered from Trinidad. Eventually, I arrived at the realization that I needed Caribbean social theories. Works such as Paget Henry's *Caliban's Reason* (2000) and Antonio Benítez-Rojo's *The Repeating Island* (1996) solidified this view for me. As I began to think through my material using the approach of Fernando Ortiz, Frantz Fanon, Édouard Glissant, Wilson Harris, C. L. R. James, Aimé Césaire, and the theoretically oriented comments of Trinidadian musicians, I found a more aesthetically pleasing fit between theory and ethnographic description than I had experienced previously. I also returned to some of the classic work on aesthetics, such as that of Susanne Langer and John Dewey, with a new reading generated by the resonances between their theories, the political-aesthetic theories that come from the Caribbean, and the musical experiences I was attempting to understand.

This raises an issue that has been well articulated by my colleague Murphy Halliburton (2004): why does anthropology turn to European and North American theories and tend to view the philosophical writings produced by the societies we study as data rather than theory? Halliburton addresses this with the centuries-old traditions of South Asia, but the same point can be made of other parts of the world, as well. The Caribbean has produced many sophisticated thinkers who grappled with Caribbean and global dimensions of postcolonialism—and many have done so while paying attention to aesthetics.

I am interested in what engages Trinidadians and how Trinidadians respond to the music that engages them. Most of the people with whom I worked are not musicians. Consequently, I do not devote much space to a musicological representation of Trinidadian music, but instead I try to capture the spontaneity one experiences in the music. Musicological approaches have difficulty in representing spontaneity—this point has been developed by Charles Keil in his discussion of "groove" (Keil and Feld 1994).

Along the way, through the various metamorphoses of this manuscript, many people have offered useful comments and advice on parts or all of the manuscript. Murphy Halliburton, John Collins, Alex Hinton, Katherine Snyder, Diana Finnegan, Donald Tuzin, Nilanjana Chatterjee, Tanya Luhrmann, Steven Parish, Krystal Roopchand, Ted Sammons, and my Music, Culture, and Society class at Queens College have read all or part of the manuscript and provided correction and encouragement. This book has also benefited greatly from the critically constructive comments of the anonymous reviewers. My friends from Anamat have continued to provide support and insight. Evelyn Silverman and the interlibrary loan department at Queens College, and the staff of the library at the Research

Institute for the Study of Man have helped me obtain many of the less widely circulated sources on Trinidad and its musics. My first fieldwork greatly benefited from the assistance of Morris Freilich and John La Guerre; my choice of Anamat as a field site would not have been possible without them. Fred Kameny has provided valuable guidance for preparing the final text for publication. In bringing this book to completion, I am indebted to Valerie Millholland of Duke University Press.

The research that led to this book has been supported by an IIE Fulbright, and by PSC-CUNY research awards #666476 and #666436. I also thank Donald Scott who, as dean of social sciences, allowed me to use the release time from teaching in the most effective way to bring this book to fruition.

Part of chapter 4 was originally published in the journal *Ethnology* 33 (1994): 165–77, under the title "Bakrnal: Coup, Carnival, and Calypso in Trinidad." I thank that journal for giving me the permission to reuse that material here, and I thank F. G. Bailey, Roy D'Andrade, James Holsten, Michael Meeker, Fitz John P. Poole, and Catherine Besteman for their comments on this early version of chapter 4.

Finally, my wife, Margaret, has played many crucial and special roles in this project, through her support, encouragement, criticisms, and valiant attempts to make my prose comprehensible.

note on music references

M any Trinidadian singers use stage names rather than their given names. This is a long-standing tradition within calypso. The given name is not a secret, but the moniker is usually a means of amplifying the persona of the performer. I have adopted a practice of referring to singers by their stage names when I discuss them. The appendix lists the given names for the performers to whom I refer by stage names. In addition, the discography includes both the stage name and the given name of the performer.

Throughout this book I cite many songs. When I quote from songs, I have chosen to provide citations for the specific recordings I used. I also include a discography of all the recordings to which I refer, with one exception: Duke's "Get on Radical." To my knowledge, a nonpirated version of this recording has not been released on any compact disc. As a consequence, when I cite lyrics from this song, I refer to a book of lyrics (L. Williams 1991), not to a recording.

In almost every case, my first hearing of the music was either in the context of a performance, on the radio, or on a pirated cassette tape. In most cases, the versions I heard are the same as those on the commercially available recordings I cite. In a few cases, however, such as Scrunter's soca parangs, the versions with which I am most familiar appeared only on vinyl, and the versions released on subsequent compact discs are not the same as the vinyl versions. In this case, I have cited the compact discs that contain the versions closest to the original vinyl.

Also, there are a variety of spellings for Sonny Mann's song "Loota La": Lootay La, Lotay La, Lota La, Loota La, and Lootala. Referring back to the original recordings, I have adopted a potentially confusing, but relatively accurate, means to refer to this song. The original version performed by Sonny Mann is listed on his recordings as "Loota La." The remixed version, which supplements Sonny Mann's singing with performances by Denise Belfon and General Grant, appeared under the title "Lootala." Consequently, when I am referring to the original version, I use the title "Loota La," and when I am referring to the remix, I use the title "Lootala." To maximize confusion, however, the version of Sonny Mann's original recording that I refer to in the discography appears on the compact disc under the title "Lota La."

introduction ❧ Initial Connections

When the Admirall sawe that he coulde by no meanes al-
lure them by gyftes, he thought to prove what he could do
with musicall instruments: and therefore commaunded that
they which were in the greatest shippe, shulde play on theyr
drummes and shalmes [a reed instrument related to the
oboe]. But the younge men supposinge this to bee a token of
battayle, lefte theyr ores, and in the twynlynge of an eye
hadde put theyr arrows in theyr bowes and theyr targettes on
theyr armes: And thus directinge theyr arrows towarde owre
men, stoode in expectacion to knowe what this noyse might
meane.

PIETRO MARTIRE D'ANGHIERA, *The Decades of the Newe
Worlde or West India*, describing the first encounter between
Columbus and the indigenous population of Trinidad

For Caribbean man, the word is first and foremost sound.
Noise is essential to speech. Din is discourse.

ÉDOUARD GLISSANT, *Caribbean Discourse*

It somehow seems appropriate that the first encounter between Europeans and the indigenous residents of what is now called Trinidad
involved a connection between music and combat. Today, Trinidadian
music still marks and sometimes instigates conflict. It creates and reflects
controversy. Music plays a pivotal role in Trinidadians' discussions about
themselves, their country, and their world. Often it is a song that inspires
conversation or a lyric that spurs debate.

To experience Trinidad and its people is to experience Trinidad's music, but Trinidadians' musical genres are diverse; they incorporate traditions from the Americas, Africa, South Asia, and Europe. In their diversity, Trinidadians are not tied to a single music. Trinidadians are not tied only to Trinidadian musical styles, either, but appreciate many styles of music popular in North America, Europe, South Asia, and elsewhere in the Caribbean. Consequently, there is value in exploring the interaction of different musics, rather than treating them as having isolated histories (Ramnarine 2001).

For many events, such as Carnival, Christmas, weddings, and funerals, music plays a central role. But music in Trinidad is not limited to festive occasions; it is everywhere. As when one watches an epic movie, where there is a soundtrack accompanying all of the action on the screen, in Trinidad much of one's daily life also is done to music in the background, if one cares to listen. Like movie soundtracks, Trinidadian music can enhance the experience of the present moment or shape one's anticipation of the future. This is most evident in calypso. It is a music that plays a prophetic role—both in the sense of criticizing contemporary events and in the sense of shaping a sense of the future (Rohlehr 2004a). Trinidadian music does not structure life, however. In discussing sound in relationship to agency in Salvador, Brazil, John Collins emphasizes the pervasiveness and the temporality of sound, including music: "It is the sound that, always present and relatively more of an envelope than a girding structure, may or may not be transformed into meaning through the interactions between people, their environments, and those sign vehicles heard only at certain, and often special, times" (n.d.: 25). Trinidadian music works in this way. The existence of music is not sufficient to determine meanings; instead, people must engage with the music and interpret it, and both the engagement and interpretation are influenced by social rhythms, including the seasonal cycle of holidays and the timing of interactions.

A great deal of Trinidad's music is heavily influenced by combinations of musical traditions from other parts of the world. This might be part of its global appeal, but it is far too easy to adopt a constrained view of Caribbean music as a mixture, hybrid, or product of creolization. The idea of hybridity and creolization seems to be struggling to represent what Huon Wardle calls the "dynamic of conflicting generative forces of which intermixture is only one" (2002, 493).

The concepts of creolization and hybridity are limiting in the way they represent a dynamic, often chaotic, process that unfolds through time, as if this process were a coherent thing. The term *creolization* has an implicit teleology in which the result of the process will be creole culture. Aisha Khan criticizes the concept of creolization as reifying how we think about culture in order to theorize mixture (2001, 294). Homi Bhabha (1994) developed the concept of hybridity with the intent of emphasizing processes that emerge out of differences. Yet the word itself seems to be an unfortunate choice in many respects. Its original field is biogenic reproduction that often produces sterile offspring—but this does not seem to be Bhabha's intended meaning. Semantically, with the suffix -*ity*, *hybridity* refers to the qualities and conditions that are products of social differences. The emphasis on product rather than on process leads to the occasional reference to "hybrid cultures." When used unreflectively in this way, the term can reify what difference produces rather than draw attention to ongoing processes.

Such reification runs counter to Caribbean social processes and perspectives. In writing about Caribbean aesthetics, Gordon Rohlehr describes the resistance of slaves to the colonial order: "In its most fundamental form it was the refusal to be a thing, an object, a tool, mere chattel: the *negation of a process of reification*" (1992a, 1, emphasis original). Caribbean music continues this tradition of resistance to reification. Music is dynamic and unfolds over time. Caribbean music is a product and a producer of the genitive forces Wardle describes. It is an art form in which rhythm and timing are crucial. Music is a topic of conversation and a means of establishing intersubjective connections—it is something to talk about when nothing else is overtly held in common, and thereby it becomes a means to establish and evolve commonalities or differences.

The purpose of this book is to explore what Trinidadian music does and how it is used. I try to address these issues by focusing on experience, and by shifting the conceptual metaphor underpinning theory from the domain of space and machinery (articulation, structure, center, periphery, and even flow), which tends to reify social processes, to metaphors based on polyphonic music—counterpoint (multiple melodies or voices going on at once) and polyrhythm (multiple rhythms unfolding over time).

Counterpoint involves simultaneous multiple themes. The movement between harmonic and dissonant relationships between themes is crucial in counterpoint (Fux [1725] 1965). The complexity of thematic interaction, along with the generation of dissonance and harmony, not only creates a complex piece of music but creates new sounds: the interacting wavelengths of sound of the harmonies and dissonances generate resonances and pulses that are not played. The resonances add additional tones to chords; the pulses emerge when two dissonant notes are played together.

Whereas counterpoint tends to be applied to melodic themes, polyrhythms follow parallel principles for percussion—they involve different rhythms performed simultaneously. Both polyrhythms and counterpoint emphasize the unfolding of colliding and colluding themes over time, with polyrhythms capturing a sense of timing or relations, and counterpoint capturing a sense of collision and collusion between parts. The shift away from thinking with a metaphor based on structure to a metaphor based on counterpoint and polyrhythm recasts the issues of agency in relationship to structure, and of individuals in relationship to collectives, in terms of the relationship of improvisation to the timing of the interaction of spontaneity and organization. In addition, the temporality of counterpoint and polyrhythm makes these metaphors less conducive to reification than the metaphor of structure. Musical, as opposed to structural, metaphors are grounded in Caribbean thought, whether it is Fernando Ortiz's explicit use of the counterpoint metaphor in *Caribbean Counterpoint* ([1947] 1995), or Antonio Benítez-Rojo's preferring to refer to the Caribbean as a rhythmical area rather than as a culture area (1996, 75).

✿ Time to Music

Trinidadian music grabbed my attention during the early stages of preparing to do my first ethnographic project—a project studying concepts of time (Birth 1999). I met several Trinidadians who generously invited me to their homes for "limes." To Trinidadians, liming is an essential social activity. The term encompasses many social behaviors and could be misconstrued as simply doing nothing, but there are two significant differences between truly doing nothing and liming: (1) one cannot lime by oneself, and (2) one can do an infinite number of things (other than "work") while liming with others. What makes an activity liming is twofold: spending time with other people with whom one likes to spend time, and doing something for the fun of it, even if the something done is absolutely nothing. My initial limes with Trinidadians in San Diego, California, were a learning experience, and, clearly for my Trinidadian friends, an opportunity to teach me about Trinidad. These limes *always* involved my friends showing off their collection of Trinidadian recordings. These records (and in the 1980s, they really were vinyl records) were cherished belongings. Since very little Trinidadian music was sold in San Diego, and since the 1980s predated Internet shopping, often these records were not merely Trinidadian music, but were indications of the struggles their owners had gone through to acquire the music—long-distance telephone calls to record stores in Brooklyn, or careful packing to protect the precious vinyl albums when one returned from visiting family in Trinidad. Given the importance of liming, and the significance of the music on these occasions, it became powerfully clear to me early on in my research that liming and music were important components of being Trinidadian. These early experiences also planted the seeds of a sense of disconnectedness between the habits of scholarship—which privileges what texts say, fetishizes structure, and even tries to treat life as if it were a structured text—versus the aesthetic qualities of my experiences with Trinidadians.

After many years of interest in Trinidad, and several years of living in a West Indian neighborhood in Queens, New York, I have heard the importance of music to Trinidadians demonstrated almost daily. To study Trinidadian society and culture means to include music. Whereas ethnographies on other parts of the world seem to be able to contain descriptions without reference to music, I know of no ethnography on Trinidad that does not address music somehow. Even works that sound unmusically inclined, such as *Modernity: An Ethnographic Approach—Dualism and Mass Consumption in Trinidad* (Miller 1994), *Capitalism: An Ethnographic Approach* (Miller 1997); *Callaloo or Tossed Salad? East Indians and the Cultural Politics of Identity in Trinidad* (Munasinghe 2001), or *Producing Power: Ethnicity, Gender, and Class in a Caribbean Workplace* (Yelvington 1995a), all contain extensive discussions of Trinidadian music. My own first book, *Any Time Is Trinidad Time* (Birth 1999), derives its title from a phrase made famous in a calypso by Lord Kitchener. Coming to understand Trinidadians entails coming to understand Trinidadian music.

☙ The Importance of Music in the Caribbean

Throughout the post-Columbian history of the Caribbean, music has served as an important forum for public discourse in the region. Studies of slave resistance mention the counterhegemonic function of music (Dirks 1987; Brathwaite 1971, 208; Liverpool 2001). Politics are often the subject of music, as has been emphasized in many studies of Caribbean societies (e.g., Averill 1997; Manuel 1995; Waters 1985).

Throughout the region, then, there has been a long historical connection between music, globalization, and the ways people think about their similarities and differences. Trinidad is part of this pattern, but with its own distinctive musical practices reflecting its complicated history of migration tied to forms of labor exploitation. The tie between Carnival musics, the history of slavery and exploitation in Trinidad, and African identity has been made clear (Elder 1967; Liverpool 2001). Helen Myers (1998) documents continuity between South Asian music and Indo-Trinidadian music and reveals how this continuity shapes consciousness of historical connections to India. Finally, a link between present celebrations and global history can be made for *tassa* drumming—a drum-based music that is presently associated with Hindu weddings and with Hosay in Trinidad. This drumming was originally associated with Hosay, the Shi'ite commemoration of the martyrdom of Hosein, but has come to be associated with Indian Trinidadian identity, not just with Muslim Trinidadian identity (Korom 2003).

Even though it seems that any Trinidadian music could be the subject of a study that links sound, politics, and history, calypso has attracted special attention. It one of the most studied musical expressions of social and political commentary in the Caribbean. Studies of calypso demonstrate close links between the musical messages and the cultural and political context (see Elder 1967; D. Hill 1993; Liverpool 1990, 2001; Regis 1999; Rohlehr 1990; Warner 1982), and such links have been embodied by individuals who have been prominent calypsonians and have held government posts, such as Atilla the Hun and the Mighty Chalkdust. Albert Gomes, a political leader in Trinidad after World War II, said, "The Calypso is the most effective political weapon in Trinidad" (quoted in Brown 1947, 251). Although calypso receives the greatest attention, the use of Trinidadian music for purposes of public political discussion is not limited to calypso. For instance, Tina Ramnarine opens her study of Indian music in Trinidad by highlighting the link between performance and political processes and concludes her study with the point "Music in Trinidad is deeply implicated with political processes" (2001, 1, 145).

Calypso inherited its political and aesthetic tone from the musics that preceded it in nineteenth-century Trinidad, particularly the music that accompanied canboulay and stick fighting. Canboulay, from the French *cannes brulée*, was an aggressively playful reenactment of burning the sugar cane. Burning sugar cane was, and still is, an important form of protest against sugar plantations. Burnt cane must be harvested quickly, or else it spoils. During the nineteenth century, canboulay became a popular Carnival activity, which involved groups of Africans marching through the streets with torches accompanied by drumming (Alonso 1990, 96–99; Brereton 1975, 51; Cowley 1996, 19–21; Elder 1967, 94–98; Elder 1998).

Stick fighting, which was accompanied by a music known as kalinda, also threatened elite control over Carnival, and police attempts to stop this practice and canboulay resulted in the Carnival riots of 1881, in which several bands of stick fighters united to resist the police (Alonso 1990, 101–2; Brereton 1975, 52; Cowley 1996, 84–90; D. Hill 1993, 37–40; Liverpool 2001, 306–12), and the Arouca riots of 1884 (Elder 1967, 104–5; D. Hill 1993, 42–43; Liverpool 2001, 315–16).

Stick fighting and the kalinda were associated with neighborhood-based groups that consisted of the fighters, vocalists, and chorus associated with particular "yards" (Elder 1966). The songs were sung in a call-and-response form. The lead singer was known as a "chantwell," but no kalinda was complete without the chorus.

The community-based organization of these groups that was echoed by the call-and-response songs was an element of Carnival participation that remained during the late nineteenth and early twentieth centuries, even as stick fighting waned and middle-class masquerade bands became common. Calypso emerged as a distinctive musical form in the context of Carnival bands known as "social unions" (D. Hill 1993, 48). The singer was closely identified with the singer's social club, whose members served as the chorus. The chantwell not only taught songs to the members of the club who would serve as the chorus but also entertained them (Liverpool 2001, 373). This audience-as-chorus actively encouraged the chantwell's lyrics (Dudley 2004, 25). Part of the preparation of a band for Carnival was the rehearsal of the music in the masquerade camps, and soon the "mas' camps," as they are now known, became venues to hear the new songs. As calypsonians gained more notoriety, they began performing in venues, known as "tents," separate from their sponsoring Carnival band. The calypso tent brought together several performers who vied for the approval of a ticket-paying audience. Before World War II, many calypso shows featured competitions between the singers, and this was done with the intent of attracting audiences (D. Hill 1993, 77). The topics of the most popular songs combined humor with social relevance while evading the silencing power of the colonial government's efforts at censorship (see Rohlehr 1990, 278–315, and Rohlehr 2004d).

Even though the contexts for the music's performance divided between what Donald Hill calls indoor and outdoor settings, and even though these settings generated different styles of music, the music continued to seek a powerful engagement between the song, singer, and audience—whether that audience consisted of Carnival revelers or the audience in a calypso tent (D. Hill 1993, 5). Writing of calypso tents in the 1920s, Errol Hill states, "It was the custom for the audience to join voluntarily in singing choruses" (1972, 65). In the tent, both then and now, that audience closely attends to the lyrics. They vocalize their approval, and if they reward a calypsonian's performance with enthusiastic applause, they expect additional verses to be performed as an encore—even if the calypsonian has to make them up on the spot (Dudley 2004, 38).

The gradual end of colonialism after World War II did not mean the end of music's political role or the antiestablishment tone of many calypsos. Rohlehr comments that "over the decades the calypso tent evolved as a sort of popular equivalent to Parliament; a privileged space that exists not because authority has willingly sanctioned its existence, but because it has, decade after decade, era after political era, fiercely asserted and defended its own right to exist as a forum for the public articulation of whatever is officially unspeakable for the public transgression into what is officially taboo; for speaking one's mind either openly or behind a mask" (2004d, 189). Instead, calypsonians sang their opinions of national politics and international events, and after independence, they collectively produced a counterpoint between progovernment sentiments and trenchant criticism (Regis 1999; Rohlehr 2004a).

Whereas the politics of music do not automatically imply nationalism in Trinidad, nationalist symbols frequently reference music. The power of music to create individual and collective sentiments and to shape political discourse and policy has resulted in Trinidadian music becoming globally associated with Trinidadian identity. In fact, Trinidad and Tobago's soccer team playing in the 2006 FIFA World Cup was known as the "Soca Warriors"—named after the popular form of Carnival music.

The importance of music in Trinidad's history enhances the complexity and significance of connections between music and the crafting of images of the nation. This complexity and significance is manifest in many forms. Every nation has a national anthem as a signifier of its nationhood, but not every nation gives its anthem the respect Trinidadians give to theirs (see Scher 2003, 174). Few nations place musical instruments on their currency, whereas the steeldrum, or "pan," as it is called in Trinidad, is on several different denominations of currency. The official Web site of Trinidad and Tobago Tourism (www.visittnt.com) used to have a musical soundtrack. The current official Web site of the government of Trinidad and Tobago (www.gov.tt) features photographs in the shape of the notes on a steeldrum at the top of its page "About Trinidad and Tobago." In 2003, if one had explored the section labeled "culture" on the government's Web site, one would have encountered the following passage as the introduction to Trinidadian culture:

> The culture of Trinidad and Tobago is a reflection of a creative and vibrant, ethnically mixed and cosmopolitan society.
>
> The rhythmic sounds of the steelband music, the pulsating beat of the tassa drums, the entertaining calypsos and chutney songs, the romantic swaying of paranderos at parang time, all tell the tale of a people emerging from four centuries of colonialism, independence and republic rule.

Such representations only thinly mask conflicts and musics with complicated traditions. For a while, the tourism Web site offered musical samples, but of the musics mentioned in the text of the government Web site, only steelband music and calypso could be heard on the tourism Web site. The musical traditions associated with Indians, tassa and chutney, and the Spanish, parang, did not provide any of the sonic backdrop for this cyber encounter with Trinidadian culture.

Even calypso has been involved in conflicts over what is national and what is ethnic. In 1979, Black Stalin, a calypsonian known for lyrics of incisive social commentary, wrote and performed "Caribbean Unity":

> One race—the Caribbean man
> From the same place—the Caribbean man
> That make the same trip—the Caribbean man
> On the same ship—the Caribbean man.   (*Roots Rock Soca*, track 1)

In the case of "Caribbean Unity," Ramesh Deosaran suggests that the song excluded Indians and women in its portrayal of the "Caribbean man." He argues that Caribbean unity must encompass all peoples of the Caribbean, not just those descended from Africans. Africans tend to view this debate as an overreaction on Deosaran's part, but Indians tend to agree with Deosaran (see Warner 1982, 83–85; Warner 1993, 282–85; Deosaran 1987; and Rohlehr 2004c). Ironically, then, Stalin's call for unity resulted in a display of the divisions within Trinidadian society—an image of harmony ("Caribbean Unity") that developed into dissonance. In an interesting twist on this debate, in 1995, Stalin sang a song called "Sundar," in which he asked Sundar Popo, a popular Indian singer/songwriter, to write a song for him—an open attempt to use the recognition of dissonance to move toward harmony.

The mid-1990s saw several popular songs that explicitly dealt with themes of multiracial identity, such as Chris Garcia's "Chutney Bacchanal" and Brother Marvin's "Jahaji Bhai" (Reddock 1999; Rohlehr 2004b). As Rhoda Reddock points out, these songs include claims of adopting all cultural heritages in Trinidad, but these claims "continue to be affected by the ethnic tensions, structures, and hierarchies that exist and that are compounded by the issues of gender and male control over women" (1999, 593). Thus, while Trinidadian music can be tied to ideas about the nation, its relational, contrapuntal aesthetic also represents ideas about the fragmentation of the nation, identities defined in opposition to the nation, and communities that, in defining themselves, do not rely on any concept of the nation at all. Still, whether one is looking at an oppositional or a unifying musical moment, one is still looking at the establishment of relations and the movement between harmony and dissonance. J. D. Elder, in a perceptive observation about musical borrowing in Trinidad, notes "the very act of borrowing from a hostile group indicates the existence of conditions favourable to intergroup communication" (1967, 195).

The images and ideas evoked by music, politics, and race create a tangled web of practices and processes. Trinidad and Tobago is a divided nation. It contains social hierarchies that were inherited from colonialism, socio-economic differences produced by the contemporary global capitalist economy, and racial categories of Indian and African that are deployed in political and social practice in multifarious ways. They can be used manipulatively to seek political support, but in counterpoint to the manipulative use of such categories are efforts at maintaining cherished traditions—for instance, the extreme efforts Indian musicians go through to master the modes of Indian music on the harmonium, a bellows-driven keyboard that has been widely adopted by South Asian musicians. The piano-like keyboard is limited to a diatonic scale and is consequently poorly adapted to the modal scales in which South Asian music is sung. Ramnarine comments about the musical compromise required to deal with this difference: "If the harmonium's part does not always correspond exactly to the singer's line, it nevertheless follows the vocal line closely, sometimes very slightly anticipating the vocal line and sometimes slightly behind the singer" (2001, 48). Such effort suggests a desire for a fusion of virtuosity shaped by South Asian music theory but manifested on a European instrument, and authenticity in South Asian music. This desire and the work and discipline required to achieve skill in this musical compromise cannot be reduced to efforts at manipulating political sentiments. This counterpoint is one dimension of what makes grappling with ethnicity in relationship to politics so difficult—it is difficult to separate Machiavellian motivations from sincere reverence of one's ancestry and heritage. As a consequence, analyses of Trinidadian politics debate whether the divisions within Trinidadian politics are based on race or class, and whether the political action is motivated by deeply held principles or by duplicitous pragmatic positions employed to achieve personal political goals. Every election produces a wave of editorials in the newspapers discussing how the votes were shaped by social categories and attempting to uncover politicians' motivations. The counterpoint of the politics of ethnic competition and the politics of ethnic celebration are built upon the ongoing legacy of the colonizer-colonized relationship as complicated by neocolonial practices of the United States, in particular.

As a result, Trinidadian identity involves a process of conceptualizing both self and others. Presentations of identity connect contested images and representations, and these images and representations can be found distributed over many contexts. As Richard Handler points out (1994), the term *identity* has implications of cultural homogeneity, which are political claims that may or may not be evident in practice. But Caribbean criticisms of identity are even more sociogenic and antiessentialist. Frantz Fanon's *Black Skin, White Masks* (1967) stresses the social conceptual processes in which people are enmeshed. Stuart Hall echoes Fanon's formulation when he describes the process of identification as being one of splitting—"this necessity of the Other to the self, this inscription of identity in the look of the other" (1997, 48). Whereas Fanon and Hall expose unconscious logics of being black in a racist world, Édouard Glissant takes the stance of demanding the "right to opacity" (1989, 2). In doing so, he argues against the perspective of peeling away the layers of individual subjectivity to find meaning but instead shifts away from the inner self to emphasize relations—a "focus on the texture of the weave and not on the nature of its components" (1997, 190). Whether the metaphor is "the texture of the weave" or counterpoint, the focus is on the relationship of the parts, and the manner in which the parts become shaped by their relationships. In the Caribbean, these processes can relate people who are different and even hostile. C. L. R. James's assertion that "It was the revolution that made Toussaint" (1963, 10) frames his exploration of the complex class and race relations amid which Toussaint acted during the Haitian revolution. This resonates with Wilson Harris's emphasis on *"involuntary* association," which he relates to the "'chasm' within humanity" (1999, 241). From a Caribbean perspective, identity and subjectivity emerge from intersubjectivities that range from supportive cohesion to demagogic hostility.

The creation of identities in Trinidad is not simply a conceptual or social process; it is also a musical one. In his book *Producing Power*, the example Kevin Yelvington provides of such awareness and symbolic manipulation is a black Trinidadian who wanted to learn to play the steel drum (1995a, 143). Since the larger context of Yelvington's book is factory work and not music, this example is telling—in Trinidad, music is an important means for making and contesting cultural claims about identities and the nation. Music is also an important means for *thinking* and generating *feelings* about such claims. Trinidadian music provides a means for moving beyond conceptualizing identity as a "thing" to looking at it as emerging from the complex interplay of a variety of cognitively dynamic and emotionally charged processes of relating—music is significant in what Holger Henke describes as the "fluidity and centrifugality in Caribbean existence" (2004, 37). Once the shift is made away from defining identity to examining the contrapuntal processes of relating, then identity ceases to be the primary concern but becomes a single theme among many.

Understanding Trinidadian music, then, involves the play of harmonies, dissonances, and multiple rhythms. Instead of coherence, there is relationship. Counterpoint is not limited to issues of identity but can subsume all experience. Trinidadian music seeks conflicts in life in order to relate their oppositions. These relationships are not resolutions—indeed, the ongoing tension is often the source of the humorous and ironic sides of Trinidadian music's lyrics. For instance, in the 1993 hit song "Bacchanal Time," the dissonance between the message of the song that Carnival revelry never ends and the reality that the police close down fetes at 4:00 a.m. makes the wish for a perpetual party and the presence of the state equally immanent and irreconcilable night after night.

🐾 Bacchanal?

Carnival is often described as "bacchanal," and this has been the theme of many songs, including Super Blue's "Bacchanal Time":

> **Super Blue**: Are you ready to go home?
> **Collective response**: No!
> Jump up (*8 times*)
> Bacchanal! (*4 times*)
> Jump up (*8 times*)
> Bacchanal! (*4 times*)
> **Super Blue**: Monday
> **Collective response**: Bacchanal!
> **Super Blue**: Tuesday
> **Collective response**: Bacchanal!
> **Super Blue**: Wednesday
> **Collective response**: Bacchanal!
> **Super Blue**: Thursday
> **Collective response**: Bacchanal!

Super Blue: Friday

Collective response: Bacchanal!

Super Blue: Saturday

Collective response: Bacchanal!

Super Blue: Sunday

Collective response: Bacchanal!

Super Blue: Everyday everyday

Collective response: Bacchanal!   (*Bacchanal Time*, track 1)

Super Blue is one of Trinidad's most popular soca artists. In 1980, using the stage name of Blue Boy, he earned his first of several Road March titles with the soca song "Soca Baptist." Soca is the music that dominates the streets and parties of Trinidad's Carnival. The Road March is the song that is adopted by the most masquerade bands and steelbands during Carnival, and it indicates one of the most popular, if not the most popular, songs of the Carnival season. Super Blue has composed many Road Marches, which ranks him as one of the greatest performers in Trinidadian music history.

In "Bacchanal Time," he asks, "Are you ready to go home?" and the response is an overwhelming "No!" In the recording, the response consists of singers in a recording studio, but in Carnival fetes or on the street, the response is large-scale and collective. An awareness of intersubjective connections is choreographed by the music, observed in the speech and physical actions of others, and sensed in one's own awareness of body and thought—"You must have the experience of dancing to it to really understand calypso," Shannon Dudley explains (2004, 49). In a crowd, shared movement and speech give sensations of shared consciousness and experience. In the recorded version of "Bacchanal Time," the lines sung by studio singers serve as an initial cue for all participants in Carnival to join in singing. But during the revelry of the Carnival season, these recorded voices become superfluous—drowned out by the learned responses of Carnival's crowds. These people do not want Carnival to end—they do not want to go home. These are not passive participants, however, but participants whose bodies, minds, and voices are willingly guided by the music, and whose past embodied actions have guided Super Blue's composition and encouraged the distribution, promotion, and sale of his recordings.

Super Blue's use of call-and-response is typical of the recorded Carnival music of the last two decades and of the street and fete styles of Carnival music from the time of the earliest descriptions of this festival (Elder 1967; D. Hill 1993; Liverpool 2001). Call-and-response must be viewed as more than lyrical antiphony, however. The response of the bystanders to Super Blue's song was physical. In another Super Blue song, the response to his call "Get something and wave!" is primarily physical rather than vocal ("Get Something and Wave," *King of the Road March Greatest Hits*, track 1). In Trinidadian call-and-response, the lyrics are often a synecdoche for an embodied, emotive response. One does not chant "jump up" without some upward movement. Such music is powerful because of its ability to guide and elicit verbal and nonverbal responses from large crowds of people. This response, which ties together emotion, cognition, and physical action, is at the heart of bacchanal.

The concept of bacchanal is pervasive in Carnival, but bacchanal is not limited to Carnival. It is also associated with arguments, conflicts, and violence—its meaning encompasses an uncanny and dynamic mixture of danger, joyful abandon, fear, elation, collective belonging, and solitary madness. Bacchanal is an inherently contrapuntal idiom playing on both the dissonances between antisocial violence and Carnival's sense of community, and the resonances between the wild abandon of Carnival and the out-of-control nature of heated arguments. The two types of bacchanal are neither contrary to one another nor consistent with one another—but they are connected to one another.

There is power in bacchanal. It is a holistic counterpoint—a place and time in which feeling, thought, power, individual action, collective action, society, culture, politics, motivation, interpretations, and reflections coincide and even collide. In musical counterpoint, it is the play of harmony and dissonance that creates the aesthetic experience. The coincidence of, say, personal feelings and public messages in bacchanalian experiences does not reflect a congruence of the feelings and messages, but reflects, instead, a spatial and temporal intersection in the unfolding of experience. Bacchanalian events are those in which connections are drawn between public and private concerns, bodily processes and social structure, national politics and personal motivations, and global and local influences. Bacchanal is a conduit in which power is embodied and bodies determine power. It is the intersection of biology, physiology, psychology, culture, and political economy, but it does not, by definition, imply shared and coherent identities.

Carnival bacchanal crescendos through music. While bacchanal ties groups and minds and bodies in a holistic counterpoint, Trinidadian music establishes relationships between disparate elements of Trinidadian life. The music exercises what Glissant describes as the poetics of relation (1997), but "poetics" is in some ways too restrictive in its implication of textuality. Rather than "poetics of relation," I prefer the broader "aesthetics of relation." Musical sound is not limited to the discursiveness implied by poetics. The sound of Trinidadian music also establishes relationships through the combination of sounds and rhythms from Indian, African, Jamaican, Hispanic, and North American musical traditions. The lyrics also relate ideas in creative ways—whether it is relating the days of the week to bacchanal, as in "Bacchanal Time," or relating the seemingly innocuous mixed drink of rum and Coca-Cola to sexual relations between American soldiers and Trinidadian women during World War II, as the Lord Invader did in his classic calypso "Rum and Coca-Cola." Relations ripple—"Rum and Coca-Cola" not only created a complex web of relationships through its lyrics, but it also became the center of a case involving female American entertainers violating the intellectual property rights of male Trinidadians through the machinations of a male American manager who was also a comedian. The Lord Invader first performed this song in 1943 to an arrangement of a Martinican melody published by the Trinidadian bandleader Lionel Belasco. In September of that year, Morey Amsterdam, an American entertainer, came to Trinidad as part of a tour to entertain American troops. He heard "Rum and Coca-Cola," and after his return to the United States, he copyrighted the lyrics in his own name, and the version recorded by the Andrews Sisters became one of the biggest-selling records of the 1940s. The Lord Invader and Lionel Belasco then successfully sued Amsterdam for copyright infringement (see Rohlehr 1990, 360–64; D. Hill 1993, 234–40). As a result, a song about a mixed drink as a metaphor for assymetrical sexual relationships between Americans and Trinidadians became mixed up in a dispute about intellectual property in the context of assymetrical global relations between American and Trinidadian artists.

When ethnographically examined from the perspective of the creation of holistic counterpoints and the aesthetics of relations, understanding music goes beyond just the sounds (Keil and Feld 1994, 122–23). In discussing music in *Philosophy in a New Key*, Susanne Langer emphasizes *"great art is not a direct sensuous pleasure"* (1979, 205), and in her *Feeling and Form* (1953) she attends to how aesthetics shape feelings. The richness of music is based not only on what it sounds like, but on what it does, and what it does is related to the connections between culture, power, social relationships, context, body sensations, and physiological processes. In his book *Art as Experience* ([1934] 1980), John Dewey castigates many who study art (music included) for creating divisions in experiences between the individual and the collective, the emotional and the cognitive, the imaginative and the practical, and thought and sensation, and then studying only a small segment of aesthetic experiences. Charles Keil, in "Motion and Feeling through Music," makes a similar point when he suggests, "it may be our own notion of the aesthetic that is crude and restricted, not that of the primitives" (Keil and Feld 1994, 57). In the dialogue between Keil and Feld, "Grooving on Participation," the dimensions of musical experience that can be explored to move beyond a restricted aesthetic become apparent: affirming Dewey's point, Feld says, "I want to keep problematizing all of the ways in which researchers separate off the psychological, physiological, musicological, text-centric, syntax-centric forms of analysis from what we are calling culture and experience" (1994, 165). Music has the potential to bring together public representations of important issues, the conversations generated in small groups, and the embodied, visceral participation in events structured by music. Music also can create specific memories of shared experiences—a particular song serving as an index of past experiences. Popular Trinidadian music is compelling to both Trinidadians and ethnographers because it does this.

Trinidadians corroborate Dewey's demand for a holistic approach to music through representations of their music. In his song "Calypso Music," David Rudder explores the power of music by invoking the political and embodied power of Trinidad's calypso genre:

> It's a living vibration
> Rooted deep within my Caribbean belly
> Lyrics to make a politician cringe
> Or turn a woman's body into jelly.   (*The Gilded Collection*, track 3)

James indicates a holistic counterpoint in recounting when the great calypsonian the Mighty Sparrow first sang "Federation," a song about the

breakup of a federation that would have united into a single country all of
the former British colonies in the Caribbean:

> I was in the tent the night he [Sparrow] returned and first sang it [the song
> "Federation"]. When it became clear what he was saying, the audience froze.
> Trinidad had broken with the Federation. Nobody was saying anything and
> the people did not know what to think far less what to say. At the end of the
> last verse on that first night, Sparrow saw that something was wrong and he
> added loudly: "I agree with the Doctor [then premier, Dr. Eric Williams]." But
> the people of Trinidad and Tobago only wanted a lead. Sparrow divined their
> mood, for henceforth he became increasingly bold and free.   (1984, 162)

James describes embodied action: "the audience froze"; he ascertains
sentiments: "Sparrow divined their mood"; and he links embodied action
and mood to political discourse about Dr. Eric Williams's decision for
Trinidad and Tobago to withdraw from the Federation of the West Indies,
thereby dissolving the Federation entirely. James also emphasizes physical movement as an important component of aesthetics when he argues
that cricket is art (1993, 205); and when it comes to the link between
cricket, art, and politics, as Sylvia Wynter commented, for James "the
aesthetics is the politics" (1981, 63).

In tying together aesthetics, body sensations, and emotion, the words
of James and Rudder strike a chord with Langer's, Dewey's, Keil's, and
Feld's shared general points about taking a holistic approach to studying
music, but James and Rudder add politics to this web of relationships. For
them, a holistic approach to aesthetics must also involve a holistic approach to politics because aesthetic experiences are political experiences.

In the Caribbean, discarding these distinctions creates not unity but
fragmentation. Any image of unity, as Harris points out, is merely a
moment preceding difference: unity is "the core of paradox. Unity appears dormant, passive, but may be fired into rhythms of differentiation
that make us aware of inequalities, jealousies, passions, that may bedevil
our world absolutely unless—by stages as it were—a transfiguration of
appearances occurs, appearances we take for granted" (1999, 186). Fragmentation and the image of any unison as only temporary are crucial
elements of Caribbean aesthetic theory, namely, that Caribbean aesthetics relate through time—they do not homogenize transcendently.
Rohlehr says of Caribbean writers that their sense of form is "based not

on the notion of a specificity of genre or aesthetic but on the inter-relationship of various art forms, aesthetics and areas of interest" (1992d, 2). Glissant describes these aesthetics as "a nonuniversalizing diversity" (1989, 253). The holistic relationship between politics, bodies, emotions, and social categories is contrapuntal—an ongoing movement between harmonies and dissonances. Based on Fanon's existential exam-ination of being a colonial black (1967), one embodied ideology can exist simultaneously with a contradictory embodied ideology.

❧ The Importance of Participation

Many studies of Caribbean music emphasize discursive connections be-tween lyrics and identity. Yet such a discursive emphasis is an artifact of a restricted aesthetic approach of the sort criticized by Langer (1953), Dewey ([1934] 1980), and Keil and Feld (1994). Paul Willis warns that such a language-based paradigm is "damaging" because language is not like the "sensuous creativity of cultural practices" (2000, 18). While many domains of experience can push one beyond complacent acceptance of approaching the world as text, music seems particularly adept at this, and African American music, in particular, has encouraged unease with essen-tializing music as text. For instance, Paul Gilroy (1993) argues for the need to expand analysis beyond the metaphor of textuality that domi-nates many interpretive models. In the context of black music, Gilroy points out, "The vitality and complexity of this musical culture . . . pro-vides a model of performance which can supplement and partially dis-place concern with textuality" (1993, 36). Developing the idea of a ho-listic and contrapuntal approach to Trinidadian music involves going beyond textual meanings and engaging with other ways of experiencing music, particularly the intersubjective nature of participating in music with a group—a key component of many Trinidadian musical events, such as Carnival. There is precedent for this. Elder's ethnomusicological approach (1967) emphasized sonic structures and qualities as much as lyrical content, and he was concerned with how emotions were encoded in sound.

Trinidadian music is used intersubjectively by people who produce, consume, and identify with particular songs at particular moments. Be-cause of the contrapuntal fragmentation of identities, rather than assuming that music and identity are mutually constituted in an essential way in a very complex neocolonial setting such as Trinidad, it is more useful to assert dynamic, changing relationships between music and these identities that unfold over time. If, as Langer argues, art expresses not "actual feeling" but "ideas of feeling" (1953, 58), then to understand what aesthetic productions do requires understanding the engagement of performers and audiences with the ideas of feeling that are presented. Furthermore, Langer describes music as a temporal art form—one in which the manner in which sound shapes passage of time is vital to the experience of the art (109–27). The created-in-time and the created-between-people connections of music and identity reveal the ability of music to create alternate visions of conflict and community. Experiencing music with other people involves the emergence and evolution of intersubjective consciousness—impositions upon individual subjectivities in ways that emphasize one's connection to others. Intersubjective consciousness can be tied to the Durkheimian idea of collective conscience—an experience that Durkheim argued emerged from festival-like ritual gatherings ([1915] 1965, 214–19).

Adopting Durkheim's perspective tempts one to assume a coherent group rather than a fragmented aggregate of people playing with mimicry, irony, hyperbole, and opposition. Trinidadian Carnival is not coherent and cannot be reduced to symbolic oppositions. Even though he adopts the framework of opposition and inversion to characterize Caribbean popular culture, Richard Burton's analyses of the Caribbean actually emphasize negotiations between people of different origins who were categorized as being of the same race in the Caribbean—"cultural creolization . . . took place primarily not between Whites and Blacks, but between one group of slaves and another" (1997, 27). In effect, in Burton's discussion, popular culture in the region, whether it is folklore, festivals, religion, or cricket, is consistently a process of evolving relatedness as well as opposition—the one does not exist except in relationship to the other. In such relationships, opposition dissolves into multiple oppositions. After all, the idea of opposition implies a position to be opposed. In a situation of fragmentation, opposition to one element can entail a tangential relationship with another. In addition, a focus on opposition or inversion can exclude all the elements of life that do not stand in opposition to something else. Shalini Puri complains that "the current emphasis on carnivalesque transgression again constricts it, for it is a very select everyday that we now study" (2004, 113). As a result, Puri advocates "attending to the often tense interplay of a given Carnival's structure, content, artistic context of performance, and historical conjuncture" (114).

Carnival is described by Selwyn Cudjoe as having a "polysemous and polysemantic richness" (2003, 175), which he then affirms as "meaning different things to different people" (176). Reducing Carnival and its musics to oppositions, then, does violence to its richness. It also takes the transient oppositions and runs the risk of making them transcendent, but Trinidad's history shows otherwise. For instance, in 1884, the police attempted to suppress Carnival; early in the Carnival of 1903, the Police Band performed at a gala event (D. Hill 1993, 52), but not long after Carnival, in March, the police shot at rioters during the Water Riots; in the 1960s, when Anthony Prospect became the leader of the Police Band, that ensemble began to play calypso and eventually became the band to provide accompaniment for calypsonians during national competitions and an incubator for calypso musicians and singers who went on to prominence; from 1988 to 1990, a member of the Police Band, Chris "Tambu" Herbert, won a series of Road March titles; and during the Carnival of 1991, which followed the 1990 attempted coup d'état, another member of the police force, the calypsonian the Watchman, was accused by government supporters of singing seditious lyrics in a song, "Attack with Full Force." This song had an apropos political observation with implications for a social theory of Caribbean politics: Watchman sang of "the opposition opposing opposition," thereby revealing the fragmentation of opposition.

During a Carnival fete, if the participants pelt the stage with bottles and stones, when only a moment before they were cheering the arrival of a major artist, what is the audience opposing? Is it a poor performance by a soca artist? Is it law and order? Is it gravity? Again, rather than a metaphor of position and opposition, the idea of temporally and polyrhythmically unfolding contrapuntal harmonies and dissonances seems much more useful. This can better capture why "Lootala" was one of the most popular songs in Trinidad in late 1995 and early 1996. This song was a remixed version of an Indian chutney song "Loota La." The remix featured a female calypsonian and a male reggae dancehall artist singing in dialogue with the original Indian singer, whose lyrics were in Bhojpuri.

The idea of a counterpoint unfolding over time also captures how the live performance of this remixed version at the Soca Monarch competition late in the 1996 Carnival season was greeted by the audience with thrown bottles and stones. Moving on several years in time, temporally unfolding counterpoint also captures why, in my neighborhood in Queens, I still hear the song. The metaphor of opposition/position limits how one can think about such fragmentary, evolving, shifting feelings and ideas, whereas the ideas of counterpoint and polyrhythm allow for thinking through such shifts, and even assert that the movement from moments of harmony to moments of dissonance in a web of relations is important for experiencing Carnival. Again, many thinkers with Caribbean roots— Aimé Césaire, Fanon, Benítez-Rojo, Harris, and Glissant—provide approaches for thinking through *and with* such fragmentation. Bursting from their works is the assertion that consciousness of one's identity is tied to the actions of others by means of efforts to define differences.

This suggests a dialogism of the sort associated with Mikhail Bakhtin (Bakhtin 1981; Holquist 1990), a parallel noted by Michael Dash in his discussion of Glissant (1995, 114); yet, because of racialized differences embedded in colonial and neocolonial contexts, it is a skewed dialogism, where the dialogue internal to self involves antagonistic voices that create themselves out of their differences. These ideas, complemented by L. S. Vygotsky's developmental psychology (Holland et al. 1998; Vygotsky 1978; Wertsch 1985), have provided fertile foundations on which to build models of how intersubjectivity is experienced and imagined. One such idea is the concept of "communities of practice" (Lave and Wenger 1991; Wenger 1998). But the communities of practice in musical settings in Trinidad are not as coherent as Lave and Wenger's work typically represents. Communities of practice in Trinidad are complicated by what Holland et al. (1998) refer to as "positioned identities"—statuses that people recognize they occupy and to which they assume others react. Three of the dimensions of positioned identities recognized in Trinidad are ethnicity, gender, and age. All of these are based on interpretations of physical features. Appearance is fodder for thinking about and perceiving such multiple and sometimes antagonistic dimensions for positioned identities. This reinforces the insight of Fanon (1967), who notes that intersubjective consciousness is not an abstract system of meaning but is found in personal encounters that involve body sensations and interpretations of one's body vis-à-vis the interpretations of the bodies of others. It involves processes acting socially, psychologically, culturally, politically, economically, physiologically, and stylistically.

The colonial and neocolonial context of Trinidad is far more fragmented than coherent—a gendered, class-inflected, sometimes ethnically charged play of traditions from Europe, North America, South America, South Asia, Africa, and elsewhere in the Caribbean. The fragmentation becomes even more apparent as one tries to trace shifting affiliations and loyalties over time. Yet this fragmentation must be viewed in counterpoint to a multitude of social and emotional ties that seek to transcend these divisions.

❧ The Audience Perspective

As a result of the current accessibility of recordings and lyrics and the promotion of particular artists, it is tempting to view Caribbean music through the eyes of the composers and singers and their lyrics as mediated by commercially available recordings. Such perspectives offer great insights not only into music, but also into Trinidadian cultural history. It is even possible to obtain great insight through such media even if one has not visited the Caribbean, as Dick Hebdige admits about his work in the beginning of his *Cut-n-Mix* (Hebdige 1987, 14). In the case of Trinidad, there have been several studies of calypsonians, including some written by prominent artists, such as the books by Atilla the Hun (Quevedo 1983), Roaring Lion (Leon n.d.), and the Mighty Chalkdust (Liverpool 1990, 2001). Studies that emphasize performers and composers produce a narrative of calypso music in terms of the relationship between different artists and the social contexts in which they worked (Elder 1967; Warner 1982; D. Hill 1993; Rohlehr 1990; Regis 1999). This body of work affirms the importance of these artists, analyzes the poetic qualities of lyrics, and explores the cogency of the songs' social insights.

Some of these works contain suggestive discussions of the importance of "the chorus," and this suggests a dimension of Trinidadian music not addressed by a focus on the lead singer. For instance, Elder writes, "Song-leader and choral-group were more or less equal partners in the performance of the songs" (1967, 184). Elder also sees a link between chorus and audience:

> At the earliest stages the singing was communal and here we may expect
> that audience involvement was natural. But even when the songs were taken
> into the streets with the public performance of kalinda and cariso the crowd
> which followed the "chantuelles" had to "answer to the chorus" just as they
> did during communal singing in the backyards. It would seem reasonable
> to expect that when the chantuelle became more or less a stage-singer he
> would dispense with the chorus. But this was not the case. Whilst the au-
> dience became at this stage purely a "listening" unit the song-leaders retained
> a token chorus to answer the refrain of the songs they were composing.
> (1967, 237)

One of the conclusions of his analysis of Trinidadian music is that
throughout the history of this music antiphonal singing remained "socially significant," and that at crucial moments, this participation of the
audience/chorus was "strategically crucial to the welfare and protection
of the singers" (1967, 238). Errol Hill wrote of the social consequences of
the engagement between singer and chorus in a Carnival band: "The
whole company was knit together by the calypso songs; singing the choruses gave band members a stake in the success of each rendition" (1972,
64). In effect, the survival of the art form depended on the sonic engagement of the audience/chorus as a form of political action.

The engagement of the audience/chorus with the music, and the social
and protective roles of these people in ensuring the persistence of the
music, hints at features of musical performance and experience not captured by printed lyrics or preserved recordings. This is corroborated by
descriptions of calypso performances. In a 1943 article for *Canada-West
Indies Magazine*, one finds the following morally condescending description of the effects of a calypso on the audience: "The music eddied under
the rayed tent. Raillery and laughter were magnified. Some in the crowd
remembering the words took up the song, a ribald offensive song upon
which a lively, catchy tune had been wasted, since obviously, it would be
impossible to preserve it in gramophone recording" (Collier 1943, 21). To
this outsider journalist, the involvement of the audience was palpable,
along with the realization that what engaged them would not be preserved outside of the memories of those who were there.

Based on his comprehensive knowledge of calypso, Rohlehr shows that
the relationship between lyrics and social issues has changed as the political and economic context of calypso has changed (1990, 1998). He points

out that calypso has been increasingly influenced by market forces in such a way that calypso now manifests contradictory "impulses":

> The first is parochial, inner-directed, quite often defensively aggressive, in which the citizens of a small "post-colonial nation" reassure themselves that they are creators by celebrating what they have created and by claiming themselves and the works of their hands and minds jealously and zealously in the face of an appropriating world that at times includes 'rival' Caribbean states . . .
>
> The second impulse is externally oriented and involves the calypso's ongoing encounter with an external market that imposes its own terms, standards and conditions of access.   (1998, 83)

The changing relationship of calypso to audiences and markets, its changing musical styles, its relationship to changing political and social conditions in Trinidad and Tobago, and the transience of many songs defy any attempt to essentialize the musical form, or even to assign a single, enduring meaning to a particular song. Studying audiences in time at particular moments in history is valuable, then. In addition, Stefano Harney warns that lyrics might not be a reliable "reflection of social formations in Trinidad" (1999, 40). He argues against confusing calypso's role in influencing ideological struggles in Trinidad with calypso as representing Trinidadian society (42) and concludes that the importance of calypso requires that it be related to social movements and institutions outside of musical contexts.

By the time calypso lyrics are subjected to scholarly analysis, they have an aura of immobility, not spontaneity; and spontaneous lyrical innovation is a hallmark of great calypsonians—one facet of the relationship of the performer and audience that resonates with Roger Abrahams's concept of the West Indian man-of-words (1983). Printed lyrics also homogenize choruses and audiences. Even when the lines sung by the chorus appear in the lyrics, the social composition of the chorus is obscure—with regard to its members, what was their age, ethnicity, class, gender, place of residence, political leanings, mood, and so on? The representation of calypso through lyrical analysis is challenged, then, by the desire to represent social spontaneity and the relative lack of spontaneity and social involvement in a published lyric. This is not a new development. In discussing the printed form of the 1926 calypso "The Landing of Columbus," Errol Hill says of the lyrics he quotes, "The above version appears in print; but as sung in the minor key the calypso is unfinished unless the singer or audience comes in at the end with *sans humanité* or some similar short refrain to complete the musical phrase, however illogical the words may seem" (1972, 63). The implication is that a calypso lyric without the response is "unfinished." Later in his book *The Trinidad Carnival*, Hill also states, "It has been observed that the impact of calypso songs can never be recaptured when they appear in print, since it is the singer's mode of presentation that gives life to his rendition. This claim is true; but it does not state the whole case against the printed calypso as a substitute for a live performance, since the underlying rhythmic harmonic base of the calypso is also an important element that cannot be satisfactorily conveyed on paper" (1972, 71). The difference between experiencing music "live and direct," as one of my Trinidadian friends would often say, and experiencing it through the printed word is substantial (Balliger 1998, 61). Musical experiences are transient and temporal in ways that printed texts are not, and the memory of musical experiences is often checked by comparison with others' memories rather than returning to an original text.

Works on the history of calypso have met the challenge of understanding the relationship between social context and lyrics by using all means possible—newspapers, photos, oral histories, advertisements, and myriad types of text—to describe the social context of the music. Ethnographic work on contemporary musical performance and consumption can play a complementary role to historically-oriented scholarship on Trinidadian music by capturing dimensions of musical experience that are not readily preserved in the historical record.

If one takes one of the most important calypsos of all time, Sparrow's "Jean and Dinah," and does an analysis of the lyrics, one can quickly realize the significance of the song in the context of Trinidadian events, but one does not capture the moment of its initial explosive significance. It is a song about power, gender relationships, sexuality, and the U.S. military's leaving Trinidad:

Jean and Dinah
Rosita and Clemintina
On the corner posing
Must be something they selling

If you catch them broken (i.e., broke)
You can get them all for nothing
Don't make a row (i.e., fuss)
Yankee gone and Sparrow take over now.   (*The Mighty Sparrow, Volume 1*, track 1)

The U.S. military had maintained several bases in Trinidad since the early days of World War II. During that time, the presence of American military personnel had altered gender relations. Lord Invader's song "Rum and Coca-Cola" expresses these changes. In the song, Invader sings about "mother and daughter working for the Yankee dollar" because the American men "give them a better price" than the Trinidadian men:

When the Yankees first came to Trinidad
Some of the young girls were more than glad
They said that the Yankees treat them nice
And they give them a better price
Rum and Coca Cola
Go down Point Cumana
Both mothers and daughters
Working for the Yankee dollar.   (*Calypso Calaloo*, track 12)

Sparrow's 1956 hit must be viewed in the context of the changing conditions that resulted from the closing of the bases. It develops the relational identities of Yankee man, Trinidadian man, and Trinidadian woman in a context of decolonization—each character has behaviors constituted by his or her relationships with the others and related to his or her nationality. Sparrow describes how, if one found the Trinidadian women Jean and Dinah "broken," "you can get them all for nothing," and he discusses through his lyrics how the Trinidadian men have things "back in control," and how he, as a man, is "seeking revenge." "Jean and Dinah" and "Rum and Coca-Cola" clearly reflect important dimensions of Trinidadian society, and their ongoing popularity, particularly in the case of "Jean and Dinah," attests to their importance to Trinidadians. A lyrical analysis can point out all of these things, but it cannot, with any certainty, describe what the 1940s' or 1950s' audiences of the songs thought and felt, or how the nostalgic memories of the song in subsequent years have evolved. An analysis of the lyrics, while necessary, is not sufficient to account for the emergence and evolution of audiences' thoughts and feelings over time during 1956 and since in a complex, multiethnic society such as Trinidad.

In Trinidad, with a few exceptions, most people forget most lyrics except for a few "hook lines" that grab one's attention through repetition and poetic function. This is particularly true when it comes to parang and chutney. Parang is a Christmas music ostensibly sung in Spanish, but many paranderos (parang musicians) do not speak Spanish, and the majority of the audiences do not understand Spanish. Furthermore, many of the lyrics have been altered by non-Spanish speakers attempting to sing them, so much so that Spanish speaking paranderos show disdain for many parang singers' poor Spanish or Spanglish. Chutney, a popular Indo-Caribbean music that combines South Asian musical traditions with soca, is sung in Hindi or Bhojpuri, or in English with Hindi/Bhojpuri inflections. For the songs in South Asian languages, again, the majority of the audience and many of the performers do not understand or speak the language. Most cannot even distinguish between Bhojpuri and Hindi (Ramnarine 2001, 60). Consequently, in the cases of parang and chutney, while lyrical analysis might be interesting, it would not illuminate the importance of the songs to their audiences—the audiences are focused on how melody and rhythm structure experience, not the semantic content of the lyrics. Even in the popular genres that contain English lyrics—some chutney, soca, calypso, and kaiso—few members of the audience remember the entire lyrical content of a song. This is even true of kaiso. Kaiso is an early form of calypso, but the term is now often used to refer to songs that emulate the early style through adoption of a tempo about half the speed of that of soca, a greater tendency to adopt a minor key than Road March and party songs, and emphasis on the lyrics, not on the melody. Even with the emphasis on lyrics, audience members rarely can reconstruct a kaiso's lyrics in their entirety. Furthermore, the importance of kaiso lyrics is gauged by audience reactions, making a focus on lyrics separated from performance inadequate for appreciating the ways in which the lyrics socially structure feelings.

As Daniel Segal has argued, however, a focus on social reception is not sufficient to understand the role of expressive culture in Trinidad (1989, 366). I choose to privilege the audience throughout most of this book, but in relationship to the efforts of the state to objectify Trinidadian expressive culture. My desire is to try to capture the consequences for political consciousness of aesthetic experiences in particular moments of time. The unresolved issue of transcendent national identity remains part of the counterpoint.

Caribbean relational and contrapuntal aesthetics emphasize spontaneity. This breaks down distinctions between participant and spectator
in ways reminiscent of Bakhtin's discussion of Carnival (1984). Whereas
Bakhtin's work is based on his interpretation of Rabelais, the work of
Caribbean thinkers such as Césaire, Glissant, Derek Walcott, and Rohlehr
is based on a lived experience of the revelry of music and movement. The
sense of subjectivity and inter-subjectivity that Bakhtin recovers in *Rabelais' World* seems, in some form, paralleled and vibrant in the contemporary Caribbean. Just as Bakhtin describes how Rabelais's views are in
opposition to the scriptocentric ideas that followed, the aesthetics of the
Caribbean also seem opposed to Europe's enlightenment heritage, as
well—not as a matter of separation from Europe, but as a recalcitrant
participation in Europe's expansion and colonial exploitation. Césaire
provokes his readers into this relation of aesthetics and struggle when he
states, "The revolution will be social and poetic or will not be" (1996,
121). A lyrical analysis begins to capture this, but even when crafted with
detailed historical analysis to describe the social context, it can feel in-
complete without living bodies and minds. One must try to capture the
intersection of state policy, public media, festive settings, intersubjectivity, subjectivity, mental states, and body sensations. This involves
viewing lyrics as one, temporally unfolding dimension of musical experience and attending to the fragmentary perception of music and lyrics by
audiences.

❧ Beyond Lyrical Analysis: Methodological Considerations

Trinidadians are critical, active recipients of the ideas and images found
in music and lyrics. In a different context, Claudia Strauss has criticized
what she labels the "fax model of culture"—her term for the simplistic
idea that public discourse becomes internalized in unmodified form
(1992, 1, 9–10). It would be a gross misrepresentation of Trinidadian political discourse to assume that calypsos determined political consciousness in a way similar to a fax model of culture. Trinidadian music's power
requires attention to the differences between determining thought, influencing thought, and instigating dialogues that then influence thought.
Critical, active musical consumers talk about their likes and dislikes, and
this influences how they think through social, intersubjective interac-

tions. Multiple audience responses are an important source of contrapuntal associations emergent in intersubjective relationships.

Remembering songs tends to involve a reconstruction out of fragments. Lyrical segments become torn from the whole, and this has a
major effect on how they become interpreted later. As Stanley Fish
showed with regard to textual symbolism, context is crucial to meaning,
and different contextual assumptions create radically different meanings
for the same phrases or symbols (1980). Meaning is not inherent in lyrics
but is provoked by lyrics instead. For instance, the calypsonian Chalkdust's song after the 1990 attempted coup suggested that Trinidadians
should act as a jury to judge the behavior of Abu Bakr, the leader of the
attempted coup. But Chalkdust's admonition in his song was that Trinidadians should act as a jury to "try" Abu Bakr—a very provocative play
on words. Since many listeners interpreted the song only as stating that
the nation should have tried Abu Bakr as their leader, Chalkdust's song
was not very popular, but its lack of popularity was due to the processes
of fragmentary perception and retention of the lyrics, followed by attempts to generate a coherent interpretation of the words. Such fragmentary recollection of music adds to the contrapuntal nature of the
intersubjective experience of music, namely, the temporally unfolding
movement of dissonances and harmonies, conflicts and collusions.

The fragmentation of lyrics is related to the fact that most Trinidadians learn most lyrics through hearing, not reading. They listen to the
radio and recordings, and they attend venues where the music is played.
In early 1991, Charles, then a nine-year-old boy, strolled down the road in
front of my house singing the chorus to Denyse Plummer's "La Trinity":
"I am your rock; I am your island" (*Carnival Killer*, track 3). Charles did
not have a set of printed lyrics, however. His singing was only of a fragment of the song, and a fragment that he found particularly compelling.

David Rubin (1995) describes how music assists memory of lyrics, and
the poetic, rhythmic, and melodic structuring of lyrics not only assists
their memory but attracts one's attention to certain powerful phrases.
Oral performance results in people remembering fragments and then
constructing representations of what they heard based on such fragments. Discussions of oral poetry traditions emphasize how these poets
hear a poem and then incorporate the poem into their own style and
repertoire of tropes, in order to reproduce it (Ong 1982; D. Rubin 1995).

The same is true in Trinidad, where most lyrics are heard, rather than read.

Since both performance and remembering are reconstructions, rather than duplications (D. Rubin 1995), remembered lyrics are not necessarily clones of the original lyrics, and even the idea of what is original must be separated from the idea of what is authentic: the former implies a process of creation, whereas the latter implies a process of objectification. When lyrics are repeated in discussion, as is the case with conversations about calypsos, or performance, as is the case with parang, they can often be altered, but continue to be viewed as authentic because of their style and form. During the 1990 Christmas season, Scrunter's "Anita," a fusion of soca and the Christmas music parang, was popular. Scrunter is a calypsonian from Sangre Grande, an area of the island in which one can still hear house-to-house parangs. In 1989, he fused calypso and parang in the "soca parang" called "Piece ah Pork," and then followed up in 1990 with "Anita." In "Anita," Scrunter describes everything he has given to Anita, and he wonders what Christmas gift to give to the woman to whom he has already given everything:

> I give you T.V.
> I give you fridge
> I give you stereo
> I give you video
> You get bed
> I give you house
> I give you land
> I give you van.   (*Decade of Scrunter*, track 9)

"Anita" became popular with one of the parang bands with whom I played guitar. The list of all that Anita received was not faithfully duplicated in this band's performances, however. In these late-night, house-to-house performances, some items reversed, such as her getting a house before the bed, and some items were added, such as furniture.

Emphasizing audiences requires paying attention to cognitive and emotional dimensions of the retention of most music. Most Trinidadians encounter many forms of music during festive occasions. Some of these occasions, such as Carnival fetes, are extremely crowded and noisy. Those participating do so in a wide variety of states of consciousness. To gloss them as "altered states of consciousness" is unfair, particularly since a "normal" state of consciousness is so poorly defined. Still, some participants were sleepy from partying several nights in a row while going to work during the day; some were sexually aroused from "wining" and "grinding" with an attractive dance partner; some were hypoglycemic from having eaten too little; some were drunk; some were violently aggressive and looking for fights; others were anxious and fearful of those looking for fights; some were hyper from drinking too many sugar- and caffeine-laden soft drinks on an empty stomach (I was often in this category); and many experienced combinations of these factors on awareness. All of these factors affect memory, and their diversity contributes to a sense of contrapuntal, rather than unitary, experiences.

Other occasions, such as weddings and wakes, are situations where the presence of music is important, but the focus of most individuals in attendance is not on the music. Still other contexts, such as house-to-house parangs, involve long periods of sleep deprivation and pain—playing a musical instrument for hours on end without a break generates blisters, sore muscles, cramps, and tendonitis. Since most Trinidadians encounter music in these contexts, and not in written form, and since these contexts are not conducive to identical performances or complete memories of songs, it is not surprising that the songs are remembered in fragmentary form and are repeated in fragments. Some songs, like "Jean and Dinah," have become folk songs. I heard "Jean and Dinah" performed at several parties, but at each occasion, instead of Sparrow's verses, I heard nonsense syllables, such as "La ta da ta da ta da da." With regard to chutney and parang, the fragmentary memory of songs becomes even more significant, since the language of the lyrics is often not spoken by members of the audience. Consequently, when I heard individuals singing "Loota La," a very popular chutney, they commonly degenerated into Hindi-sounding nonsense syllables rather quickly. A similar thing occurs with parang, when one takes into account the fragmentary memory of the audiences, and then one realizes that any interpretation of their reactions to these songs must be an interpretation of their reactions to these song fragments.

The same image can have different meanings to different participants (Fish 1980; Iser 1978). Glissant describes the "poetic force": "We see it as radiant—replacing the absorbing concept of unity" (1997, 192). To take into account audiences' experience, one must also note diversity within the audience. Race, gender, and age are notable culturally recognized dimensions of diversity in Trinidad. The same lyric can create different reactions based on such identities.

The lyric that I appreciate the most in this regard is probably "Any time is Trinidad time." This is a good example of a phrase from a calypso composed by Lord Kitchener in the early 1970s that has entered everyday speech and gained significance far beyond its use in the original song. As I argued in *Any Time Is Trinidad Time* (1999), Trinidadians use this expression in many ways, have many different views about its significance and meanings. This can be seen in the following statements from five individuals about the phrase:

Twenty-something year-old: "That expression means like, you know, like everybody liking their own stylin'—they don't care nothing and thing—any time is Trinidad time."

Thirty-something year-old: "Any time is Trinidad time is more pertaining to a party. The average Trinidadian, when he say he have to reach work for seven o'clock, he reach at half-past-six, quarter-to-seven, but any time pertain to any time is Trinidad time, it more pertaining to having fun."

Forty-something year-old: "Well, the slang is good, but the attitude is bad."

Fifty-something year-old: "That goes to punctuality. That really was, that calypso had compose, it was really a calypso compose, you know, any time is Trinidad time."

Sixty-something year-old: "I think the expression there is really, it's something that should not—any time is Trinidad time—it is very wrong. And it was a calypsonian who brought that. And anything that you hear a popular calypso say in Trinidad, that is it—which is very, in my opinion, wrong."

These individuals have a shared familiarity with "any time is Trinidad time" and a diversity of opinions and views. One could break down such discourse into shared meanings and dissonant meanings and even argue that the shared meaning is the cultural meaning, but the cultural processes at work when these people encounter one another and use the phrase "any time is Trinidad time" are processes that relate their shared understandings of the phrase to their different feelings and thoughts about it. The multiple meanings potentially associated with "any time is Trinidad time" show that the relationship of spontaneity and organization is manifested in the potential for both divergent and similar ideas and feelings in personal encounters. The power of Trinidadian music involves playing with these contrasts—the double meanings often associated with calypso lyrics symbolize this form of play.

The same images can generate different interpretations and meanings on subsequent exposures, thereby forcing a recognition of time and timing. In literary criticism, this was powerfully shown by Roland Barthes's multiple readings of Balzac's novella *Sarrasine* in the book *S/Z* (1974). It is also apparent during the annual cycle of soca music during Carnival. This is another, less explored, dimension of diversity. Interpretations evolve over time *and* differ between people. When Chris "Tambu" Herbert's "No No We Ent Going Home" began to get frequent exposure at fetes in 1990, it was greeted with enthusiasm. Not only had Tambu won the previous year's Road March, but his 1990 song seemed his strongest effort yet. The catchy chorus about a party that had been taken over by women who demanded that the revelry never end excited crowds. By the late Carnival season, some of those with whom I attended fetes began to play with the song in ways that suggested waning popularity. One night, when the fete ended at 4:00 a.m. with the disc jockey blasting "No No We Ent Going Home" at high volume, one of my friends began singing "Now now we are going home; we are leaving!" By Carnival Tuesday, many openly expressed boredom with Tambu's song. Even though it won the Road March by a landslide, its overexposure tarnished its appeal.

Cognition and feeling include relational, social processes. With regard to music, audiences are more than collections of individual minds. Compelling songs generate conversations, and these conversations create interpretations of the music. With repeated exposures over time, more and more fragments are remembered and reassembled in social situations. They become linked to personal stories. One night in 1991, I was with a group attending the "pan around the neck" semifinals in Arima. This is a competition for small steelbands in which the musicians carry their instruments. That night a band was playing their rendition of "Fire" by the calypsonian Bally. Suddenly, a middle-aged member of the group grabbed me, waved his arms, and shouted above the music, "You hear that—that real ol'-time rhythm, poom poom, poom poom poom!" Another member of the group then recalled playing the same rhythm years earlier when he played with the pan-around-the-neck ensemble Trinidad Nostalgic. The contemporary performance was thus reinterpreted in terms of past musical styles and past musical experiences. The attractiveness of the arrangement to the group shifted away from a discussion of virtuosity to a discussion of nostalgic memories. This connected the past to the present, and individual memories to collective knowledge and sentiment.

An important facet of the social process of the social interpreting and intersubjective sharing of music involves shared, embodied processes. Césaire represents this in his *Notebook of a Return to the Native Land*: "And not only do the mouths sing, but the hands, the feet, the buttocks, the genitals, and your entire being liquefies into sounds, voices, and rhythm" (1983, 41). Why else would a soca singer's order to "jump up" have a unifying physical effect on an audience? What happens in many musical contexts involves physical actions, as well as cognitive response.

Still, as Gilbert Rouget warns in his study of possession trance and music (1985), one should not view music, or a particular kind of music, as automatically having a specific physiological effect; cultural ideas about physical responses must be explored. In the case of Trinidad, Trinidadians describe several musics, such as soca, chutney, and parang, as generating an embodied state of "heat," or as "hot." The idea of heat is linked to ethnophysiological ideas. Roland Littlewood suggests that heat is related to heightened activity, such as sex, dancing, or mental exertion (1988, 132; 1993, 34). He adds, "To say that disputes, sex, music, and Carnival are 'hot' is not just to speak in conscious analogy: when engaged in them, one's body is physically heated, with possible risks to health" (1993, 34–35). In West Indian ideas about the body, heat opens the body up, allowing impurities to enter (Sobo 1993, 45–46). Consequently, heat can cause sickness. Heat can also lead to violence, thereby causing conflict. The residents of Anamat, the rural community where I do most of my fieldwork, described Port of Spain, the capital city of Trinidad, as "hot" because of the crime found there. In effect, if certain musics generate "heat," then the implications of this "heat" must be explored in the context of Trinidadian ideas about physical and mental processes. These ideas are cultural interpretations of physiological states. The musics that generate heat are also musics to which people dance and sweat. The culturally expected response to these musics is dancing, jumping, and singing. In the case of some soca and chutney, there is a clear erotic element as well, manifested most powerfully in the dance style known as wining. In addition, since heat can cause madness, so can music. Ideally, however, the madness is a euphoric and social madness, rather than a violent and solitary madness.

Since the Trinidadian ideas of Carnival events and calypso music include ideas of body states, such as "hot" and "cool," then attention must be paid to dimensions of experience beyond the words of the songs played during Carnival. The most powerful Trinidadian musical events are multisensory—they typically involve hearing, vision, touch, balance, and body sensations that include fatigue and excitement. Among the senses, there is a redundancy of the messages perceived: the movements one sees, and the physical sensations one has, are both coordinated by the music one hears. Importantly, each of these senses is processed in different parts of the brain, but the neural pathways that would result in their connection meet in the limbic system. The limbic system is important in the generation of emotion, and linkage with a powerful emotional experience can strongly encourage memory (Damasio 1994, 1999). Consequently, the experiences that Carnival fetes generate involve not only the coordination of the senses in perceiving messages, but also an increase in the likelihood that such powerfully coordinated moments and messages will be remembered.

The congruence of neuroscientific and endocrine models with Trinidadian ethnophysiological models calls for exploring the connections of physiology, culturally elaborated physical experiences, and cultural cognitive processes. By prompting an attempted synthesis of science and subjectivity through blurring the boundaries between the study of culture, the mind, and the body, such approaches turn scientific models of physiological and psychological processes into interpretative frameworks for understanding individual and collective cognition/emotion (itself a problematic dualism—see Lutz 1986). This is done not by assuming the authority of experimental science, but by exploring the resonances between laboratory-generated scientific knowledge and other types of cultural knowledge encountered in humans' natural habitat (which is usually not a laboratory).

The structure of the musical context and the ways in which music and lyrical instructions coordinate the activity of audiences creates shared physiological responses. This is not a reductionist stance; it in no way implies that psychobiological factors cause social processes. Quite to the contrary, as Iain Edgewater (1999) argues about music in general, I am arguing about Trinidadian music: namely, that certain features of the cultural and social environment found in many Trinidadian musical events affect audiences' ideas by establishing complementarity between discursive messages and psychobiological mechanisms. If, as Thomas Csordas argues, "behavioral dispositions are collectively synchronized as attuned to one another through the medium of the body" (1994, 10), then it is worth exploring how these behavioral dispositions are synchronized and attuned to one another through biological processes—basically, to explore how social and cultural processes influence psychobiological rhythms. Or, as Fanon points out in discussing the cultural and anticolonial significance of storytelling, that it "gives rise to a new rhythm of life and to forgotten muscular tensions, and develops the imagination" (1967, 194). Once again a thinker with roots in the Caribbean (and rhizomes far beyond) compels us to take a vision connecting sensuality with the imagination.

✿ Situating the Participants' Participation in this Book

An emphasis on participation involves identifying particular places and times. While on maps Trinidad looks like a relatively small island, it feels much larger than it looks. This is because of three mountain ranges that cross the island and prevent views from shore to shore. These mountains can result in the shortest distance between two points being impassable, and the terrain forces roads to weave around mountains and valleys. Driving between two points separated by five miles can involve twenty-five miles of road. Consequently, identifying the place from which I construct my ethnographic reflections is important: this is the village of "Anamat"—a pseudonym first applied to the location by Morris Freilich (1960).

Anamat consists of several hamlets in the heart of one of the cocoa growing regions of Trinidad. The hamlets are connected by roads, kinship, and intermarriage. Until the late 1990s, the boundaries of the community were marked by particularly bad stretches of road—this creates a sense of the hamlets belonging together, since the road that connects them is in better shape than the roads that connect them to the rest of the island. The historical origin of the community is legally obscure—the area was probably settled by Venezuelan and African squatters on land belonging to the Crown during the nineteenth century. The land records provide no direct account of settlement but instead document that in the 1890s several plantations and a multitude of small holdings appeared with legal titles to land; these records also document an odd pattern in which much of the plantation-owned land was not contiguous but existed in shreds and patches—indirect evidence of land claims and transfers that preexisted legally recognized titles. The plantations were dedicated to cocoa, coffee, and rubber, and they employed large numbers of indentured laborers from South Asia and free laborers from the Lesser Antilles. Many of these workers settled permanently in the area, thereby defining the dimensions of diversity that currently define Anamat: the ethnic categories of Spanish, African/Creole, and Indian, and the religious categories of Catholic, Hindu, and Muslim, to which have been added Presbyterian, Missionary Baptist, Pentecostal, and Seventh-Day Adventist. These categories are somewhat negotiable, in part because of the flexibility of categories such as Spanish (Khan 1993), and in part because of kinship and marriage ties that crosscut and undermine ethnic categories (Birth 1997).

The location and heritage of Anamat influence the people's participation in music. As is the case with many parts of the island in which cocoa is king and Venezuelans settled, the musical tradition of parang has a strong local, family-grounded manifestation. Because Anamat is a place where Indians settled, Indian musics, such as tassa drumming and bhajans, can be found preserved in the groups that organize around the local Hindu mandir (temple). Because Anamat is in "the bush," most residents' exposure to Carnival music and commercial chutney is through radio and television, or through attending parties in the suburban and urban areas of the island.

The study of a specific group of people who live in a specific location, Anamat, allows me to place their ideas, opinions, and reactions in the social context in which they live, and it allows me to document the development of their ideas with regard to certain songs or genres of music and the development of their association between music and other issues of social importance.

This book also examines particular moments. Instead of tracing the history of Trinidadian music, the treatment of music is episodic. Each episode is placed within the larger context of Trinidadian history, but the focus is not on that history, but on the experience of the moment. A Trinidadian idiom, "now-for-now," is often applied to the lifestyle associated with immersion in Carnival. This immersion in the moment is not a denial of history or the future. Quite the contrary, despite the seeming emphasis on transience, living "now-for-now" also has an element of living to make every moment memorable. In this perspective, the future and the past submit to present concerns. In some ways it is akin to the saying "eat, drink, and be merry, for tomorrow we die"—this statement is conscious of a future fate, but the consciousness of the inevitability of one's future fate motivates a focus on the present. Many musical experiences in Trinidad have this now-for-now quality. This is similar to the "conjunctural approach" taken by Puri (2004). Her frustration with the study of Carnival in terms of inversion and opposition is that it insufficiently captures both the relationship of Carnival to everyday life, and the relationship of a particular Carnival to a particular moment in time. Since most calypsos are not played after the Carnival for which they were composed, clearly an approach to music in terms of the moment of which it is a constituting element, rather than in terms of where it is located in the more general history of Trinidadian music, is worthwhile. This does not diminish the importance of work that takes a diachronic, historical perspective—without such work, the episodic context would be incompletely understood. The ethnographer does not bring to the musical context the same sedimented musical memories of other participants and relies on the complementarity of ethnographically collected memories and historical scholarship to meet this challenge. In many contexts, Trinidadian music creates memories for the future, and people who are regularly and annually engaged with Trinidadian music have memories of the past that were shaped by past music, and which influence present experience.

The plan of this book is to explore contrapuntal subjectivities and intersubjectivities through specific events and cases. The first constellation of events is based within the early independence period, in which the state played a major role in crafting policies about music and Carnival. During this period, the government attempted to appropriate music for purposes of defining a national identity and creating nationalist sentiments, and, in this process, the governmental desire to suppress contrapuntal voices in favor of unitary images is apparent. The effort expended on this task is notable, but what is remarkable is the way in which this project emerged from theories of development and was explicitly linked to economic development. The government sustained this effort and even institutionalized it as part of a cabinet-level ministry. Chapter 2 completes this picture by looking at the experience of music by Trinidadians in those contexts the state has attempted to appropriate. This provides the first glimpse into the intricacies of how experience is influenced by public discourse, powerful music, and collective contexts, and it offers the first contrapuntal themes—themes that move between harmony and dissonance with governmental efforts, and that connect national identity and music. Coupled with this is participation in Carnival—an event labeled as "national theater" (E. Hill 1972) but that, in practice, defies such a label. This chapter also begins to explore aspects of annual social rhythms that are punctuated by musical participation.

The third chapter, which focuses on the Christmas music parang in Anamat, develops the spatial and temporal context of musical expression and political discussions in Anamat. Parang involves a highly structured and exhausting practice of moving from house to house throughout both the day and the night. The connections that emerge from the relationships that form and the physiological states that one may experience during parang are crucial for understanding the unfolding of an awareness of belonging and community. It also provides a context to explore how ideas that are held to be locally laudable become inculcated through embodied means in a context where the messages of community belonging and solidarity are never explicitly stated. This chapter explores how community relations form intersubjective themes in contrapuntal experiences as part of an annual cycle anchored by Christmas. This annual cycle is not entirely synchronized with cycles promoted by the government's policies, and the cycle of Carnival, and consequently forms part of the annual polyrhythmic feel of the yearly exposure to music.

Music and politics are further explored in the following two chapters. In chapter 4, the experience of music is examined in terms of feelings and images of Trinidad that emerged in response to the 1990 attempted coup d'état, and how they changed among Carnival-goers in early 1991. Chapter 5 also refers to an enigmatic event—the 1995 parliamentary election that resulted in a tie between the major political parties. In this case, music plays a role in the way in which Trinidadians discussed and contemplated political events, and the significant issues of race relations and party politics, thereby playing a role in how the experience of the events was constituted.

Music exists publicly and intersubjectively. In relationship to the context of its performance, it evokes conventionalized responses that are clearly culturally shared and shaped. From such cultural responses can emerge powerful emotional and cognitive experiences that, because of their power, often become converted into long-term memories that are individual, but because of the intersubjectivity of the setting, collective, as well (Clark 1997, 165). Music creates contrapuntal relations between subjective and intersubjective processes by tying together body and mind, and individuals and groups. This is an organic, vibrant complexity in which the relationship between ideas is not merely complex, but a result of timing of the interaction of recurring issues—such as race or community—and novel, unexpected events—such as an electoral tie or an attempted coup.

chapter one ❧ Governmental Organization
of Spontaneity

> In this nationalist struggle I am confident . . . that the man of
> culture has an important role and that the political leader can
> only succeed by enlisting culture in the struggle and placing it
> in the vanguard of the nationalist movement.
>
> ERIC WILLIAMS, *Nation*, November 20, 1959

The international image of Trinidad and Tobago is tied to its music.
This is the product of the skill and innovation of Trinidad's musicians, and the government's efforts to use music to define the
nation locally and globally. This chapter examines the nation-building
strategies adopted by the government early in the process of gaining
independence. These policies emphasized the institutionalization of musical and cultural competitions in order to invoke and inspire national
unity. These competitions were not only a means of celebrating national
identity but were also a part of the policy of mobilizing the population to
develop the country's economic infrastructure without having to use
large amounts of government resources during the early independence
period. By the 1970s, as government patronage evolved, the government's economic strategies shifted from local development toward con-
centrated, state-sponsored industrial development, which resulted in a
separation between cultural competitions and local economic development. The competitions remained, and even proliferated, but as the subsequent chapters will show, while the showpieces of government cultural
policies are still the competitions, they are only one of many influences
on Trinidadian musical participation.

✼ Forging Independence

A crucial moment in the political history of Trinidad and Tobago was the formation of the People's National Movement (PNM) in late 1955 and early 1956 with Dr. Eric Williams at the helm. Williams had an impressive background. He had won one of the very competitive colonial Island Scholarships to study in Great Britain; he had earned a doctorate in history from Oxford and established himself as one of the leading thinkers on the political economy of slavery; he had taught at Howard University; and he had served on the Anglo-American Caribbean Commission. Williams's participation in the decolonization process revealed his ability to transform spontaneous popular fervent into an organized political movement and to impose his will on the party, the government, and the nation. The emergence of the People's National Movement and the leadership of Williams happened so quickly that they seemed driven more by their own effervescence than by careful planning. Williams's effort to control the process of defining national identity linked spontaneous enthusiasm to planned policies.

The founding of the University of Woodford Square played an important role in the formation of the PNM, the political party that led Trinidad and Tobago into independence. Woodford Square is a park in the middle of Port of Spain, the capital city. The University of Woodford Square consisted of popular political meetings in which Williams, among others, gave speeches from the bandstand in the park. These political gatherings began in 1955 under the auspices of the People's Educational Movement, an educational organization. In July of that year, Williams stated: "Somebody once said that all that was needed for a university was a book and the branch of a tree; someone else went further and said that a university should be a university in overalls. With a bandstand, a microphone, a large audience and slacks and hot shirts, a topical subject for discussion, the open air and a beautifully tropical night, we have all the essentials of a university" (quoted in Oxaal 1982, 113).

The climate of nationalist and anticolonial fervor associated with the political rallies at the University of Woodford Square was transformed into the inauguration of the People's National Movement as a political party in January 1956. Later that year, the PNM won thirteen of the twenty-four elected seats on the Legislative Council—an advisory group to the colonial governor that, since 1946, had been increasingly allowed by the British to be in charge of Trinidad and Tobago's domestic policies. Since the governor still nominated four members of the Legislative Council, the PNM's thirteen elected seats were not a majority. Playing into the gradualist logic of British decolonization policies that saw the emergence of political parties as a necessary step toward independence, the PNM argued that it was a coherent political party, and that since it had won a majority of the elected seats, it should be given the power to rule. The British governor, Sir Edward Beetham, with the reluctant support of the British Colonial Office, then allowed the PNM to choose two of the four nominated members of the Legislative Council, thereby giving the PNM the majority on the council.

Once the PNM gained control, consolidating its grip on power clearly was an important goal, made all the more pressing when the PNM lost the elections for the parliament of the Federation of the West Indies in 1958. During this time, the vision was not for Trinidad and Tobago to be an independent nation, but for it to form part of a regional federation. Based on the recommendations of the Moyne Commission (West India Royal Commission 1945), the British Colonial Office's plan was for the colonies in the West Indies to gain independence under a single, federal government. During the 1950s, this led to fragmented systems of governance in which individual colonies formed their own governments while, at the same time, they participated in the creation of the federal government. Daniel Segal notes that as Trinidad and Tobago moved toward independence, "'the nation' was referentially ambiguous" because it referred to both the British colonial unit "Trinidad and Tobago" and the proposed Federation of the West Indies that included all of the British colonial possessions in the Caribbean (1989, 158). In Trinidad and Tobago, the 1958 elections were for the Federal Parliament and did not influence the composition of the Legislative Council. While the PNM's affiliated federal party, the West Indian Federal Labour Party, lost the federal elections, the PNM retained control over the government of Trinidad and Tobago. This created a situation in which the group that lost the federal elections consisted of those who were in charge of negotiating Trinidad and Tobago's political relationship to the Federation (see Mordecai 1968).

Even though a West Indian Federation would presumably craft a pan-Caribbean identity, the PNM consolidated its position by shaping a policy of national identity for Trinidad and Tobago that was inextricably linked to the PNM, and not to the Federal West Indian Federal Labour Party, of which the PNM was part (Oxaal 1982; Ryan 1972). A subtle indication of the choice to promote local identity over pan-Caribbean identity was the PNM's emphasis on the organization and promotion of national "culture," by which it meant, specifically, musical, folkloric, and Carnival traditions distinctive to Trinidad (and not even Tobago).

The version of nationalism found in the work of several prominent Caribbean thinkers indicates that some perspectives viewed nationalism as a constructed, even contrived effort of political elites from the middle class. Long before Benedict Anderson's emphasis on the nation as imagined (1983), Césaire situated its imagination in terms of class by stating "the *nation* is a bourgeois phenomenon" ([1972] 2000, 74), and Fanon described efforts to create sentimental support for a national consciousness as "the result of the intellectual laziness of the national middle-class, of its spiritual penury, and of the profoundly cosmopolitan mould that its mind is set in" (1963, 149). The words Walcott puts into the mouth of the spectral calypsonian the Mighty Spoiler strikes a similar tone, by suggesting that independence did not end colonial-style domination, but that it only changed the "colour and attire" of those locally implementing systems of domination ([1980] 1986, 433). Rohlehr says that Walcott "noted how after Independence, folk culture had been exploited politically by both the local bourgeoisie come to power and their fake-radical opponents of Black Nationalist persuasion" (1992b, 172).

The association of nationalism with a particular class position had some credence based on the network of ties between nationalist leaders. In the 1950s and 1960s, other colonies were also moving toward independence, and the personal relationships cultivated between many colonial scholarship winners in England became the foundations for diplomatic and consultant relationships. James recalls that, during his youth, there were three such scholarships awarded in Trinidad and Tobago every year (1993, 22). The scholarship winners often became connected to extraordinary networks of immigrants in Great Britain. A 1959 edition of the *Nation* newspaper printed an article titled "The Doctor Says: My University Generation" (March 27, 1959, 3), in which Williams mentions people with whom he associated during his years in England: W. Arthur Lewis (the noted development economist), Patrick Solomon (a medical doctor who served in several cabinet posts for the PNM), Hugh Springer (Governor-General of Barbados, 1984–90), Learie Constantine (a famous cricketer and the first chairman of the PNM), Jawaharlal Nehru (first Prime Minister of India, 1947–64), Kwame Nkrumah (the first head of state of Ghana, 1957–66), Nnamdi Azikiwe (the first premier of Nigeria, 1963–66), George Padmore (a noted Pan-African leader), Jomo Kenyatta (Prime Minister of Kenya, 1963–78), Amy Ashwood Garvey (Marcus Garvey's first wife), and C. L. R. James. In the case of Trinidad and Tobago, the PNM leadership boasted several scholarship winners, including Eric Williams, Patrick Solomon, and A. N. R. Robinson. As early as 1956, Williams used his educational background to legitimize himself and the PNM by arguing that the new leadership of many countries consisted of well-educated scholar-politicians. He contrasted such qualifications to those of one of his opponents, T. U. B. Butler, one of the leaders of the 1937 labor strikes in Trinidad and an elected member of the Legislative Council. About Butler, Williams said that "agitation, militancy and graduation from jail do not equip a man for the tasks of government, legislation and planning" (quoted in Rohlehr 1997, 866). This attitude is consistent with what Lloyd Braithwaite described as the "illusion of greatness" shared by scholarship winners: "The student knew and conceived of himself as exceptional. The emergent nationalism which resulted from the personal identification with the West Indies did not prevent an exaggerated opinion of the social role he would play on his return home" (2001, 67).

In the process of gaining independence, then, it is not just a matter of new states, such as Trinidad and Tobago, absorbing abstract expectations of independent statehood, but it is a dynamic process in which the leaders of new states would interact with one another on a personal basis as more abstract principles of government and development emerged. In the case of Trinidad and Tobago, the contacts that Eric Williams had with the Marxist-Leninist orientation of C. L. R. James, the Pan-Africanism and Marxism of George Padmore, and the economics of W. Arthur Lewis were personal. Indeed, in his autobiography, Williams suggests that a trip to Europe while working for the International Confederation of Free Trade Unions (ICFTU) had an additional motive related to organizing the PNM: "From Brussels I proceeded to London, where my principal concern, apart from my routine work for the ICFTU, was to discuss our draft party programme and constitution with George Padmore, C. L. R. James and

Arthur Lewis" (1969, 143). Such ties and consultations clearly contributed to the sense of excitement and innovation that accompanied the
emergence of the PNM, but such ties were also victims of the PNM's
attempts at consolidating its position, and Williams's desire to be in
complete control. Padmore died in 1959; C. L. R. James resigned from the
party in 1960; and W. Arthur Lewis's economic planning models were
abandoned by Williams and the PNM during the 1970s, in favor of using
petroleum revenues to encourage economic expansion.

The image of personal greatness built on competitive achievement
gave Williams and his associates the sense of authority to define the
nation. Nationalism was crucial to achieve independence and a cornerstone of early state policies. Trinidad and Tobago accrued the symbols of
nationhood—a national anthem, bird, flower, seal, and currency. It even
gained a written history with Dr. Eric Williams's *History of the People of
Trinidad and Tobago* (1964, originally published in 1962)—his gift to the
people of Trinidad and Tobago upon independence.

✿ Forging a Nation

The state's attempts to create a sense of nationhood had to contend with
sources of division between religious, class, and ethnic groups, as well as
between rural and urban areas. The "culture" with which the national
identity would be forged included the dynamism of Carnival and calypso.
In the case of Trinidad, the link between music and political discourse was
well established before independence. The popular significance of both
Carnival and calypso included their ability to challenge hierarchy and
criticize authority. Early calypsonians engaged in political commentary
(Rohlehr 1990, 2004a, 2004d; D. Hill 1993; Regis 1999; Warner 1982),
and politicians used music in their representations of Trinidad. At the
same time, Trinidad and Tobago's colonial government had tried to impose order on music for purposes of control and propaganda (Rohlehr
2004d). This took many forms: censorship of calypso, but also, less often
explicitly noted, the use of music in governmental ceremonies, such as the
pomp and circumstance given to the arrival of colonial dignitaries, and the
singing of "God Save the King/Queen" at the beginning of the school day.

Music played a role in the formation of middle-class imaginings of the
nation. For instance, Albert Gomes, one of the major power brokers in

1950s Trinidadian politics, emphasized the value of Trinidad's music in defining its cultural contributions to the world and its creative differences from Great Britain (1974, 82–83, 95). In discussing the embracing of folklore by the Trinidadian middle class after World War II, Ivar Oxaal notes: "Before the war, from all accounts, the Trinidad middle classes, taking their cue from the European snobbery of the colonial elite, tended to view the local folk culture as something shameful. The mentality of the PNM leadership was entirely different, the product of a major transformation in social consciousness. In the post-war period the educated Trinidad middle class discovered the *artistic validity and prestige* of local folk culture" (1982, 151).

Gomes represents this as an important transformation in Trinidadian middle-class consciousness:

> It was the illiterate and semi-illiterate Negroes who kept the ancestral fires burning . . . who filled the Calypso tents with song and music in the early days before this Aristophanic art form became a tourist attraction, favoured by British and American alike, and so won at long last the approbation of the middle class educated Negro; who invented the steel band and fought and died to keep it alive so that it would become eventually a status symbol proudly adorning the drawing-rooms of the same middle-class who during its embryonic period joined forces with British officialdom in the effort to stamp it out as another culturally retrogressive influence.   (1974, 82)

Stephen Stuempfle notes that during this period, advocates in favor of the steelband, in particular, promoted the music as art rather than noise (1995, 82), and in 1949, the colonial government formed the Steel Band Committee to study steelbands and make recommendations to curb the violence associated with the bands, and under the leadership of Canon Farquhar, to urge public acceptance of steelbands (see Stuempfle 1995, 88–91).

Writing in the early 1950s on the results of this process, Braithwaite documents an important change in attitude by the colonial government that was the result of the efforts of "far-seeing individuals in the community" who worked to give the steelband "recognition by the upper classes of society" and succeeded in getting government and public support to form the Trinidad and Tobago Steelband Association in 1949, and to send a steelband to the Festival of Britain in 1951 (1954, 94).

Paralleling the growing acceptance of local music among the middle class was the proliferation of competitions sponsored by local businesses—middle-class respectability and competition seemed to arise in tandem. J. D. Elder, a folklorist who played an important role in the PNM's policies to preserve and promote folk music, said of the transformation in how local Trinidadian elites began to view calypso: "Confined at first to Negro lower class groups the calypso has grown into a song socially accepted at all levels of the Trinidad society and has become a recognized Caribbean Negro art-form in the wider world. Performance of this song in the main centres of the world's largest cities and mass-media dissemination through television and the radio transmission have captured for it a universal listening clientele" (1967, 296).

Music served as more than a means to define identity and to mobilize political support across class lines, however. Segal emphasizes that "the idiom of 'development' applied to the forging of 'national society'" and not just to economic policies (1989, 316). Segal made this point with material from 1984 to 1985, but as far back as the period of the PNM's ascension to power in the 1950s, it viewed culture as playing a crucial role in fostering economic development and political stability. While in the 1950s, the field of economics was just becoming aware of the need for models for third world development, the Caribbean had already produced two prominent pioneers in this area: Teodoro Moscoso of Puerto Rico and W. Arthur Lewis of St. Lucia. Williams admired both men, but he had been a friend of W. Arthur Lewis since 1933, when they were both students in England. Like Williams, Lewis was a winner of a colonial scholarship and earned a doctorate in Great Britain. Lewis's specialty was economic development, and his distinguished career included winning the Nobel Prize for economics in 1978. Moscoso was the architect of Puerto Rico's "Operation Bootstrap," a then-highly regarded development program. The economic models of Moscoso and Lewis were initially adopted by Trinidad and Tobago, with the PNM asking them to jointly conduct a survey on industrial development (Legislative Council 1956, 149). In addition, Williams often read extensive sections of Lewis's writings to the Legislative Council as a means of rebutting the opposition's arguments during budget debates.

In addition to his economic insights, Lewis was concerned about the type of leadership and popular support required to develop the economy of a newly independent state. According to Lewis, "Apart from government action . . . a strong sentiment of national cohesion may be helpful to economic development" (1955, 79). Uncannily anticipating Williams's leadership style, Lewis added, "The cohesive, authoritarian group will also have superior economic growth, *if the chief knows better than the individuals* the measures which growth requires" (1955, 80, emphasis original), thus laying a foundation for what Ryan calls "maximum leaders" (2003, 309). Williams was the leader of the PNM, and his control over the party seemed complete.

The challenge facing the new government of Trinidad and Tobago was great—according to Lewis's model, the country needed decisive leadership and national cohesion. A threat to both government stability and national cohesion was the fact that Trinidad and Tobago did not consist of a single people who shared a common history. Indigenous diversity predated the arrival of the Europeans (see Whitehead 1997; Figueredo and Glazier 1982; Glazier 1980; Boomert 1984; Forte 2005), and despite many claims to the contrary, the indigenous population survived (Forte 2005). Spain's colonial policies encouraged the immigration of French planters and their slaves during the late eighteenth century—a policy that was so "successful" that the predominant language in Trinidad became a French-based patois; Great Britain's policies also contributed to Trinidad's diversity, through reliance on immigrant labor—enslaved Africans, then indentured laborers from Asia, and free laborers from the Americas—that brought people to the island from the Middle East, China, Africa, the United States, other Caribbean islands, South America, and South Asia. In the early 1800s, Trinidad was also a destination for people fleeing political upheavals rendered by revolutions in France, Haiti, and on the South American mainland. Tobago and Trinidad were very different islands that did not share a common colonial history until they were unified into the same colonial administrative unit in 1889. The colonial history consequently involved conflicting political, economic, class, religious, linguistic, geographic, and ethnic interests. Even the plantation economy could not be characterized by the hegemony of the sugar industry but instead involved the political and economic competition of sugar, cocoa, and rubber plantation interests with a large number of small-scale farmers who cultivated both cash and subsistence crops and often supplemented their incomes by working on plantations. Sugar was not always the most important agricultural export. At the end of the nineteenth century through the early part of the twentieth century, cocoa overshadowed sugar. Indeed, in contrast to sugar, Trinidadian cocoa is famous, and one species of high-quality cocoa is named after the island—*Theobroma trinitario*. The plantation economy was further fragmented by ethnic and economic differences among the elites (Brereton 1979; Wood 1968). There were divisions between the British creditors and the Trinidadian planters (Lobdell 1972), as well as competition between French, British, German, and Venezuelan planters. The educational system relied on parochial schools that often created and institutionalized conflict and competition among the country's diverse religions. The attempt to "unify" the people of Trinidad and Tobago into a "nation" in the context of this overwhelming number of disunifying factors attests to the power of the idea of nationhood in the minds of those leading the two islands to independence (Segal 1989), and of those in the governments of Great Britain and the United States who had significant political, economic, and strategic interests in Trinidad, and significant influence, even control, over the move toward independence. The fact that the need for unity was then a part of widely accepted theories of economic development—theories advocated by Williams's longtime friend Lewis—created additional pressure on the PNM to create such unity.

The question of how a sense of nationalism would be created in this situation was important. As Puri observed, "If Williams is to legitimize a Trinidadian nation, he must produce it as both hybrid *and* homogenous" (2004, 48). Williams and the PNM chose to emphasize a model of the nation as defined by a negation of colonialism—an ideological act to define what the nation is not, but to beg the question of what it is. In defining nationhood based on differences between the colonizers and colonized, as Partha Chatterjee argues nationalisms commonly do, there were not the other common components of nationalism described in Chatterjee's model, namely, "'spiritual' or 'inner' aspects of culture, such as language or religion or the elements of personal and family life" (1993, 26). Instead, a very politically persuasive theory in the Anglophone Caribbean, particularly in a country such as Trinidad and Tobago that included a large South Asian population, was the cultural pluralism model articulated by the anthropologist M. G. Smith (1965). Smith was a Jamaican whose approach to understanding societies suffering from the legacy of colonialism emphasized their fragmentation and lack of shared values. The assumed lack of spiritual and inner aspects of culture among those who agreed with M. G. Smith did not diminish their politically felt need for cohesion, however.

Williams's astute choice was to define cohesion on the basis of negating colonialism with a clear, local aesthetic component. This strategy was powerfully and poetically manifested in his speech "Massa Day Done." In this address, he said, "Massa day done connotes a political awakening and a social revolution" (Williams [1962] 1993, 239), and then he continued to contrast the PNM's progressivism with "massa," whom he associated with racism, plantation monopolies, and exploitation. As Cudjoe says of this speech: "Williams contrasted the old era of slavery and colonialism with the new era of internal self-government" (1993, 79). Yet, while rejecting "massa," massa's cultural heritage was still present. Instead of accommodation, though, there was adoption, with stylistic modifications, of European cultural forms and traditions. This was coupled with attempts to be innovative and to achieve supremacy at these forms. Such is the case with the Nobel Prize–winning writers Derek Walcott (a St. Lucian with close ties to Trinidad) and V. S. Naipaul. In another example, James's discussion of West Indian cricket (1993) documents an example of this process in which the colonized, through skill and innovation, beat the colonizers in their own game. Rather than ancient monuments or revolutionary heroism, the image of Trinidad and Tobago crafted by the PNM emphasized aesthetics as its substance—music, literature, poetry, and Carnival were held up as artistic contributions equal to those of any nation in the world.

Early Cultural Policy Goals: Defining a Nation Aesthetically

The transformation from collective innovation and spontaneity to obsessive control through hierarchical organization took place during the period between 1956 and the late 1960s. The integration of culture and economics is striking in this process, as is the gradual move away from an emphasis on economic planning to an emphasis on organizing and controlling music and folklore. Popular culture thus became a central concern of governmental planning. Writing of Williams's legacy as a political leader, Gordon K. Lewis said, "Dr. Williams' more unique contribution was to engineer a remarkable marriage between the creole intellectual and the colonial crowd, founded on his belief that in colonial societies searching for a new identity politics and culture must travel hand in hand, so that the political leader also feeds the infant indigenous culture" (G. Lewis 1968, 213).

The tone of this effort was set by the *Nation*, the PNM's party newspaper. James became editor of this paper in 1958 and changed its name to the *Nation* from the *PNM Weekly*. On the first page of the renamed paper was a list of goals, including: "We wish to make ourselves the centre of those artistic and creative activities which will be the inevitable result of the intense political life through which our Federation is passing" (*Nation*, December 8, 1958). Elder described the PNM government as one "whose policy recognized popular song as 'culture of the people' and viewed the calypsonian's art as a national asset" (1967, 132). The links between economics and popular culture for the PNM-led government were explicit, as the draft of the Five Year Plan for 1969–73 states:

> The promotion of culture and the creative arts as in the specific circumstances of Trinidad and Tobago has both instrumental and intrinsic value. The instrumental value of the creation of a national culture is that it promotes the feeling of a national identity and sense of solidarity which provides the basis for achieving the goal of purposeful national economic and social development. . . .
>
> The intrinsic value of national culture derives from two main considerations. First, a tiny country such as Trinidad and Tobago can never, and should not hope to make its mark in the world by its economic accomplishments alone. That kind of achievement can safely be left to other countries. *Our accomplishments as a Nation will have to be judged in the main by other criteria such as the excellence of our unique cultural achievements.* Second, and more important, we have for historical reasons been deprived of a secure sense of identity deriving from the awareness of a coherent widely-shared collective past. Only the conscious development of a collective culture can under these circumstances give the individual a feeling of identity with and participation in the wider society.   (Government of Trinidad and Tobago 1969, 400, emphasis added)

By the promoting of the national anthem, the fostering of folk musical traditions through the Best Village Competition, and the managing of

Carnival, calypso, and steelband music through the state-run Carnival Development Committee, the state, led by Williams, followed a complex path that linked aesthetic achievement to economic development and to crafting an international reputation.

The prominence given to culture faced early opposition. In 1956, legislative councilor Victor Bryan complained about the emphasis given to the Department of Culture seemingly over old-age pensions:

> Even $1.00 would have helped; but no, "we have got to have more research on this," but at the same time you come down arbitrarily with a Department of Culture. No research necessary for that one!
>
> What do you do with a Department of Culture? Where does that come in? It comes in after, not before. That culture thing is one that can stand some examination instead of the Government being so haphazard about it.   (Legislative Council 1956, 450–51)

The importance of music and Carnival was not simply political but a melding of political expediency with personal sentiments. It is clear that leaders within the PNM were fans of calypso and steelband music (Stuempfle 1995, 116–18) and that some had actively participated in Carnival. Such personal tastes led to calypso and steelband music being represented as "national" musics, while Indian and Spanish musical traditions were not granted a similar status. This practice persisted and continues to create controversy over what is included and what is excluded from what is presented as the "core or 'official' cultural ensemble" of Trinidad and Tobago (Ryan 1999, 26). As with many issues, Williams set the tone for the party. On the eve of independence, an amusing interview between the *Nation* and Williams demonstrates the significance of Carnival (even above cricket!) in his presentation of himself:

> **The Premier**: Everything has been subordinated to the preparation for independence at three levels: government, community, and party.
> *The Nation*: Will you have any time then for international cricket?
> **The Premier**: Sorry, but that is how it is. There is a time for everything and everything must be in its place. So if it happens that cricket is on during the period when everyday must be given to the preparation for independence as the first priority . . . As a matter of fact, I have been invited but have written to express my regret at not being able to attend, for all social engagements must be cut to the bone until this first priority is cleared out of the way.

The Nation: And what about Carnival Mr. Premier. Does this mean that you will also miss the Carnival weekend celebrations?

The Premier: Well, I have never missed any of the functions and in view of the emphasis placed on the promotion of indigenous culture . . . I shall not miss this year's functions either. As a matter of fact, I can well recall my own masquerading days, when in Robin Hood and His Merry Men ours was the band of the year, though I as Robin Hood never got to know who was my Maid Marian for the day.   (February 9, 1962)

The emphasis on steelbands and calypso involved a complex mixture of factors that included commercial interests and the reputation these forms of music were gaining in Great Britain and the United States, the countries that identified themselves as having a paternal relationship to all English-speaking Caribbean nations. In the case of Trinidad, the emergence of the PNM and the beginning of self-rule occurred at the same time as the growth in global awareness of steelband music and calypso. By the time Trinidad and Tobago's constitutional convention met, Harry Belafonte had gained popularity in the United States by performing Caribbean songs, including calypsos, and steelbands were beginning to go on international tours.

It is no surprise that the PNM's leadership adopted these musics as the core of cultural traditions presented internationally (Stewart 1986, 305). This included the use of steelbands in official ceremonies to greet foreign dignitaries (Stuemfple 1995, 120). The international presentation of certain cultural traditions had effects within Trinidad, namely, in that international recognition reinforced local promotion and financing of calypso and steelband music. With regard to steelband music, Stuempfle describes a master narrative in which the music was transformed "from a widely condemned form of grass-roots leisure into a respected national art and symbol" (1995, 3), and as he notes, it was not simply the government appropriating the music, but also the musicians asserting their cultural significance (1995, 124).

As Gayatri Chakravorty Spivak (1988) and Chatterjee (1993) have argued, the elites who promote national identities often are influenced by ties with European or North American societies. The growing global market for calypso and steelband music gave them international legitimacy, and thereby influenced the PNM leadership's decision to adopt them as important components of national images. At the same time, there were other forms of postcolonial paternalism and mentoring tied to other global economic and political interests, such as multinational corporations and the U.S. government. While these influences affected Trinidadian policy makers, they did not work directly on the Trinidadian population. Instead, both the internal and external policy makers worked on the assumption that state directives and state-appropriated symbols conveyed meanings that were internalized by the population. This was a naive psychological model about the motivations and attitudes of Trinidadians, particularly about the Indian Trinidadians who felt disenfranchised by the PNM.

The use of music in defining national identity was part of a tangled web of personal ties between colonial scholarship winners, increased valuing of popular culture by the Trinidadian middle classes, the need to affirm the PNM's and Williams's legitimacy to lead the nation, anticolonial sentiments, pride in certain musical forms because of their growing international recognition, and the desire to enter the community of nations with symbols of nationhood—a distinctive and proud history, internationally renowned contributions to the arts, a flag, a national anthem, a national bird, and a national flower. Resonating with James's analyses of cricket (1986, 1993), becoming a nation involved appropriating the forms that other nations employed, but combining them with a distinctively Trinidadian aesthetic that emphasized both Trinidad's uniqueness and its international importance in music and art. This was important because, as Segal notes, "with decolonization, the 'mother country' and 'the colony' became 'foreign' nations to each other" (1989, 169). This created a contradiction between a hierarchical logic that was colonial but persisted after independence, and a logic of equality based on the idea of joining the community of nations as an independent country (1989, 174), and this fostered a drive to present to the world a distinctive Trinidadian aesthetic, and the aesthetic practices that were privileged in this presentation of the nation to the world were those associated with Carnival. To borrow a distinction created by Daniel Miller (1994), this involved transforming Carnival from a transient aesthetic that emphasized the moment, to a transcendent aesthetic that captured the past, present, and future of the nation. The use of Carnival in this way is at odds with how most Trinidadians participate in Carnival (Segal 1989, 255–56).

❧ Aesthetic/Political Institutions

These multiple influences seemed, for a short period in the 1950s and 1960s, to create a comprehensive policy for fostering national unity and identity. The elements of this model are a mixture of Williams's creative mind, ideas he obtained from friends such as Lewis, Padmore, and James, emulation of how nationhood was modeled in countries such as the United States and Great Britain, and the political and economic support from those countries and multinational corporations. The model for defining the nation that Williams and the PNM promoted, then, was produced in a dynamic, structured global environment in which other political and economic entities, such as the United States and United Kingdom, assumed themselves to be in a paternal, mentoring role (see Pastor 1992). The model set about constructing symbols of nationhood but also emphasized institutions for communicating these symbols to the populace. The symbols emphasized Trinidad's distinctive aesthetic traditions, and the institutions emphasized local organizations, such as village councils and adult education centers.

The policies adopted by Williams during the early independence period reflected Lewis's ideas about local development—a concern about balancing rural and urban needs. Lewis (1955) warned that lack of balance between economic development in rural and urban areas would generate uncontrollable inflation, movement of people to the cities, and food shortages that would result in greater importation of food and loss in foreign exchange. Recognizing that newly independent governments had a shortage of capital with which to finance rural development, Lewis suggested voluntary community development as an alternative to large government expenditures—as he said, "An alternative way of getting capital works done, without inflation or taxation, is to persuade people to work on them without payment . . . this is indeed feasible in rural areas, if the works in question are of strictly local interest, and if they are likely to benefit nearly everyone in the village" (1955, 219). In this model, the government provides supervision and raw materials, but a community-based organization provides the labor. Such community-based organizations could also serve as the basis for building national cohesion out of local cooperative efforts.

These policies also allowed for government to influence local affairs through patronage. This affirms the cynical view of nationalism in relationship to "culture" found in Césaire and Fanon—a perspective that sees such cultural policies as shallow efforts at manipulation. Echoing this cynicism, Rohlehr states about Trinidad, " 'Culture,' as perceived by Williams as 'commandant' of the intellectual ruling class, became a manipulable lever in an elaborate machinery of patronage on the part of the controlling elite and clientelism on the part of the common folk" (1997, 868). Folk culture, particularly music, took on a large, practical political significance.

In the PNM's plans, village councils filled the roles of fostering economic development and being conduits for political patronage to flow to the local level. These local governance bodies brought together local economic development initiatives, community improvement initiatives, adult education programs, and the cultivation of "national culture" through folklore. To encourage these functions and to support the councils, the government constructed community centers. These buildings were to be used by village councils to integrate local communities to encourage participation in national cultural celebrations, and to link local economic development to national development (Williams [1964] 1981, 219–20, [1970] 1993, 277; House of Representatives 1953–64, 240–48; National Planning Commission 1963, 1; Government of Trinidad and Tobago 1969, 379–81; Craig 1985, 181). These centers served as the seat of village councils that were to organize the infrastructural and cultural activities associated with community development: "community centres, by virtue of their function, became widely used and helped to integrate the villages, promote them, and express village solidarity" (London 1991, 256). During this period, Elder played an important role working on community development for the PNM government. He took on many roles that linked music and community development. He worked with the government's Adult Education Centre; he conducted research for the Community Development Department of the Ministry of Local Government on the relationship between youth gangs and steelbands in Port of Spain; he organized for the government an exhibition titled *Origin and Development of Carnival Calypso and Steelband in Trinidad*; and he was a field organizer for the Best Village Competition.

In the 1958 address of Governor Beetham to the Legislative Council—a speech often written by the ruling party—the government articulated the policy of linking the Education Extension Service to fostering village councils. These local councils encouraged the development of handicrafts, promoted local folklore, and, as the governor's speech noted, "The Village Councils have dòne much to promote unity and harmony in the villages on a non-party, non-sectarian and non-racial basis" (Beetham 1958, 45). Williams saw these councils and community centers as playing fundamental roles in, as Williams said, "developing the art and culture of the place" ([1964] 1981, 221). Furthermore, the community centers were supposed to integrate villages and to incorporate villages "into the nation" (221). Multinational corporations such as Texaco, and Tate and Lyle provided monetary assistance for the building of community centers, and Chase Manhattan provided advisers and money. In addition, then, as now, the village councils often coordinated local development projects and recruited the workers for these projects. Consequently, the community centers and village councils played an important part in integrating local communities into national economic and cultural development.

Shortly after independence in 1962, Williams undertook his "Meet the People" tour, in which he promoted the role of village councils in economic and cultural development. This tour seemed to indicate a comprehensive approach to rural development that would use local community centers as bases for operations, and village councils as managers of educational, vocational, and cultural programs. Associated with the tour was the proposal for the Better Village Programme. As the *Second Five Year Plan* (1964–68) describes this project, it is "designed to improve village amenities (principally by mobile services in the field of health and libraries), to dignify community life and strengthen community organizations and to stop the drift from village to town" (National Planning Commission 1963, 1). The construction of community centers played an important role in the Better Village Programme: Williams, in addressing Parliament, stated that "the new policy is that the Government through the Better Village Programme will deliberately go out of its way and start a large-scale construction of community centres" (House of Representatives 1963–64, 243–44). For a short period, community organizations were viewed as linchpins in a comprehensive political and development plan that tied together industrialization, infrastructural development, foreign capital, improved and expanded free education, and the celebration of folkloric traditions.

Williams modeled his economic plan on Operation Bootstrap, the development program applied to Puerto Rico by Moscoso and synthesized into the development models associated with W. Arthur Lewis. Operation Bootstrap encouraged foreign industries to build plants in Puerto Rico through significant tax and labor incentives (Carrington 1971; Thomas 1988). Lewis's model emphasized such industrialization by invitation (1950, 1954, 1955), and as one economist put it, Lewis's "one big idea" was theorizing that one major resource that "less developed countries" could use to attract industrial investments was their unlimited supplies of labor (Findlay 1982, 3).

While Williams's emulation of Operation Bootstrap is well known, there are also striking parallels between Puerto Rico's Operation Serenity and Williams's efforts to exert state influence over music and control in Trinidad and Tobago—a policy of connection between cultural aesthetic traditions and economic development. In this, he also had agreement with Lewis, who argued that "a society without creative arts is a cultural desert. I would commend to our statesmen that they put a lot more money into the creative arts department of our secondary schools" (1973, 302). Arlene Dávila describes Operation Serenity as "Operation Bootstrap's cultural and social counterpart" (1997, 34). This government program promoted and consequently attempted to define Puerto Rican culture through folklore, music, and festivals. It led to the founding of institutions to support and guide "national culture," and it created structures by which sponsorship from multinational corporations could be attracted. The efforts made by the PNM government were quite similar.

Since Carnival, dance, and musical traditions represented Trinidadian creativity and resistance to foreign domination, these traditions were to be fostered at the community level, in order to integrate communities into the nation (Williams [1970] 1993, 277, 308–10; Williams-Connell 1993, 382; Prime Minister's Best Village Trophy 1967). A particular pattern would soon emerge, in which the government obtained funding from multinational corporations in order to fund aesthetic competitions, which would lead to impressions that the competitions received greater attention and support than rural development. This was most prominent in the steelband movement, where many steelbands became known not only by their names but also by the names of the corporations that sponsored them (e.g., the Amoco Renegades), but this approach was also applied to policies directed toward rural areas such as Anamat.

✿ From Better Village Programme to Best Village Competition

The Better Village Programme, implemented in 1963, was grounded in Lewis's ideas of rural development. From the outset, the program encouraged local initiative through village councils to improve local communities in many ways ranging from infrastructural improvements of roads and water supplies to educational initiatives and cultural celebrations, and the village councils became the managers of the government's "crash" programs to reduce unemployment (Stuemfple 1995, 143). An important component of this program was the Best Village Trophy. One component of this trophy was competitions related to Trinidadian traditions and folklore. In fact, the use of the Better Village Programme to create jobs and improve rural infrastructures came to be overshadowed by the Best Village Competition and similar cultural contests that emphasize talent and artistic performance rather than infrastructural improvements. Susan Craig reports, "The officers in the field were 'bogged down,' as one supervisor put it, with organizing the various competitions initiated by the Prime Minister: Best Village Trophy Competition, National Youth Arts and Craft Exhibition, Village Olympics, Food Fair. This left little time for what they understood by community development, and resulted in what a senior officer called the 'malaise' of the Division" (1985, 181). Indeed, Craig's indictment of the Better Village Programme was that it produced "bread (crumbs) and circuses" (1985, 181). Offering a more positive interpretation of the legacy of these competitions, London argues that they "brought about a renewal of folk activities," including parang, drumming, dance, and Carnival characters (1991, 257–59). Elder noted the effect of the increased exposure of "night-club entertainers" to folk music led to experimentation (1967, 267). The innovative use of folk music traditions by Trinidadian musicians continues—an example is Super Blue's use of Shango and Spiritual Baptist rhythms in his popular socas.

Williams's eventual emphasis on cultural competitions above Lewis's initial vision of community development is consistent with the government's practices of harnessing cultural traditions to define national identity and to increase national cohesion. Rohlehr describes this emphasis on cultural traditions: "Partially located in the program for Community

Development, culture fitted into the system of local government as *real-politik*, in which the party in office dispenses jobs, contracts, and training for the price of political support" (1997, 868). Rohlehr continues,

> "Culture" was also aligned with Education and later with Sports. Fostering "culture" involved the recovery and rehabilitation of the steadily waning pastoral folk culture which had declined with the spread of education in English during the last quarter of the 19th century when the older languages of Creole French and Spanish went out of currency. Languages in which most of the folk music, narratives, and humor of Old Trinidad had been conducted had virtually died or gone underground or become the property of cloistered rural communities such as Lopinot, Paramin, or the deep South. While dying languages could not be resuscitated, old traditional folk dances were rescued and taught to younger generations albeit in stylized form.   (1997, 868)

In the February 21, 1959, issue of the *Nation*, James wrote that there was a link between "entertainment," "sport," and social and economic development, and he concluded that entertainment and sport were "a necessary part of civilized life" (5).

The cultural competitions succeeded in creating local pride and cohesion where the development programs failed by creating local competition and division. The shift to emphasize "cultural policy" was possibly a response to a weakness in Lewis's model of fostering rural development through community organizations and voluntary labor: even if labor is voluntary, local competition for the managerial positions and resources the government provides tends to undermine local cohesion—this was a pattern in village councils throughout Trinidad and Tobago (Craig 1985). The success of the cultural policies no doubt contributed to their growing importance in relationship to the local community-development policies that were fraught with conflict.

The Best Village Trophy was given to a village thought "to be the best in Trinidad and Tobago in some particular field of village activity which is designated by the Prime Minister" (Prime Minister's Best Village Trophy 1967, 2). In 1967, this trophy evolved into the Best Village Competition, in which villages competed against one another for prizes in folk literature, folk music, folk dance, local foods, and folk art. Rohlehr describes this as Williams's "first grand attempt in the post-Independence era to enact part of what he had dreamed of in his 1962 statements on nation building and the creation of a coherent multiethnic society" (1997, 875). In discussing these categories, Williams stated, in his foreword to the brochure describing the competition,

> In fulfilling these categories, villagers will find themselves doing what comes naturally in a Country where people love to sing and dance; where there is opportunity to create and design each year for Carnival; where our humour and zest for living have given us a wealth of expressions and sayings, where the true flavour in the melting pot of our many races may be tasted in our cuisine.
>
> I think it is only fitting that villagers throughout Trinidad and Tobago join hand in hand to forge a common link in our nation, and preserve our traditions, beliefs, and customs.   (Prime Minister's Best Village Trophy 1967, 1)

The back cover of the brochure also reveals the interest of international financial corporations in this project:

> Presented to the People of Trinidad and Tobago by
> The Chase Manhattan Bank
> The Bank of Nova Scotia
> Canadian Imperial Bank of Commerce
> Bank of London and Montreal LTD.
> First National City Bank
> The Royal Bank of Canada
> Barclays Bank D. C. O.

Aesthetics, economic development, and nation building became linked through the Best Village Competition. This connection of aesthetics, politics, and economics also linked localities to international finance capital through the medium of cultural competitions.

Carnival Competitions

The PNM-led government took charge of the administration of Carnival, by creating a "venture in cultural patriotism" directed by the Carnival Development Committee (CDC) (Stewart 1986, 306). The CDC initiated many competitions with preliminary rounds beginning several weeks before Carnival. The CDC offered financial, logistical, and marketing support for these competitions. The competitions encouraged participation, and through standards set by panels of judges, the competitions also attempted to improve the quality of the art forms. As a result, the money necessary for competing in Carnival events made many calypso tents (and consequently, many calypsonians), steelbands, and mas' bands dependent on corporate sponsorship, much of it from multinational corporations, such as Amoco, W. R. Grace, Coca-Cola, and their local subsidiaries. This sponsorship took several forms: some steelbands had corporate sponsors, many calypso tents augmented revenues with corporate advertisement, and community-based organizations sometimes obtained corporate support in the form of donations or relied indirectly on corporate support through government programs or competitions that used corporate monies. Williams used his influence on corporations and wealthy Trinidadians to encourage them to provide financial support, if not formal sponsorship, to steelbands (Dudley 2004, 84–85; Johnson 2002, 98; Liverpool 2001, 396). Control over Carnival was not merely to impose organization on it, but also to gain control over the various competitions associated with Carnival traditions. Judging moved from the hands of private interests into the supposedly unbiased hands of government appointees. As Williams stated to the Legislative Council on February 22, 1957: "A dispute has arisen between many of the leaders of Carnival bands and the persons who in the past have sponsored Carnival competitions. This dispute has threatened the disruption of the entire festivities and as Chief Minister I was approached with a request that I try to find some solution" (Legislative Council 1957, 911). This was used as the justification for the government to intervene and to put H. O. B. Wooding in charge of a committee to "put forward proposals for the re-organization of the festivities, improvement of seating accommodation, and question of prize money and so on" (911).

This did not end controversy, however. Wooding, a prominent jurist and, like Williams, a former colonial island scholarship winner, was an impressive appointment. By this period, he had served as mayor of Port of Spain, and on the board of British West Indies Airlines. Later, he would become Trinidad and Tobago's chief justice and serve on the Privy Council, the highest court in the British Commonwealth. It did not take long for conflicts over Carnival judging to emerge between Williams and Wooding. In 1958, the newspaper the *Trinidad Guardian* ceased to sponsor the Carnival Queen Competition. This contest was between the queens of masquerade bands and was a beauty competition, and it had a notorious reputation for judging "beauty" in terms of complexion. It was very different from the subsequent government-sponsored competitions, which emphasized costumes. When the *Guardian* withdrew sponsorship, Wooding's Carnival Development Committee backed a plan put forth by the Port of Spain Junior Chamber of Commerce to take over the competition. Patrick Solomon, the PNM's Minister of Education and Culture, opposed this plan, with the strong backing of Williams. Wooding and the CDC members resigned in response to what they perceived as government meddling in their development of Carnival policy. Williams then publicly berated them in the Legislative Council for supporting racial discrimination (Ryan 1990a, 117–19). From the beginning, then, even the official, government attempts to organize Carnival quickly became divisive, and concerns over racial divisions became intertwined with personal rivalries.

﷼ From Economics to Aesthetics

As many have noted, Williams's regime slowly gave up systematic economic policy planning, particularly in the wake of greatly increased oil revenues in the 1970s (Hintzen 1989; Ledgister 1998; Ryan 1989). While the government moved away from the planning models that came to be the hallmark of Lewis's work, the emphasis on cultural institutions as a means to foster national sentiments remained. This is partly because Williams remained prime minister until his death in 1981 and his party retained power until 1986. The persistence of government involvement in "culture policy" is also related to the seeming success of cultural policies, and, by the late 1980s, a shift in government economic policy toward neoliberalism, with decreasing governmental economic interventions.

In 1986, the PNM was soundly defeated by the National Alliance for Reconstruction (NAR). As the PNM had done in 1956, the NAR campaigned on a platform of national, multicultural unity. The phrase "One love," taken from Bob Marley's reggae hit of the same name, became a campaign theme for the NAR. This campaign for unity seemed publicly persuasive due to the political union of several political parties with different class and ethnic associations: the United Labor Front (ULF), an Indian-dominated party led by Basdeo Panday; the Organization for National Reconstruction (ONR), a largely middle-class and Creole party led by Karl Hudson-Phillips, a probusiness, law-and-order, former PNM official; and the Action Committee of Dedicated Citizens (ACDC), led by A. N. R. Robinson, a Tobagonian and another PNM outcast. The NAR appeared as a truly multiracial party, and its campaign based on racial equality, national sentiment, and fairness resulted in a landslide victory in which the PNM won only three seats in parliament, and one of the seats showed some signs of electoral irregularities. By 1988, the coalition of Indians and Creoles had fallen apart, and by 1989, the Indians had formed a new party, the United National Congress (UNC), led by Basdeo Panday (see Ryan 1990b). The remnants of the NAR that maintained power turned to the International Monetary Fund (IMF) to solve the government's fiscal problems, and the IMF prescribed a harsh restructuring plan, which raised taxes through a value-added tax (VAT) and continued to cut at the public-sector workforce (Ramsaran 1994). The NAR, in fact, gave up control over large components of economic planning to the IMF and was left with the greatest control over the development of sports, music, festivals, and art. Given the long-term commitment of the government to the IMF, this pattern has been continued in the subsequent governments of the PNM and the UNC. As civil services were cut due to economic restructuring, cultural competitions increased, as did attempts to provide greater temporal control over Carnival, in order to market it to tourists. Under the NAR government, the Carnival Development Committee was changed to the National Carnival Commission and given more autonomy from the government.

The involvement of the government in promoting certain Trinidadian musical forms has persisted even as different political parties have controlled the government. In 1996, the minister of culture and gender of the UNC-led government advocated that primary schools teach calypso (Ryan 1999, 67). While the government had the power to suggest such a policy, it was met with some resistance. Whereas the government funds primary education, the direct administration of many schools is in the hands of religious organizations, some of which do not wish calypso and education to mix. In Anamat, the two primary schools are sponsored by the Presbyterian Church and the Sanatan Dharma Maha Sabha, respectively. In the 1997 budget speech to parliament, a degree in music with a specialty in pan was proposed for the University of the West Indies at St.

Augustine (Ryan 1999, 64). In 1999, the government formed a Carnival Institute to encourage research on Carnival.

The issue of the relationship of music to government presentations of the nation also continues to be of interest. Before the 1995 parliamentary elections, the PNM government declared the steel pan as Trinidad and Tobago's national instrument. This was met with strong opposition by some Indian leaders. Late in 1995, the parliamentary elections resulted in a tie between the UNC and the PNM, with the NAR winning two seats. The NAR threw its support behind the UNC in order to create a coalition government led by Basdeo Panday, Trinidad and Tobago's first Indian prime minister. Soon afterward, the debate began over whether the UNC should strip the pan of its designation as the national instrument, but the UNC kept the designation and promised to promote both pan music and Carnival music (Ryan 1999, 64).

The tradition of government fostering of cultural traditions through competitions is now well established in Trinidad and Tobago and has survived several transitions. The emphasis on calypso and steel pan, in particular, has also continued. The competitions receive a great deal of media attention and often attract large crowds. Whereas the existence of these policies can be tied to the leadership of Trinidad and Tobago, these competitions and related institutions are sites of counterpoint between the people's participation in festivals and music and the government's policies. As chapter 2 shows, these policies and the events they create are not sites of the people's complicity or resistance to the policies, but of a movement between attitudes that include but are not limited to support for government's efforts, criticism of the government's rules and officials, and participation in ways that ignore the government's role.

chapter two 🐾 Bacchanalian Counterpoints
to the State

> But always you have to watch what the people do, and not
> what *you* think they ought to do.
>
> C. L. R. JAMES, *Party Politics in the West Indies*

> This consideration of violence has led us to take account of
> the frequent existence of a time lag, or a difference of rhythm,
> between the leaders of a nationalist party and the mass of the
> people.
>
> FRANTZ FANON, *The Wretched of the Earth*

Chapter 1 explored the state's effort to use music to define identity.
This chapter develops one set of contrapuntal themes—local participation in the domains the state attempted to appropriate and
control. The state emphasized particular types of institutions—community centers, Carnival competitions, and the Best Village Trophy. These
institutions became part of the fabric of Trinidadian society, and central
in the annual cycle of musical events. Rohlehr notes, "State policy, despite its obvious political pragmatism and its habitual brutality, has been
beneficial to both folk and oral traditions, raising to the surface what had
in the colonial era been submerged" (1992b, 174). The government's
various competitions focused attention, for those in Anamat, on particular musics at particular times of year: steelband music and calypso during
Carnival, then the folk musics of the Best Village competition, and finally
parang music at Christmas.

When I arrived in Anamat in 1989, the community center was the headquarters for the efforts to support and prepare a local woman for the finals in the Best Village Queen Competition, and residents built my anticipation for Carnival with tales of Panorama, the national steelband competition that takes place during the Carnival season. Even though these government-created institutions now temporally punctuate the year, this does not mean that local participation in these institutions adheres to the government's intention of forging a comprehensive, unified national identity. In fact, the residents of Anamat participate in these institutions in ways that make the government's intentions peripheral.

The state also emphasizes particular musics—the national anthem, steel band music, and calypso—but in Anamat, other musics such as parang and chutney are also socially significant. This chapter shows that the institutions on which the state relied in its projects were contexts in which old antagonisms played out. It was not the state's policies toward music that had the greatest influence on shaping musical consumption in Anamat, but educational and economic policies that prompted Anamatians to distinguish between local musical traditions and national traditions and to develop a spatial differentiation in how they participated in these traditions. "National" music, such as calypso and soca, was consumed by means of recordings, radio, or venues and competitions far outside of Anamat. Local music, such as hymns, parang, and Indian music, was consumed by means of live performance in the home, church, or mandhir (Hindu temple). The state's efforts intersect with the musical participation of the residents of Anamat only at particular times and places. Outside of mandated contexts such as primary education, these times and places are at the choosing of the people in Anamat, not the state. These times and places generally involve groups of people participating, not sole individuals, so the state's efforts get refracted through the already patterned participation of people in groups.

The government's attempt to organize culture, as documented in the previous chapter, was defined early in the PNM's rule and sustained by subsequent administrations. The importance that the leaders of the Trinidadian state attributed to music was not created by them but was part of their images about Trinidad and the relational aesthetics of music embedded in these images. Through government efforts, music became central to images of the nation. Because of this, politicians' efforts to harness the power of music seem reasonable, but in many ways, they were grabbing a tiger by the tail. While political elites valued music, Trinidadian music does not have a history of adoration for political elites and their efforts at manipulation and control. The Carnival riots of the nineteenth century were a clear indication that when the government took an oppositional stance toward Carnival and its music, the government failed (Alonso 1990; Brereton 1975; Cowley 1996). The colonial government's attempt to quash the use of drums created a context for creative innovation in percussion instruments, which lead to the invention of the pan (Stuempfle 1995). Censorship efforts encouraged creative innuendos and double entendres in lyrics (D. Hill 1993; Rohlehr 1990, 2004d). Williams and the PNM were fully aware of the ability of music to elude political control, and it is part of the legend around Williams that when he heard something he did not like, he turned down the volume on his hearing aid.

Still, the PNM's leaders assumed that their legitimacy based on anti-colonial efforts would give them influence that colonial officials lacked. They were wrong, but instead of being opposed, their efforts at control-ling and organizing Trinidadian music were often ignored or circum-vented. In fact, as Segal notes, "in exercising authority over Carnival . . . the state has appeared not as an agent of 'the people,' but as an intrusive 'power' engaged in acts of illegitimate appropriation" (1989, 238). Indeed, it seems that music continued to have greater power over shaping the politicians' images of the nation than politicians had in shaping the image of Trinidad through music. To represent this pattern as power and resis-tance is too conceptually constraining. Instead, it is better described in terms of dialogues in which one or both parties occasionally chose to keep speaking but stopped listening. Based on his work on Trinidadian music and artistic expression, Rohlehr says: "My maps into the interior universe of feeling, desire, perceived horizons, and dreams were the remarkable flowerings of poems, plays, short stories, and pamphlets which pointed towards directions and choices that were diametrically opposite to or, at the very least, startlingly different from the cultural preferences of the State" (1997, 869). Rohlehr's representation attributes more catalytic agency to people than to the terms *resistance, response,* or *reaction.* It also covers both cooperative, complicit relationships and openly hostile ones. The relationship of people to music and music to the state is not one-dimensional but is a counterpoint of a wide range of feelings and ideas.

Studies of government appropriations of aesthetic production suggest that the goals of these policies are rarely achieved in the way they are originally conceived. Instead, the goals evolve and the policies produce unintended consequences. For Puerto Rico, Arlene Dávila (1997) shows that the diversity of popular experiences does not consistently reinforce but often contradicts state-sponsored messages. For Venezuelan festivals, David Guss (2000) demonstrates how the state's entry into efforts to support and define festive performances generates conflicts over authenticity and the relationship of particular folkloric forms to particular segments of the population. In discussing Costeño music in Colombia, Peter Wade (2000) demonstrates that while the government formed a cultural policy that viewed and promoted music and folklore as a source of cohesiveness, the success Costeño music has reaped from this policy has occurred because it can have multiple meanings associated with it— because under a veneer of homogeneity is diversity. This diversity is not just between people but is something that unfolds over time among the same people.

The vantage point from which I was immersed in this play of organization and spontaneity is the rural community of Anamat from 1989 to 1998. The governmental change from NAR to PNM to UNC during this time, punctuated by an attempted coup d'état in 1990 and an electoral tie in 1995, makes this period fascinating, even though my timing was purely accidental. The locale of Anamat is a marginal and seemingly unusual vantage point for this process. Located in the bush, Anamat is a place about which most Trinidadians are unaware. Still, the nature of power is to find its way into even the nooks and crannies to which some have escaped to hide from its reach. A vantage point located in the seemingly marginal locale of Anamat allows one to see the energy of the government's efforts and how this energy becomes dissipated at the local level. Yet, there is another dimension of significance to viewing these processes from the bush rather than from town. The significance given to cultural politics in rural development that emerged out of Lewis's models and was honed as the Better Village Programme became more focused on folklore than on economics. This process is not seen as easily in the cities as in the rural areas.

Anamat's community center was constructed with great fanfare and was commemorated by the personal presence and blessing of Eric Williams during one of his "meet the people" tours in the early 1960s. The center soon became a major prize in the conflicts among Village Council members. It eventually became a place to hold occasional meetings, the Roman Catholic Harvest festival in October, and usually an Indian-sponsored fete sometime during May, June, or July—a fate marginally better than how Louis Regis describes that of most centers: "The centres were systematically looted leaving only open spaces for interested parties to rehearse for the prime minister's Better Village Competition" (1999, 142). The center's gradual deterioration was a symbol of the deterioration of the function of the Village Council, primarily due to racial bickering and personal animosities that began soon after the group was first formed (Freilich 1960, 98–100). As one former Village Council member said to me in 1990, "If you run for an organization in [Anamat], everyone will complain and cuss at you." Others recalled that whenever the Village Council was active, it favored one ethnic group over another.

The period from 1956 to 1998 saw major changes in the local participation in musical events. During the 1950s, music in Anamat was extremely local in origin—the parang tradition of string band music was particularly strong. Based on Elder's study of musical change in Trinidad, the link between music and community was strong throughout the island (1967). Even Carnival was celebrated within Anamat, rather than with masses of residents traveling throughout the island. The development projects that improved the road from the 1950s through the 1970s and provided electricity to most of the community by the early 1970s altered the ways in which people living in Anamat were exposed to music. Travel throughout the island became easier, and more people began to attend parties outside of Anamat's immediate surroundings. Radio and television provided additional means of listening to music, but these media were quickly recognized as being under state control and thereby not playing music critical of the government. To learn of this music, residents turned not to attending calypso tents but to reading the weekly newspapers, many of which took political stances critical of the government and savored reporting politically critical calypsos. This practice has continued for many who engage in a weekly ritual of acquiring these newspapers and discussing the stories in them, particularly around Carnival time and elections. These papers, particularly the *Mirror* and the *Bomb*, are known for their critical tones. *Punch*, another weekly that focused mostly on entertainment news, was also a major source of information during Carnival. When the residents of Anamat decided to protest the poor condition of the main road in 1991, it was to this weekly media that they turned. They were particularly interested in reporters from the *Bomb*, since that paper, at the time, was particularly critical of the government and interested in covering grassroots protests.

The government's educational and economic policies also had unintended effects. The policy of providing free secondary school education to those who passed the Common Entrance Examination was a cornerstone of Williams's educational policies. The hegemony of the importance of education motivated many children and their parents to work very hard to pass the test and to secure a spot in one of the island's secondary schools, but Anamat had no secondary schools. This meant that children had to attend these schools outside the village, but since the road was bad and transportation unreliable, for many children this meant leaving Anamat to stay with people who lived near the school. Sometimes these houses were owned by relatives; sometimes they were not, and often the arrangement involved paying money for the child to stay.

In the 1970s, the government's investment of oil revenues to subsidize industry further enhanced this trend of youth moving away from Anamat very early. The generation that had first benefited from the policy on free secondary school discovered that the best-paying jobs were located in Arima or Port of Spain, not in Anamat, and often this led to their beginning their working life in their midteens with jobs of an hour or more commute from Anamat.

These residential consequences of governmental policy also influenced the way in which Anamatians participated in music. Many developed allegiances to steelbands where they lived and worked, and attendance of Carnival parties increased immensely during this time. During this time, the celebration of Carnival in Anamat waned in favor of traveling to celebrations outside the village. In terms of how music was consumed, this was important. The localized identity of the factory workers in Arima made Arima-native Kitchener a favorite and turned his song "Trouble in Arima" into a favorite sung at parties. The early 1970s Road Marches associated with Sparrow, such as "Drunk and Disorderly," became the most cherished songs that were also quickly adopted to cuatro, a four-string relative of the ukulele associated with the traditional Trinidadian music of parang.

The current consumption patterns were set by the forced mobility associated with work and education during the 1960s and 1970s. The demise of local Carnival celebrations in favor of traveling throughout the island dates to this time, as well. This turned the revelry of Carnival from a community celebration to an outward-looking celebration where awareness and ties to family, friends, and neighbors in a sea of strangers became important. While Carnival received a boost from state patronage, other musical traditions, particularly parang and traditional Indian music, remained profoundly locally oriented. Government sponsorship was typically tied to national competitions, and calypso music was increasingly oriented toward making commercially successful recordings. The local traditions had their own competitions, but these tended to be sponsored by local businesses, such as recreation clubs or rum shops. They also emphasized the live, participatory performance, rather than the crafting of recorded versions of songs.

This is reflected in the commentaries on Carnival music versus local music. As musical products that are both Trinidadian and external to the community, calypso and soca have become subject to critical attention and evaluations that are not applied to the localized folk music forms. As the political economy of calypso and soca drove the music toward marketable formats and themes (Rohlehr 1998), and as the state continued to try to appropriate music for the purpose of defining a nation (Scher 2003; Regis 1999; Rohlehr 1998), the local engagement with the music as a means of defining local identity dwindled. At the same time, there was sustained concern for the preservation of local musics. When the local Hindu youth formed a musical group for the performance of bhajans, it was greeted with support and local pride from both Hindus and non-Hindus. With regard to parang, another locally performed music, the musicians expressed great concern that the distinctive local virtuosity— which includes a particular strumming style attributed to one local man— be maintained. To play the chords on the cuatro was not sufficient; one needed to be capable of playing the chords in the local style.

Many of those from Anamat with whom I discussed soca music said that they were tired of songs calling on revelers to wave their flags, roll their bam-bams, and jump—attitudes that, based on Scher's work in Port of Spain (2002, 2003) and Rohlehr's close analysis of calypso (1998), seem to be shared by people in other parts of the island. At the same time, it should be noted, calypsonians and musicians feel pressure to record songs about waving flags, rolling bam-bams, and jumping, because these songs sell more copies more widely than local Trinidadian themes— indeed, most of the recording and distribution of soca music takes place outside of Trinidad (Liverpool 1994), and increasingly, the major markets are outside of Trinidad, as well. This seems like a contradiction: if the music-consuming public is tired of songs asking revelers to wave flags, roll bam-bams, and jump, then why are these songs the ones that are purchased and played with great frequency? This is part of the counterpoint of Trinidadian music as it exists at the level of consumption, and this parallels the distinction between calypsos to which one listens and music to which one dances.

The global market for Trinidadian music has also had its role to play in consumption. In fact, more people participate in, or are spectators at, the soca-dominated Brooklyn Carnival (about 2 million) than reside in the entire country of Trinidad and Tobago (estimated at 1.3 million by the Central Statistics Office of Trinidad and Tobago). The attempt of the National Carnival Commission to exercise control over Carnival was also met with derision. One man told me, "They [the NCC] don't comply with regulations, yet they blame steelbandsmen and calypsonians, which isn't a fact at all—they should never be blamed. I was hearing them saying they was going to charge the steelbandsmen something like $100 or something like that for fifteen minutes or thirty minutes after starting time. One commentator was saying, 'I wonder how they going to do that.'" This man's opinion is confirmed by Scher's description of a sit-down strike by members of the masquerade band Poison. This band is large, and on Carnival Tuesday in 1999, a large segment of the band was waiting in the judging area for the arrival of one of their sound trucks. As Scher describes it: "After some exasperated minutes the NCC decided to issue a warning to the revelers to move on and let the next band on the stage. In response, the mass of mostly women revelers simply sat down in an impromptu strike. After some pleading by Carnival authorities and much confusion three mounted policemen herded the reluctant band members off the stage" (2002, 474). The jaded responses to government efforts to control music and Carnival echo the cynicism found in the writing of James, Césaire, and Fanon about the ability of political elites to lead in the domain of aesthetics. The divisions between local and national music that government policies unintentionally fostered make the government's nationalistic musical goals seem disconnected from locally embedded musical experiences.

🐾 The National Anthem

Even the stately national anthem indicates a counterpoint of division and unity. In keeping with the global ideas of how a national anthem should sound, the melody and rhythms of the song are staid, even, and subdued, in contrast to the vibrant polyrhythms of Trinidad's other musical forms. The lyrics are hymnlike, as opposed to the wordplay found in calypso. Its solemnity does not seem to represent Trinidadian musical identities. In addition, the temporal unfolding of the song is, itself, a play in contrasts—a minor key modulated into a related major key as the memories of the past become modulated into future possibilities. The process by which the anthem was selected is an interesting case of an attempt by the state to define national sentiment.

As Trinidad and Tobago was approaching independence in 1962, choosing all the accoutrements of independence was an issue (Mohammed 2002). Among other things, the new nation needed a flag, a national bird, a national flower, a coat of arms, and a national anthem. To generate pride in the nation and to encourage popular participation, the creation of a national anthem was turned into a competition in which people would craft lyrics and submit them for review. The competition was followed nationally, as lyrics that had been entered were printed in newspapers, along with editorials on what characteristics the anthem should contain.

In August 1962, the winner of the national anthem competition was announced: Patrick Castagne. The anthem that was chosen musically charted the movement from fragmentation and colonialism to diversity, solidarity, and independence. Musically, the anthem has two parts. The first lyrics are accompanied by music in a minor key:

> Forged from the love of liberty
> In the fires of hope and prayer
> With boundless faith in our destiny
> We solemnly declare

The second and largest part of the anthem parallels the first portion, but instead of being in a minor key, it is in the related major key. In addition, while the first portion of the anthem begins in the past tense, the part sung in a major key is entirely in the present tense:

> Side by side we stand
> Islands of the blue Caribbean sea
> This our native land
> We pledge our lives to thee
> Here every creed and race find an equal place
> And may God bless our nation
> Here every creed and race find an equal place
> And may God bless our nation

The musical shift from minor to major keys is a clever marker of transformation from the past of colonialism, in which the nation was "forged from the love of liberty," to present independence based on cooperation and equality, but not on homogeneity.

National anthems are supposed to evoke nationalist sentiments around a shared image of the nation. The national anthem of Trinidad and Tobago is no different. Yet, as is the case with popular calypsos, only fragments of the anthem seem to elicit a patterned response. The most important fragment of Trinidad and Tobago's national anthem is "where every creed and race find an equal place"—a line in the major-key portion of the anthem that is repeated twice for emphasis. This line would have little significance in a homogenous society. Its profound significance arises from the perceived and felt ethnic and racial divisions of the people of Trinidad and Tobago. Through this fragment, Trinidad's diversity is presented as a symbol of nationalist pride. This form of national representation is far different from that found in many European and North American presentations of nation; namely, instead of neglecting diversity in the service of representing homogeneity, Trinidad and Tobago's national anthem foregrounds diversity of religion and race. This contrast can be played out in representations of history, representations for tourists, and representations made to businesses (see Segal 1994).

But is the national anthem effective? Does it generate nationalist sentiments? By itself, the answer is no—it represents an idea of unity that many desire but that many feel has not been achieved. As Deosaran says of the anthem, "we received this national ideal in 1962 but since then we have been struggling day by day to put it into full practice" (1995, 176).

The use of the idea of cosmopolitanism in heated racial disputes does not calm but heightens tensions through accusations of "racialism." Indeed, these two ideas are closely conceptually linked. The phrase "Trinidad is a cosmopolitan country," which schoolchildren repeat as a mantra, and which many people use to represent the nation, is often accompanied by a discussion of racial diversity and tolerance. Sometimes discussions of cosmopolitanism do not lead to the idea of unity the government's discourse implies. One "old head," as elderly Trinidadians are often called, commented to me: "The whole island is mixed, and that is why they call it a cosmopolitan island. Long time, everyone lived as brother and sister, but now, the island is cosmopolitan and mixed up. There used to be plenty unity, but now there is so much hatred." Later in the same interview, this man concluded, "Williams shit up the country." Charges of "racialism" emphasize racial diversity but indicate intolerance. In these two representations, diversity is the common thread, with tolerance as a moral dimension, and with cosmopolitanism at one end and racialism at the other.

The national anthem cannot overcome the well-documented racial basis of political party support. Since universal adult suffrage in 1946, politics have been profoundly influenced by racial antagonisms. As John La Guerre (1972) shows for the 1946 elections, even at this time, candidates began to use their racial backgrounds in explicit appeals for votes. In districts dominated by Indians, Indian candidates explicitly made reference to their race as a qualification for representation. In districts dominated by Africans, African candidates made similar appeals (Ryan 1972; Hintzen 1989; Oxaal 1982).

By the late 1950s, Trinidadian politics was dominated by two political parties, each one with a political base based on racial affiliations. The People's National Movement (PNM) claimed an initial multiracial appeal as a nationalist party, but within the party there was mistrust of Indians and white Creoles by the African leadership, expressed in overt attacks on these groups (Ryan 1972, 138–46). When the Democratic Labor Party emerged in close association with Trinidad's Hindu leadership, the politics became enmeshed in racial divisions (Ryan 1972; Oxaal 1982; Hintzen 1989). In addition to anxiety about the PNM's hostility, Indians were concerned over being a minority in the proposed West Indian Federation (Bahadoorsingh 1968). In the context of charges of racism and racially contentious politics, Trinidad and Tobago achieved its independence, and the government, led by the PNM, tried to forge a national identity, as discussed in the previous chapter.

It is against this history of conflict that the contexts in which the national anthem comes into awareness must be explored. Discussions of race relations span many more contexts than performances or discussions of the national anthem. They predate the anthem, and in many ways, by drawing attention to equality among creeds and races, the anthem is a response to the pervasiveness of concerns over racial and religious divisions. The pervasive ideas about racial differences and race relations influence the interpretation of the anthem, rather than the responses to the anthem influencing attitudes about race relations.

Internalizations of the anthem as a symbol of national identity are contextually enacted—the anthem is found in most public ceremonies, schools, national festivals, calypso tents, and sporting events. In these contexts, the singing of the anthem is a very serious matter, and all are expected to be deferential during its performance (see Scher 2003, 174). Despite the respect with which the anthem is treated, and its widespread performance, its ubiquity actually results in many contexts in which it is performed containing relatively ethnically homogenous audiences. For instance, the anthem is always played before major sports events, but such events sometimes manifest some of the ethnic divisions within Trinidad. In the case of cricket, the West Indian team consists mostly of Creole players, and in some cases, this is interpreted by Indians as a form of racism, particularly when there are some very gifted Indian cricketers. In addition, when the team from India visits the Caribbean, some Trinidadian Indians support the Indian team, rather than the West Indian team (see Yelvington 1995b). The other major sport is soccer, and in 1989, when the Trinidad and Tobago team was on the verge of qualifying for the World Cup tournament, there was widespread support. Even then, however, many Indians were quick to point out that the team was dominated by Creoles and associated with Creole music, namely, the "Soca Soccer" style that the team had claimed to invent, which was further urged by soca songs composed for the team, such as those by Super Blue and Sound Revolution. Several Indians expressed to me—albeit therefore to an American ethnographer—that they were supporting the U.S. team in the match.

Emotional response is an important component of these different contexts. The performance of the anthem at an event in which the national team is pitted against an international rival, such as in World Cup Football qualifying matches, is very different from the performance found as part of a daily routine in school. In the former, the juxtaposition of the anthem with a team that is serving as symbol and synecdoche of the nation generates far greater passion than the classroom does. Yet the passion must be understood in terms of the participants. Many of the state-sponsored sporting events are attended primarily by Creole crowds. The more homogenous the crowd at an event, the stronger the sense that every creed and race present has an equal place. The anthem's ubiquity demonstrates the respect it is given, but many of the events at which it is sung have crowds that consist predominantly of a single ethnic group.

Outside the stadium, back home, where Indians and Africans encounter one another on the road, and usually in a context outside a shop, there is widespread approval of the sentiments expressed by the anthem. The phrase "where every creed and race find an equal place" is at the forefront of many people's consciousness of the anthem. Yet there are recurring disputes over whether different creeds and races are indeed equal within the nation. Standing in counterpoint to the anthem are debates over racial equality that are frequently fodder for weekly columns in the newspapers. These debates make their way into the scholarly publications of Trinidadian intellectual leaders, as in the case of Winston Dookeran's argument concerning economic inequalities and Indians (1985), or Selwyn Ryan's edited volume on the relationship of social stratification, occupation, and race (1991).

In effect, because of the national anthem's association with either state-sponsored ceremonies or national sporting events, and because both activities are closely associated with Creoles, even though many Trinidadians approve of the sentiments expressed by the national anthem, there is ongoing discussion and debate about whether every creed and race in fact do have an equal place. While this indicates the anthem's failure to overcome conflict, such a view reflects a function-oriented view of the anthem and of public policy, in general. The anthem does affect people—its aesthetic power and attraction are built on the religious and ethnic divisions it notes. The connection of aesthetics to politics is not formed in the way the government seems to assume, namely, by serving as a unifying panacea, but instead, the power of aesthetics in the anthem and much Trinidadian music is in the power of relating, not in the achieving of unity. The anthem, through its lyrics and musical transition from a minor to major key, relates conflict and change to nationhood.

✾ The Best Village Competition

The most direct connection between the government's policies on music and Anamat is the Best Village Competition. Devised in the 1960s, when Williams drew connections between Village Councils, community centers, and the fostering of national pride, this competition celebrates folklore. From a disengaged perspective, it appears as a means of encouraging contributions from Trinidad and Tobago's diverse mosaic of traditions. No doubt, this was and is part of the government's intention. If one is personally engaged in the competition, the goal of celebrating the diversity and quality of Trinidad and Tobago's folk traditions is inextricably tied to manifestations of ethnic differences, local conflicts, and long-standing competitiveness between neighboring communities. Indeed, this idea of a policy that combines folklore, ethnic diversity, and competition contains the seeds of a contest between groups in society, with groups being defined along many dimensions—ethnicity, religion, class, gender, and locale.

Some Creoles from Anamat take great pride in their participation in the Best Village Competition—it is mostly Creole youth who participate in these competitions. Despite Anamat's large Indian community, and despite its active Hindu youth group, only the youth group from the Catholic church chooses to participate in the Best Village Competition.

In 1989, local pride swelled to include even many Indians when a young woman from Anamat reached the national finals of the Best Village Queen Competition. Normally, the participation of the Roman Catholic youth was little noticed among non-Catholics in Anamat, but with a local success story, local pride overshadowed ethnic and religious differences. The new effervescence of local pride fostered amicable discussions. "Unity" would be far too simple a term to use in this context, however. It was not that everyone in the village "became one" or "united," as "unity" implies. Instead, the topic of local success in the Best Village Competition brought people together in expressions of support and pride—more a sense of association and connection than a sense of unity.

While the climate of connectedness amid Anamat's diversity emerged around discussions of the competition, the maxi-taxi that carried supporters to the finals at the Chaguaramas complex northwest of Port of Spain included only those associated with the Roman Catholic youth group and me, the recently arrived ethnographer.

Having the finals at Chaguaramas was a juxtaposition of the past and the present, the global and the local. Chaguaramas was the site of a U.S. naval base. This base took shape out of a deal between the United States and the United Kingdom, in which the United States was granted ninety-nine-year leases on land in British territories in exchange for destroyers. In Trinidad, the U.S. military decided on the land it would appropriate for the construction of its military installations. This included the scenic area of Chaguaramas, a harbor with beaches near Port of Spain. The colonial government protested, but the U.S. military won out.

About twenty years later, as Williams was galvanizing support for independence, Chaguaramas became the centerpiece of a confrontation. Williams, the premier of a nascent nation, acted as the anticolonial champion of the Federation of the West Indies—a governing body that had been convinced by Williams to make Chaguaramas its capital. Williams's ideological foe was the United States and its Cold War policies. Further stoking American Cold War anxieties was Williams's appointment of C. L. R. James as the editor of the PNM party newspaper. James was a known Marxist, who, even though he was highly critical of the Stalinist government of the Soviet Union and the Communist Party (see James 1986b), was still viewed as a potential communist threat by United States officials. In this context, as James took on a leading role and as revolution swept Cuba, Williams demanded that the United States relinquish its claims to Chaguaramas. Williams's effort climaxed in the "March in the Rain" in April 1960, when he gathered supporters in Woodford Square for a protest against colonialism that culminated with a march on the U.S. consulate to present the demand for the return of Chaguaramas to Trinidad. As Oxaal describes this event, "The March in the Rain was, perhaps, the militant high point of Trinidad nationalism" (1982, 133).

Thus, the Best Village Finals were held in a complex built by the United States Navy, a place that was one of the most contested places in the PNM's displays of anticolonialism, and a place that was returned to Trinidad and Tobago, thus providing Williams with a major diplomatic victory and a symbol of the United Kingdom's and the United States' recognition and respect of Trinidad and Tobago's sovereignty and the legitimacy of its leadership. The historical significance of Chaguaramas might not have been in the minds of the youth who went to the finals that night, but the adults who supervised the excursion were old enough to remember not only Williams's protest, but also the "base days" of World War II. Such was the setting for celebrating local culture.

The 1989 finals show included a costume and talent competition for the contestants, as well as calypso performances by Black Stalin and Tambu, and dance performances by several dance troupes. Black Stalin is a calypsonian known for his political lyrics. By 1989, he had won the Calypso Monarch title three times—in 1979, 1985, and 1987. Tambu was a police officer and a trombonist in the Police Band who had achieved great success singing soca music and winning the Road March in 1988 and 1989 (he would win again in 1990). Stalin sang from the stage; Tambu sang from the area in front of the stage where the Police Band was set up. The costumes worn by the Best Village Queens were supposed to be from the cultural heritage of Trinidad. During the 1989 finals, five queens wore sub-Saharan African costumes, two wore Egyptian costumes, one wore an Ethiopian costume, two wore Indian costumes, two wore East Asian ("Chinee") costumes, two wore French costumes, and one, Anamat's contestant, wore a Spanish costume. Without exception, all the costumes were extravagant. They all included lace, and many had large quantities of gold trim. The contestants chose to perform talents that included singing calypsos or spirituals, dancing, and poetry recitations about the evils of drugs or slavery.

The program for the 1989 finals included several dance routines, as well as the Queen competition. All of the dance companies used drums meant to emulate traditional African drums. Only three dances left an impression on the group from Anamat, there to support their own contestant for Best Village Queen. The first of these was a belair. The belair is considered to be a traditional Trinidadian dance derived from a slave adaptation of the dances of elite plantation owners. The dance company that performed the belair consisted of several drummers, four women dressed in long white dresses, and one man in white with a red sash. The dance involves spinning and playing with the length of the skirts to create fluid motions. The second dance that left a real impression seemed to represent a Shango Baptist service with women going into possession. Again, this dance was memorable to my companions because it clearly linked a spectacular dance to a tradition that was specifically Trinidadian. The last dance, and the most memorable, was the limbo, a dance Trinidadians claim to have created. The performance was extremely erotic, frequently using women and men with their legs spread wide into human limbo bars for dancers of the opposite sex who were able to limbo *very* low.

The following year, I attended the preliminary round of the Best Village Competition for the region around Sangre Grande, a town in eastern Trinidad. This preliminary competition was known as a *gayap*. *Gayap* is a Trinidadian term referring to the tradition of a community coming together to achieve a common goal. This competition took place in late 1990, after the attempted coup d'état led by Abu Bakr (see chapter 4). Not surprisingly, the coup attempt was a major theme. My friends from Anamat who accompanied me reacted the most to one skit that featured a caricature of Abu Bakr telling female members of the audience that they had to "wear clothes from your nose to your toes." After this, a young man came on stage and began to sing a calypso titled "Put Down Your Gun Young Man." In the end, the youths in the skit triumphed over Abu Bakr.

Again, at this preliminary round, mostly Creole traditions were represented. This was despite the large numbers of Indians who live near Sangre Grande (including those from Anamat). Creoles dominated the audience. In effect, while the Best Village competition was designed to forge a national identity at the community level, in eastern Trinidad, the Indian population did not take part, a pattern that is islandwide (Stuempfle 1995, 143–44). The Best Village gayap ended with performances by several calypsonians. One of them "who ent easy," as my friends said, sang a song about interracial sex. He complained that Indian women would have sex with Indians, whites, Syrians, and Chinese, but as soon as an Indian woman "went" with a Creole man, it was a scandal in the family. This sung complaint served as a dissonant counterpoint to an occasion meant to celebrate national unity.

What is to be thought of this? The Sangre Grande gayap provides a context of a contrapuntal encounter between the diverse traditions of northeastern Trinidad, but in 1991, if this counterpoint of different traditions existed, it was clear that Creole traditions provided the loudest themes, both in terms of what was presented and performed and in terms of who attended. In Trinidad, a government-sponsored event to celebrate the nation's cultural heritage is viewed by some in terms of who does not participate. The fact that such public displays also imply who is not present is as much a part of local-level celebrations as of national events. The politics of absence send an important message that is strongly felt at deeply personal events, such as wakes. When one prominent Hindu Indian man in Anamat died, many Creoles stayed away, claiming that the man was miserly and cheated Creoles regularly. On the other hand, one man, remembering his father's funeral, said with pride about his father, "That was a real nice man. The average person will tell you that, because when he die, it was all the biggest funeral they ever had in [Anamat]." Absence implies a refusal to acknowledge a relationship, but in the racially charged climate of some events, it is also a statement that one's own presence will not be acknowledged. Such is the case of the Creole men who were not served food at an Indian household in the festivities leading up to a wedding (see Birth 1997).

The predominant participation of a single group in the Best Village Competition is just one indication that the Best Village idea has not resulted in widely shared sentiments and ideas about the nation that explicitly include all traditions, but that, instead, it creates a complicated representation of the politics of participation, competition, and absence. This lack of inclusive display is one based on the choices made by people to participate or not, rather than a well-crafted, explicit state policy, but the need to choose to be present or absent is a consequence of state policy, as is the interpretation of such presence or absence.

Except when somebody from Anamat was in the Best Village finals, the competition did not create locally strong sentiments. On the other hand, there are many traditions and practices that the people of Anamat eagerly await: Divali, Christmas, Carnival, Phagwa, Eid, and the harvest festival. The Best Village Competition is not among these events. Indeed, it is only a very small segment of the population of Anamat—mostly Catholic women—who invest both emotionally and financially in participating. This lack of general enthusiasm and interest does not apply to folk traditions as a whole, but to this particular forum for their display. Outside of direct government sponsorship and its associated climate of competition, local traditions continue.

The Best Village Competition is structured to promote Trinidadian traditions. As such, it is a vehicle for the promotion of government-fostered images of the nation, rather than a context that locally reworks these images. It is also an event in which the boundaries between audience and performers are very clear, and this limits audience participation and makes the event most powerful for the relatively few who compete. The competition emphasizes juxtaposing ethnic costumes and traditions with discursive messages in the form of songs or poetry. In sum, the structure of this event emphasizes symbols and messages that are performed to be perceived by an audience, but perception of a message is not the same as its internalization or its fostering strong sentiments.

🐾 Carnival Music: Steelbands and Calypso

The most important and most heavily marketed musics used to encourage nationalist sentiment are those of Carnival—calypso and steelband music. The seeming chaos of Carnival is actually structured (Stewart 1986; Mason 1998). Different masquerade bands represent class and ethnic differences in their membership. Steelbands have close neighborhood, and consequently class, identities (Stuempfle 1995, 183–91). Every year, there is a set of calypsos that addresses a variety of political issues, including racial conflict, gender conflict, and "nation-building" (Regis 1999). The approach to festivals derived from the work of Victor Turner (1967, 1974, 1977, 1987) and Max Gluckman (1969) emphasizes symbolic opposition through concepts of antistructure or symbolic inversion. Such an approach is inadequate to the task of capturing Carnival's complicated play of multivalent significance (Alonso 1990). Moreover, some suggest that Trinidad's Carnival does not stand in an oppositional relationship to Trinidadian social organization at all (Burton 1997, 157). In models emphasizing antistructure, the festivals invert normal social behavior—for example, men dress as women, streets become devoted to pedestrians rather than to cars, and activity peaks at night rather than in the day. Some elements of inversion do exist in Trinidad's Carnival, but to characterize Carnival as inversion is to oversimplify it. Instead, many of the staged events of Carnival are closer to what MacAloon calls a spectacle than a Carnival: spectacles emphasize visual experience and "institutionalize the bicameral roles of actors and audience, performers and spectators" (1984, 243), whereas festivals and carnivals emphasize physical experience in which the boundary between performer and spectator is blurred. Those Carnival contexts in which the state plays a major role are particularly oriented toward spectacle, complete with stages, judges, and television coverage. Yet Carnival is more than these state-sponsored presentations and parades. Away from the stage areas, and on the streets of the major towns in Trinidad, Carnival is not a spectacle, but is more like Bakhtin's representation of the carnivalesque: "Carnival is not a spectacle seen by the people; they live in it; and everyone participates because its very idea embraces all the people" (1984, 7). Carnival has multiple, shifting conflicts and collusions—this movement between conflict and collusion is contrapuntal.

There is an interpretive tension between applying MacAloon's ideas and Bakhtin's ideas to Carnival. Making a rough phenomenological distinction, I would suggest that spectacle emphasizes visual and aural experiences, whereas Bakhtin's carnivalesque includes and engages all senses. Bakhtin's choice of Rabelais as evidence of a pre-Enlightenment carnival tradition is telling, as the characters in Rabelais's *Gargantua and Pantagruel* take pleasure in excesses of body experience—noises, smells, tastes, touch, sexuality, and defecation. In effect, for Rabelais, the carnivalesque must engage all sorts of body sensations, particularly those associated with debauchery and its associated body effluvia.

But there is something even more important in understanding the ebullient seriousness or serious revelry of Trinidadian Carnival aesthetics. The idea of structure and antistructure is based on a categorical logic that pits order against disorder and seriousness against revelry. Carnival is very serious. Lent and Carnival are not opposed but are physically and psychologically tied to one another. The Trinidadian ideology that Trinidadians love to "fete," and even have a "Carnival mentality," is coupled with admissions that Lent provides a time of recovery and rejuvenation after Carnival, and that the culmination of Lent—Easter—is a time for a "cool" event, such as a "beach lime," for family and friends. There is no quarrel between Lent and Carnival, but a relationship linked by temporal sequences. Instead of the reinforcing antagonism implicit in the structure/antistructure model, one finds a lived symbiosis. Carnival is not a reversal or a negation of Trinidadian social structure but is an important phase in the annual cycle of Trinidadian life.

The state-sponsored portions of Carnival are organized, televised, and defined temporally and spatially, and they emphasize sound and sight. In these respects, they are similar to the Best Village Competition. In fact, there is a recurring pattern of how state-sponsored events emphasize the senses of sight and sound, clear delineations of performers versus audience, spatial and temporal organizations, and competition. In contrast, Carnival transcends the senses of hearing and sight, distinctions of audience and performer, and spatio-temporal organization, and it blurs the line between competition and cooperation. It is playful in the sense that Bateson discusses play—serious and creative, but with few serious consequences (1972).

The Carnival season starts after Christmas and lasts until Ash Wednesday—a day that shifts from year to year. Most Carnival events—mas' camps, steelband rehearsals, and parties—are not for presentation on television, but are designed for intimate physical participation, whether it be the feverish making of costumes, the all-night rehearsals, or the exhilarating and exhausting pace of dancing at fetes. Throughout the Carnival season, Carnival is represented through media such as newspapers, radio, and television. These representations are more spectacle than festival. Combined with corporate and state involvement, they make parts of Carnival into a spectacle. The state and corporate competitions require judging areas that include stages. The stages are defined spatially, and a performer's time on stage is limited. The stages are flanked by stands where spectators sit, and where television cameras and commentary booths are placed. The structure of the event in these areas is created for purposes of competition and broadcasting, and is different from the structure of Carnival outside these areas, in the same way that spectacle is different from Bakhtin's description of Carnival. In a strange way, though, such organization and government practices heighten the comedic irony of Carnival. In the middle of the playful, egalitarian unfolding of Carnival, competitions spatially define stage areas, temporally define presentations in those areas, and give power to judges to rank participants. As a result, schedules get broken; competitions criticized; and, as with the Best Village Competition, the absence from competition of certain groups and people sends a powerful message. This is profoundly embodied in mud mas'—a "costume" that consists of covering oneself with mud, slime, and sometimes body paint. This costume is anticompetitive, disorderly, dirty, and aesthetically interesting because of its beautiful grime. How does one judge mud and slime? How would a spectator discern high quality from low quality? The beauty of mud mas' is as much in its feel, texture, and movement as in its appearance.

There is a big difference between the televised images and mud mas', but such divergence indicates Carnival's contrapuntal complexity. It involves many avenues of participation, probably the least important of which is radio and television airplay for calypsos and their videos. Until the 1990s, the radio and television stations were government-controlled. As a result, calypsos critical of the government were rarely played, whereas "nation building" songs received extensive airplay. Listeners from Anamat, like other Trinidadians, were acutely aware of this. Their awareness stemmed from reports in weekly newspapers such as the *Bomb*, *Punch*, and the *Mirror* that documented the scandalous and politically critical calypsos. News also traveled by word of mouth from those who attended calypso tents. Consequently, even though the residents of Anamat rarely attended calypso tents, they were aware of the politically scathing calypsos, and they looked forward to the live broadcasts of the Calypso Monarch semifinals and finals on television and radio to hear these songs.

The disorderly social organization of Carnival also challenges the worn distinction of collective versus individual. Carnival crowds are not collectives. There are too many differences and conflicts played out during Carnival to think of any large collection of Carnival revelers as a single group. Carnival crowds are not aggregates of individuals, either. I know of no one who participated in Carnival alone. Carnival relates individuals to groups, identities, differences, and conflicts. Participation begins with one's relationship to a group that is participating and is influenced by the relationship of that group, or "posse," to others.

Despite the seemingly chaotic nature of the festival to the outsider, there are clear social patterns in Carnival. Groups are clearly defined in such a way that a group of fifteen friends finds one another amid 20,000 people. There are defined social roles that emphasize group membership: drinks are bought and shared; fights occur between groups, as well as individuals; and groups' territories are protected against unwanted incursions by other groups and individuals. In addition, group definition is raised in situations that are viewed as "hot," and lowered in situations that are viewed as "cool." At the level of these groups, or "posses" as they are called, the experience engages all five senses. The structure imposed on Carnival by the state dissipates, and the nationalist character of the season dissolves into more immediate concerns of drink, dance, friendship, and occasionally fighting. Whereas it is tempting to view the idea of the posse as emerging from the influence of cinematic Westerns, Selwyn Cudjoe quotes a reference to a Carnival posse made in 1880 (2003, 231), suggesting a long association of the concept with Carnival groups. As Jankowiak and White found for Mardi Gras in New Orleans, a "restricted communitas" (1999, 347) emerges that emphasizes friends and kin, rather than a communitas that emphasizes general unity.

During the Carnivals of 1990 and 1991, I attended several large Carnival events with a group of individuals from Anamat. After Christmas, corporate-sponsored fetes are held. Corporations such as Nestlé, Amoco, and Carib Beer construct huge enclosures with multiple stages. The fetes are advertised on radio, on television, and through newspapers. They bill popular soca bands and disc jockeys. Often, guest appearances by popular calypsonians are advertised, as well. Within the fete enclosures are bars and booths serving food and drink. The fetes begin during the early evening hours, and by midnight, thousands (at one fete, organizers reported over 20,000 people in attendance) are drinking and are dancing to the music. The fetes usually end at 4:00 a.m., because the police do not protect fetes after that hour, and a police presence is required at all fetes that sell alcoholic beverages. In addition to fetes, the Anamatians who I accompanied attended the preliminary round of Panorama (the national competition of steelbands), J'ouvert in Port of Spain (the official beginning of Carnival before sunrise on Monday), and other Carnival celebrations in Arima and Sangre Grande—two towns closer to Anamat than is Port of Spain.

Consequently, my coverage of Carnival fetes is not exhaustive but follows participation by those residing in Anamat. This allowed me to study how members of a particular community participated in Carnival— an approach adopted recently by Scher (2002, 2003)—rather than trying to essentialize Carnival as a whole. There is great diversity in Carnival participation, and the texture of this diversity requires focusing on the microlevel attitudes, relationships, and forms of Carnival involvement. Scher's description of the prominent mas' band Poison as providing a means of expression for middle-class women, while at the same time acknowledging that theirs is just one position out of many forms of participation in Carnival, is a window into the unfolding of Carnival at the level at which revelers experience it. Scher moves beyond attempts to describe Carnival as an entirety and, in the seemingly more modest goal of understanding one small component of the celebration, opens up a Pandora's box of grappling with how Carnival's participants relate—in ways that are both conflicting and colluding.

Another important dimension of Carnival consists of the minions of nonmasquerading participants. Included in this overly broad category are people from rural areas such as Anamat, who immerse themselves in a celebration that is quintessentially of "town." Little has been presented concerning the participation of non-masqueraders, non-calypsonians, and non-pannists in Carnival (Birth 1994; Miller 1991, 1994; and Balliger 1998 are exceptions). This group of nonperforming participants forms the greatest number of participants in the festival.

These participants in Carnival challenge the state's organization through displays of freedom (Miller 1991). These displays reach their pinnacle when they encompass all the senses, which, again, are in situations that are labeled "hot"—situations of dancing, drinking, and infectious music.

This display of freedom, as Miller points out, is not limited to young adult males but includes all those who participate. Still, there are subtle gender, ethnic, and age distinctions manifest in these displays. The audiences for events dominated by pan music tend to be older than the audiences of the large-scale soca fetes. Some fetes are viewed as Indian fetes, based on their location or on the artists performing. Some occasions are viewed as cool and thereby are attended by more women and couples than the really hot fetes. Other events are viewed as extremely hot and are dominated by young adult male posses. Consequently, underlying the collective display of freedom are subtle displays of difference—these then structure the ways people think about their Carnival experiences.

Since Anamat is a remote village, about a two-hour drive from most of the major fetes, finding transportation is a major challenge in attending these events. The problems do not arise from getting to them—Trinidad has an effective, inexpensive transportation system consisting of route taxis and maxi-taxis (small buses), but most taxis and maxi-taxis are not working at four in the morning when fetes end. Commonly, cars leave Anamat already full, with six to seven passengers, and when the fete is over, usually two to four new passengers will be added for the trip home. These new passengers got to the fete by other means, but have no recourse for getting home except to squeeze into an already-full car. For these individuals, finding others from Anamat is a very important component in attending fetes.

As the following two cases will show, the emphasis on revelry and group maintenance during fetes defies the dichotomy of collective/individual. It creates a particular kind of contrapuntal intersubjectivity that is quite different from the government-promoted image that Carnival creates collective, national unity. The relational, limited communitas of the intersections of body, thought, feeling, groups, and participants in Carnival thus challenges not only social scientific categories, but also the ways in which such categories and accompanying assumptions form models for government policy. At the same time, the seemingly chaotic encounters of groups based on friendship, kinship, and locale foster the bacchanalian aesthetic appeal of Carnival participation.

❧ Steel in the Brain: Panorama

Invented in Trinidad and associated with calypso and Carnival, the steel drum, or pan as Trinidadians call it, serves as a powerful icon of Trinidadian music. Even though the instrument was invented in the living memory of many old heads, pan music evokes a sense of nostalgia and history. When attending the preliminary competition of steel orchestras, known as Panorama, two brothers, separated in age by fifteen years, both told me that the large concentration of steelbands found at Panorama was like the way Carnival was for their mother. Its association with the Caribbean has led to its widespread use in popular media representations of the tropics, whether this be in movies or orange juice commercials. This global recognition pan receives enhances the local sentiments Trinidadians feel toward the instrument and its music—as one resident of Anamat said, "that one place where we have a lot of broad talent."

From the perspective of how music connects disparate issues, pan is an extraordinary example of how music serves to relate mind, body, material, social consciousness, and political conflicts. The instrument's construction from fifty-gallon oil drums connects Carnival and Trinidad's petroleum-based economy. While tenor and double-tenor pans are used as solo instruments, pan is at its most compelling when part of a steel orchestra. These ensembles tend to be neighborhood-based, and the large, competitive bands attract prominent sponsors, such as Amoco or VAT19 Rum. Playing the instrument is extremely physical, and playing the bass can involve extremely acrobatic movements between a dozen or so pans mounted around the musician. Paradoxically, pans are tuned with hammers in a process that requires a careful touch and a discerning ear. The sound of a steel orchestra combines counterpoint and polyrhythms: basses that rumble the earth beneath one's feet, tenor pans that pierce one's body like arrows, and the middle-pitched pans—known as the guitars and cellos—that cause one's body to vibrate to the calypso and soca rhythms these particular pans tend to sustain throughout a piece. All of this is layered on top of a percussion section consisting of trap drums, scrapers, bells, and "iron" (steel wheel rims struck with metal bars) engaging in polyrhythmic relationships. Moving through the streets with a skilled band is like riding a wave of musical energy. Pan thus brings together oil production, national identity, neighborhood affiliations, corporate sponsors, and powerfully embodied musical experiences.

Given the international recognition of pan, its Trinidadian origin, its ability to serve as a vehicle for extraordinary virtuosity, and its local importance as a result of neighborhood-based pan yards and orchestras, it is not surprising that the state has tried to organize and harness the power of pan. Kim Johnson observes, "[Eric Williams] saw the steelband movement as both the seedbed of national culture and a link with urban grass roots communities" (2002, 61).

Steelband music has been adopted by the state as one element of Trinidadian national identity (Stuempfle 1995), so much so that steel drums are featured on currency. Even so, the participation in steelband music has always involved intercommunity conflict. In the early days, this led to fights; more recently it has involved musical competition. Anamat does not have a steelband. Its loyalties are strongest to the Sangre Grande Cordettes, but many people from Anamat have personal ties to other bands, or have played in other bands at times when they lived outside of Anamat. Consequently, the participation of those from Anamat in steelbands is not presently in the role of performer, but in the role of audience.

At the same time, people from Anamat make up an audience attached to some performers through ties of friendship and kinship. These social ties radically change the nature of the audience. An audience of a commercial recording may have a relationship to the performer only through the commoditized performance. In the case of pan audiences, the relationships to many performers are determined by highly personal ties. During Panorama, as the steel orchestras are lined up waiting to move into the judging area, Trinidadian audiences go back and forth between ensembles with friends or kin and perennial favorites in the competition, such as Desperadoes and Renegades, known for their complicated arrangements, outstanding musicianship, and aesthetic qualities. Ideally the two are combined and publicly acknowledged when the ensemble that includes friends and relatives is successful in the national steelband competition, Panorama. Pan's persuasiveness as a national symbol is at least partially due to these personal ties. National competition thus links communities to their orchestras, and the orchestras to national pride. Because the demands of education and job opportunities led almost everyone in Anamat born since 1950 to have lived in several communities during their lives, it is typical for residents of Anamat to have ties to two or three competitive orchestras. Steel orchestras serve as nodes in interwoven social networks that encompass the entire country—even a location such as Anamat that has no steelband and no panyard within ten miles.

During my fieldwork in 1989–91, many men from Anamat in their thirties and forties enjoyed attending one of the preliminary rounds of Panorama. They enjoyed this round because the most steelbands are there, and the lime is "cool and nice"—meaning that the setting and crowd are festive and exuberant but not violent or uncomfortably out of control. Because of the large numbers of steelbands there, it is also a good place to meet old friends. As a result, attendance of the preliminary rounds often involves searching out bands that contain friends in the band or among the supporters. This round is held at the Queens Park Savannah in Port of Spain, a long car trip from Anamat. The trip and the nature of participation indicate important features of this event. The enactment of these ties related to pan is thus more than just the music. Not only does pan relate communities, music, nation, and state, but the enactment of these relations also brings into association gender, generational, and intercommunity relations.

Traveling from Anamat for Panorama seems to follow a script—itself part of the holistic counterpoint of the event that relates many aspects of Trinidadian life to pan. In this profane ritual, the cars full of people (mostly men) traveling to the Panorama preliminary round leave several hours after the agreed-upon time. This delay reflects one of the dimensions of audience participation in events like Panorama that is not captured by a focus on the music. While it is mostly men who travel from Anamat to Panorama, women have their own way of participating and thereby disrupting their exclusion. The delay in leaving is because the men wish to take food and expect their wives to cook for this excursion, and the food is never ready when the men wish to leave. The delay then prompts discussions among the men about the reasons for their late start. In 1990, it was the driver who initiated the topic: "Is the women," he explained, and then he began a story about how his wife was slow in cooking the food that we were taking with us. The women who cooked were not coming—they were not invited. Confiding in my wife, the implicated women defended themselves by stating that, if they are not invited, they do not feel inclined to wake up early and cook so that the men who are going can get an early start. The women cooks' subterfuge of the men's plans goes beyond not getting up early, however. There is always an ingredient missing: "What you want me to do—you bring home no chicken las' night, and you expectin' chicken curry for your little lime!" The counterpoint of Panorama—the conflict between men and their wives—begins long before arrival at the Queens Park Savannah. The preliminary conflict over cooking and food unfolds into general discussions about women during the long car ride.

In both 1990 and 1991, as the car continued its travels on the winding, narrow road, the conversation shifted slightly away from the reason for the delay to the reason women are not invited to come in the car. Even though women do not frequently and explicitly communicate why they are slow in cooking the food, through their delay, accompanied by the sound of sucking their teeth when men express impatience, the men in the car seemed aware that the women resented not being invited—hence, the male justification of female exclusion. In one homily from the front seat, that was greeted by affirmations from some of the others in the car, one man commented, "You can't take women on limes. They want to stop when you don't want to stop, and they want to go when you want to stop." It is not that women do not attend Panorama; it is simply that they usually go separately. As I would discover, while the car would take only men to Panorama, there was nothing wrong with bringing women back. To begin, however, the lime was for men.

In fact, gender relations are an important component of many limes, and the women that men exclude are family members, spouses, and girl-friends. In some cases, once at events such as Carnival fetes, men actively seek "outside women." One man confided that the reason he did not want any women from Anamat along on the lime was that, if one saw him with a woman other than his girlfriend, his girlfriend would find out. In other cases, men are concerned about the reputation of the women in their lives, particularly since damage to these reputations would damage the man's reputation. Some limes are thought to be "hot," and consequently, not for "respectable" women. Other limes are thought to be "nice" and "cool," and appropriate for respectable women. The latter limes would often include women. Sometimes, however, a group of women would travel to a fete independently, surprising their brothers, husbands, and boyfriends by their sudden arrival. Limes involve a constellation of gen-der issues that prevent the fete from serving any homogenizing hege-monic purpose. This constellation is not stable over time, however. The Carnival season is a prolonged period of movement between household harmony and dissonance. Some fetes bring couples together, and others create dissent. Sometimes men want to lime only with men, and women only with women.

Panorama is part of this complicated constellation, and in some re-spects is an exception—a cool lime to which men with whom I worked did not take their girlfriends or wives. None of the men I was with seemed to be seeking amorous relationships there. Instead, the lime was more along the lines of informal all-male gatherings in rum shops, with an additional dimension of encounters between men who knew one another but who had not seen one another in a long time. In a sense, Panorama brought together men from all over the island. Stephen Stuempfle suggests that the "pan life" is dominated by men (1995, 178), and not only are the orchestras dominated by men, but many of the social activities that de-velop around the bands are also male-dominated. From the perspective of Anamat, this seems to be true of attending Panorama. But the male domination of pan life hides a hidden counterpoint of gendered relationships that is revealed through the means by which women are excluded or choose not to participate.

As part of the standard sequence of events of attending Panorama, we stopped at a snackette (a type of rum shop) in Valencia, a town halfway between Sangre Grande and Arima. Valencia is not a particularly big place, nor are its facilities out of the ordinary when compared to other places along the route to Port of Spain, but Valencia is an important point of transition between eastern Trinidad and the residential sprawl that follows the Eastern Main Road from Port of Spain to Arima—it is the last easy stop before leaving the Eastern Main Road and taking the highway into Port of Spain. During World War II, Valencia was a town heavily involved in servicing the American military bases of Fort Read and Waller Field. Between Valencia and Arima, there is very little development—mostly chicken farms and squatter's villages. This land is the former site of the military bases, and the entrance to the site remains marked by two masonry pillars. When traveling to Port of Spain from Anamat, shortly after Valencia, one can leave the two-lane Eastern Main Road and take the divided four-lane Churchill-Roosevelt Highway, which was constructed for the use of the bases.

In the 1990 trip to Panorama, when we stopped at the snackette in Valencia, everyone got out, some heading to the bathroom and some to the bar. We limed there and chatted with the bartender some, and, when we left, someone had bought everyone in the car a beer. Revisiting the earlier conversation, somebody commented that, when women are on the lime, one cannot make such stops, although on the few gender-mixed limes I observed, such stops were made anyway, and in every lime that included women in which the final destination was Port of Spain, the car stopped at this same snackette.

About an hour after stopping for drinks, the car arrived at Panorama, which was located in a large Port of Spain park called the Queens Park Savannah. At Panorama, part of the field outside the stands is set aside for parking. We parked the car, noted its location, and began to wander about.

One of the characteristics of a lime at Panorama that sets it apart from other limes is the degree to which people wander—the space outside the judging area encourages this, with food and beer vendors lined up along the queue of steelbands, themselves overflowing out of the Queens Park

Savannah onto the streets of Port of Spain. As will be discussed below, at Carnival fetes, groups of people tend to stake out territories and stay there for the duration of the fete. This behavior is also true for those who witness Panorama from the viewing stands. For those who are not in the stands, however, Panorama involves wandering about and sampling the various steelbands that are lined up waiting to enter the judging area.

Such wandering results in encountering friends and acquaintances from outside the village. People split from the initial lime; others join and buy drinks in celebration of these encounters. Through kinship networks, most Trinidadians have relatives throughout the island, and through these relatives, they have a wide network of friends. The educational and work histories of most men from Anamat also have resulted in islandwide networks of friends. Since Anamat contains no junior secondary or secondary school, all local youth seeking education beyond primary school must leave the village. Some move out of the village entirely during this period—this was particularly common in years past, when the transportation out of Anamat was less regular than it is now. After completing their education, many young men and women from Anamat obtain jobs outside the village. This was particularly true during the oil boom of the 1970s and early 1980s, when an entire generation of men obtained jobs in the manufacturing or construction industries and left Anamat to reside elsewhere. Many of these men moved back to Anamat after losing their jobs, and their coworkers returned to their homes. Panorama provides an excellent context for seeing old friends from both school and work. Since Panorama brings together steelband associations, which are community-based throughout the island, audiences from throughout the island come, as well, to support their local band and to evaluate the competing bands. The wandering of limes about the rehearsal area for Panorama results in encounters that reaffirm or reestablish these wide-ranging social ties. It also involves seeking particular bands to which one has ties. In the case of the group with which I traveled, they always gravitated to the Sangre Grande Cordettes, the competitive steelband near the secondary school that most of the group attended. One man with whom I limed at Panorama would also stop by the Solo Harmonites from Morvant, since one of their pannists was married to his cousin. The lime also listened to Amoco Renegades and Desperadoes, perennial favorites to win Panorama, but bands to whom nobody in the lime had a social connection. These bands come closest to serving as national steelbands to my friends. The high, consistent standards of musicianship in these bands, combined with the innovative and complex arrangements of Jit Samaroo and Robert Greenidge, the respective arrangers for each ensemble, are counted on by those with whom I limed to represent the pinnacle of the pan art form, and by implication, to represent something that is intrinsically Trinidadian. Occasionally, another steelband would capture the hearts of my friends with a spectacular arrangement, but part of the ritual of Panorama was always to visit Renegades and Desperadoes as they rehearsed.

Consequently, the experience of the spatial organization and social dimension of liming at Panorama involves affirming community allegiances among men, through choosing steelbands to support, reestablishing islandwide social networks; and, for particularly important relationships, sharing food and drink as a mark of solidarity. This dimension of Panorama, which takes up most of the lime, coexists with a hope for a burst of nationalist sentiment generated by hearing Renegades or Desperadoes. Since the arrangements are not complete by the preliminary round, and since the top orchestras "save something" for the semifinals and finals—some set of arpeggios, counterpoint, furiously played runs, or ornaments that will grab the attention of the judges—sometimes the prominent bands disappointed my friends at the preliminaries by playing well enough to move on in the competition, but not well enough to inspire their audience in the preliminary round.

As an event, Panorama is viewed as cool in comparison to other Carnival events. There is little or no fighting, and the drunkenness is much more sedate than at other events. During Panorama, there are bursts of heat, when a particularly proficient steelband is playing an excellent arrangement that drives all around to dance and chip (a shuffling, semi-dancing walk). The heat lasts for the duration of the song, after which people settle back into their limes. For those not in the stands, there is not the constant music that is found in fetes or on J'ouvert.

While pan music and Panorama are used as national symbols, the contrapuntal experience of Panorama displays ethnic, gender, and generational differences, while at the same time it tends to reinforce solidarity among Creole men of about the same age. Again, the metaphor of counterpoint allows for movement between harmony and cohesion at one moment, to dissonance and conflict at another. From the beginning of a Panorama lime, with the dissonance between men and the wives, to the wandering from band to band while invoking past and present social ties, the significance of Panorama is not that it presents a single unified theme about the nation, but a place and a succession of moments where ideas and social relationships intersect. In many respects, the relationships that developed during the oil boom years, when one generation of men comprised a highly mobile workforce, are maintained by meetings that occur at Panorama. Old friends know they will find one another there. The structure of the event encourages these encounters. The bands are lined up, and each band has a banner identifying it. The crowd is not dense except near the judging area. Consequently, those who regularly attend have a clear cognitive map of how the event is arranged, based on prior experience. These old friends do bask in the nationalist pride of steelband music, but this nationalist imagery does not integrate them into a larger population, and the competition, in fact, fuels conflict and, often, anger at incompetent judges.

On the other hand, Stuempfle has noted for the rest of Trinidad, both Indians and women often feel disenfranchised from the steelband movement. While both participate, pan is still associated primarily with men and Creoles, and this hinders its nationalist appeal (1995). As is the case with other state-sponsored events, the emphasis of the state-imposed structure is to communicate steelband musicianship as a symbol of the nation. Again, this communication occurs in competition marked by a stage area, flanked by stands, with the clock running on each performance. Outside of the state-sponsored areas, the event has a very different structure where the boundaries between bands, kin, and friends are blurred. The issues of musicianship and images of the nation are mingled with sentiments generated by kinship, friendship, shared experiences, and cherished memories. The sentimentality that emerges is, consequently, not simply due to the music, but due to the company one keeps and the ease with which one can find family and friends.

This is not really a case of the state appropriating pan. Appropriation implies an attempt at possession, and pan, like most Trinidadian musics, defies such efforts. Instead, the state's involvement is a deliberate attempt to insert itself inside the social connections and sentimentality that pan evokes. Pan preceded independence and has spread in ways over which the state has little control, but also in ways in which the state, like many Trinidadians, wishes to participate. In this way, the state is enmeshed in the counterpoints pan creates, but the state is rarely a dominant theme, except when the audience disagrees with the judges' decisions.

🐾 Brass in Me Brain

While the media pays the greatest attention to the spectacular masquerade bands, the inventive lyrics of the calypsonians, and the musicianship of the steelbands, a large number of participants in Carnival choose large fetes as their yearly initiations into Carnival. At these fetes, the disc jockeys and brass bands rule—*brass bands* meaning ensembles that play soca. This context is a major inspiration for soca music, as the number of songs about parties attests (Rohlehr 1998; Scher 2002). Likewise, it is in this context that the soca bands hone their skills and develop their material during Carnival, and for many it is the participation of the crowds at these events that begins to hint at which song will claim the Road March— the song that is most played during Carnival Monday and Tuesday.

The Carnival fetes are not explicitly part of a program to promote nationalist pride. The large fetes are sponsored by organizations, government agencies, or corporations: the Water and Sewage Authority (WASA), Nestlé, Carib Beer, and Amoco, for example. The small fetes are sponsored by local rum shops, recreation clubs, and civic associations. Such fetes do not communicate nicely articulated discourse about the nation, but rather express a raw, physically encoded set of sensations and memories. The language about parties emphasizes temperature, for example, "hot" and "cool"; it emphasizes activity and movement, for example, "wine," "grind," and "get on"; and it emphasizes mental states, for example, "head bad," and "madness." The experience of these fetes involves dancing until four in the morning, sometimes in the last great rains of the wet season—a welcome relief to cool one's hot and sweaty body. Understanding fetes is crucial to understanding the sentiments that emerge around Carnival, and understanding fetes requires a broadly phenomenological approach, rather than a discursive approach. The state's fixation on "messages" limits the state's influence in fetes and the fete-spawned activities that spill out onto the streets during Carnival.

The holistic counterpoint created by fetes—generated by the combination of music, lyrics, and body movement—becomes a means for remembering key themes of a particular Carnival season. The feelings of the moment become tied to the music so that, even years later, the music provokes the feelings to come back. This element of Carnival is based on the aesthetics of the relation of lyrics, emotions, and situations to one another, not on the poetics of lyrical messages. So I learned in 1990 when one of my friends heard the onomatopoeic refrain of David Rudder's 1986 Road March, "Bahia Girl": "Pi lim pim pay bee dee bam bam" (*The Gilded Collection, 1986–1989*, track 2). My friend suddenly began chipping as he relived J'ouvert of 1986—four years before. While the lyrics of calypsos will become a historical record of the time, they will also serve a more visceral function, namely to remind the fete-goers of particular sensations at particular events—a Carnivalesque version of Antonio Damasio's somatic marker idea (1994). Damasio suggests that such visceral sensations play an important role in memory. He argues that for memory to be adaptive, it cannot be limited to conscious, calculating cognitive processes. In situations that require rapid response based on prior experience, Damasio suggests that remembering relies on memories that were encoded viscerally, rather than just cognitively. These memories are related to the body sensations that are commonly noted in ethnophysiological systems around the world—for instance, feelings in one's "gut." This visceral encoding serves to limit the number of responses to a situation that one considers, and it is learned. Since it is learned, it is cultural in origin. The extension of this model is that any practice that creates extensive body sensations will create powerful somatically encoded and triggered memories. Once these experiences become somatically marked, then similar experiences in the future will trigger both a somatic response and memories. As such, the songs indicate the experience and memories of small groups and individuals.

Whereas Damasio's treatment seemingly emphasizes adaptation and decision making, there is no reason to think that the somatic and emotional encoding of memories is limited to such functions. While the mechanism might be adaptive, an implication of the theory is that any event that involves profound multisensory somatic experience is somatically and emotionally encoded. Consequently, a sense of embodied joy that emerges in anticipation of Carnival need not be viewed as adaptive or functional but simply as a result of a cultural trigger to memories with powerful somatic and emotional elements.

The nondiscursive dimensions of this are driven home by my friend's remembering J'ouvert of 1986, triggered by the sounds "pe lim pim pay bee dee bam bam"—a set of nonsense syllables. When sung by David Rudder to the melody and rhythm of "Bahia Girl," these syllables create a memory in my friend that is manifest in his body movements, and not just in his spoken recollections. The song, itself, tells the story of an encounter between the calypsonian and a Bahian woman, in which a fusion of soca and samba rhythms emerged from their dancing.

While, presumably, the psychobiological foundations for remembered responses are a shared, universal element of human biology, since this is a mechanism highly responsive to environmental cues in the embodiment of memory, and since people have different memories, there is no reason to assume that the results of somatic marking are uniform. Instead, they become a domain for the play of counterpoint—the same music (a shared, harmonic theme) generates different, powerful memories in different participants (potentially dissonant themes). With regard to experiences and linked memories of Carnival, there are important social and generational elements that enter into the play of harmonic and dissonant themes. The fete-going groups I studied consisted of young adults and their relatives who were visiting from the United States, Canada, or Great Britain. Members of the former group were perennial participants in fetes, but many of the latter group said that they had not experienced Carnival for many years—in one case, almost twenty years. As will become apparent in my description of particular fetes, the experience of these events emphasizes individuals' involvement in group actions. Consequently, the somatic marking that occurs must be viewed potentially as a group phenomenon—a shared embodiment—rather than simply as an individual one. Attending fetes is a group activity. Even if one did not travel with a group to a fete, one would meet one's friends at the fete, and once at fetes, those people with whom I went would find one another and form a group, called the posse. The posse stakes out a territory and limes together for the evening. At different times, individual members or small groups from the posse will travel to the bar and buy drinks, or travel to a food booth and buy food.

Recalling fetes is also a group activity. One evening there was a "cook" at my neighbor's house. A group of men who had worked together at the Amalgamated Automobile factory during the 1970s gathered for a lime that included fish soup, beer, and a cuatro. In between beers and bowls of soup, the men sang songs of the Carnivals they had attended as young, gainfully employed factory workers. It is easy to get the impression that calypsos remain in people's consciousness for only a single Carnival—for, after Carnival is over, the songs often disappear from regular radio airplay in Trinidad (although not from more nostalgically driven playlists in New York City). This night proved otherwise. As one man strummed chords, they all sang the choruses—the verses had been forgotten. The singing spurred group remembering—details of past events and people were collectively reconstructed. Fetes and calypsos live on, not as discourses, but as fragmentary memories.

The memories should not all be viewed as nostalgic, however. They are often conflicted. One of my most powerful memories (and one of the more often recollected memories of my participation in Carnival from those who were present that night) was of my first Carnival fete. This powerful memory imprinted in me the counterpoint of conflict and social cohesion in these fetes.

When I attended my first fete, I did not know there was a posse, or how people from Anamat attended fetes. I made arrangements with a friend in the village, Curtis, to travel to the fete early on the maxi-taxi system. He wanted to go early because a friend of his was one of the disc jockeys at the fete, and we had complimentary tickets from this man. When we arrived, we positioned ourselves in front and just to the left of this disc jockey's speaker column. There we began to lime—drinking rum and beer. Without my realizing—partly because I did not know everyone in Anamat at this time—as the crowd grew, so did the number of people from Anamat standing around us. Somehow, they managed to find us in the increasingly dense mass of people. By the time the fete started to get "hot," there were about twenty-five people from Anamat liming in front and just to the left of the speaker column. Two popular bands were appearing, Blue Ventures and Shandileer, in addition to two popular disc jockeys. We were in front of Blue Ventures. Curtis said he wanted to hear some of Shandileer, so I dutifully followed him. We walked briefly through that crowd, stopped by a bar to buy drinks for our friends, and brought the drinks back with us. Curtis then disappeared again into the crowd. Midway through the evening, I witnessed one of the reasons why people from Anamat lime in posses, when a man tried (unsuccessfully) to pick my pocket, and I caught him. The scene unfolded quickly after that.

"What the ass is this? I'm goin' to kill you," my antagonist exclaimed as he grabbed my shirt. One of his friends came up to support him in his threat.

Curtis's cousin liming nearby saw all of this, tapped the would-be pickpocket on the shoulder and said, "Don't mess with him. He limin' with me."

"He limin' with you—fuck dat. He put a razor in his pocket an' cut my hand." (I had not.) Then, turning to me, the antagonist said, "Give me all of your money."

The best I could do was to meekly reply, "I'm sorry, but there was no razor in my pocket."

My friend from Anamat continued to argue that I was liming with him, and that the would-be pickpocket should leave me alone. After what seemed like hours, but could have been only seconds, I noticed that familiar faces from Anamat had completely circled my two antagonists and me. My antagonists were seemingly not yet aware of this.

Another man from Anamat, very tall, and very strong from agricultural work, said to my antagonists, "What's the problem here? He limin' with us."

My naive antagonists, apparently not dreaming that their target was with a group of about twenty-five, tried explaining again that I had placed a razor in my pocket, and therefore I should give them $20.

My friends replied, "Nah, cool yourselves."

The argument continued with the request dwindling from $20 down to buying them a beer.

The crowd of people from Anamat was now pressing on them, and a woman who worked as a taxi driver came up to the would-be pickpocketer and whispered something in his ear.

The posse continued to press, and my antagonist displayed a look of fear, turned to his friend, and said, "Let's get out of here," then turned to me and said, "Sorry, breds [brother]. Have a good time." The members of the posse let them out, and my antagonists ran through the crowd toward the exit.

Shortly thereafter, Curtis returned. The story was related to him, and he replied, "Boy, if I was here, there would have been real licks." At the end of the fete, at 4:00 a.m., he then led me to the car that he had arranged for us to travel home in—somebody who had driven from Anamat. Seven people squeezed into the car built for five, and the conversation soon turned to the incident. One man said that the two men had been lucky that the "cooler" heads were in the posse at the time. "With some Anamat boys, they would have given them licks right then and there, then put them in the trunk and taken them back to Anamat to teach them a lesson."

What is the Anamat posse? First and foremost, it is a group of people who are bound to one another by coming from the same village, but it is also a group in which collective Carnival memories get formed, reworked, and set. An important aspect of social organization in Trinidad is the power of neighborhood allegiances. Steelbands are organized around neighborhoods, and their history is intertwined with that of neighborhood gangs. Posses also are derived from this history. A posse is a group of people from the same neighborhood who "ride out" to a fete. The functions of the posse are multiple.

The core of the posse is a group of young adult men. These men are those who frequent fetes. Some, particularly old heads, talk of these individuals as examples of the "Carnival mentality" that Trinidadians view with ambivalence. Usually, these young men are economically marginal—existing in a state of underemployment. Their marginal status is frequently viewed as simply a life stage, however. Men grow out of this phase and become "respectable." Curtis is an example of this. Before I met him, he had held a lucrative job at an automobile assembly plant. The factory had retrenched him and many others, forcing him into a state of "scrunting"—looking for any sort of work to make a living. By the following Carnival, Curtis was no longer in Anamat but had left, having secured a work contract elsewhere.

When others attend a fete, they usually associate themselves with this core membership of the posse. The relationships in posses have multiple dimensions involving kinship, affinal, economic, and other social ties. Membership in the posse is marked by liming in the informally defined territory of the posse at a fete, by buying drinks for posse members, by consuming drinks bought by other posse members, and by wining with opposite-sex members of the posse.

Sometimes the posse has as many as seventy members. On occasion, it joins with other posses to create a huge posse. The inter-posse allegiances that I witnessed were between posses with affinal and consanguinal relationships (see figure 1). In these cases, the posse from the neighborhood into which women from the other posse married lime in the location of the posse from which the women came.

The Anamat posse almost always staked out the same territory relative to the stage area. This made it easy for members of the posse arriving in different cars to find one another in the throng of revelers and to mobilize the posse when necessary.

An important aspect of posses is wining. The best description of this dance is found in calypsos about Trinidadians teaching foreigners how to wine. In Colin Lucas's classic song "Dollar Wine," he gives the following instructions:

> Put a cent piece in your left pocket
> Five cent in your right
> Ten cents in your back pocket, safely out of sight
> In front, under your belt, stick a dollar.   (*De Trini Party*, track 7)

And then he tells his foreign, female wining student to move to the money, so to speak: "Cent, five cent, ten cent, dollar." To complete the joke, the woman replies, "Leave out the small change. Give me big money wine—dollar, dollar . . ." at which time she pulls out a "Yankee dollar" and adds, alluding to the then-exchange rate between U.S. and Trinidadian currencies in the early 1990s, "Is five wine to one!" While this captures the basic movement of wining, there are many variations and different movements. Not all wining serves the same purpose. While wining has an autoerotic dimension, as Miller (1991, 333–34) notes, wining can mean much more. It is a densely packed condensation of body movement, sexuality, and social relationships. It is an activity varyingly motivated by desire, anxiety, protectiveness, and jealousy—an embodied counterpoint of mixing emotions. It has multiple uses in establishing posse membership and the relationship of individuals within the posse.

Most wining within the posse serves to define posse membership. In such contexts, men and women dance with one another for portions of songs. The regular fete-goers participate in this the least, and those who only occasionally attend fetes participate in this practice the most. In particular, this seems to be a practice that marks women as members of the group, since, in general, women do not attend as many fetes as men. Within a short time of the formation of the posse in the territory, the women have wined with several members of the posse. This wining,

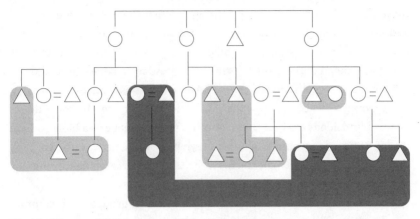

1   **Kinship diagram of Carnival posses.** Those circled in light gray are on the Anamat posse; those circled in dark gray are in the non-Anamat posse.

which I call social wining, seems to indicate a social relationship between the men and women of the posse internally, and it displays this relationship to non–posse members.

A second form of wining has a protective function. Typically, men play the active role in establishing sexual relationships at fetes. This role involves wining on potential partners. Women do not wish such attention from every man who tries. Indeed, they reject many men by simply not providing the men an opportunity for wining. If a man is persistent in his pursuit of a woman, then members of the posse will begin to wine with her to foil his desires. The members normally are men but can also include women. If the man is particularly troublesome, people will wine both in front of and behind the woman.

A third form of wining can best be described as flirtatious and involves acrobatic wining, wining low, and particularly animated wining. Flirtation sometimes leads to the development of an exclusive wining situation with potential sexual intent, but other times it is used to establish or display a particular informality between the man and woman involved.

Finally, intimate wining anticipates a sexual relationship. Wining can be particularly erotic, and it is possible for both men and women to have orgasms on the dance floor. In rare instances, it will lead to heavy petting, and even sex, if the partners are of complementary statures.

Most typically, though, one finds social or protective wining. Indeed, these wines are a major strategy through which the posse protects itself and avoids conflict. It is not always successful, however. At one fete, a man unknown to the posse members was persistent in trying to wine with one woman in the group. Social wining and protective wining did not deter him. Eventually, one of the members of the posse pushed him away. He responded by attempting to throw a punch, but before he could do so, he was blindsided by a blow from another posse member—a blow so hard it sent him to the ground. As he was trying to stand, he was hit again. By this time, he apparently got the message, and he retreated hastily outside of the territory the posse had defined.

Posses are, thus, kinship and community-based groups, with community loyalties. They are marked by the sharing of drinks, and by wining between men and women, and less frequently, between women and women. They defend their members through a variety of strategies involving utilization of space, wining, and violence. Within the confusing mass of Carnival revelers, these groups reaffirm local allegiances. They revel, feud, and fight. Whether the activity is drinking, wining, fighting, or fleeing, it is a group activity. It is also a multisensory activity that includes cultural expectations of physical activity and even exertion. These posses also provide a basis for collective remembering later. The posses of today, structured as they are around kin and friends, become the cool reflective limes of the future, during which events are reconstructed out of the personal memory fragments each person carries, and during which old social ties become reenacted.

While the common physical and sensory experience creates bonds within the group, antagonisms with other groups can also emerge. Such is the counterpoint of conflict and cohesion in Carnival. Indeed, this element of Carnival is not new, as the repeated conflicts between stick bands in nineteenth-century Carnival (Brereton 1975; Cowley 1996), and steelbands in the 1940s (Stuempfle 1995, 70–75) demonstrate. As is the case with Brazilian Carnaval (see Linger 1992), Carnival has this violent undercurrent. This undercurrent does not foster a sense of national unity or a coherent image of the nation—the structure of the setting and the intent of the participants are not related to such concerns. Furthermore, the experience of fetes involves all five senses, and except for occasional conversations yelled over the music, and occasionally echoing the lyrics of a popular song, fetes are also profoundly nondiscursive. The exhilarations and anxieties associated with this context are connected to physical experience—the heat, the sweat, the wining, and the fighting. The wining and the fighting play complementary roles of bodily establishment of belonging to a group, and of its boundaries. In the context of the posse, the state's project of musically defining identity is solely reliant on soca lyrics that attract the posse's attention. The highly physical experience of fetes overflows into the streets on J'ouvert.

﹡ J'ouvert

Carnival itself, beginning early on the Monday morning before Ash Wednesday, is described as "national theater" (E. Hill 1972). The links between the government and Carnival are strong, but the government's control is weak—most Carnival participation takes place outside the government's reach. The popular participation in the event again suggests that any concerted effort to fuse a national image with the festival, whether through government effort (Stewart 1986), private interest (Green 2002), or tourist development (Green 2002; Scher 2002, 2003), does not correspond to many people's experience of it. Petrus Koningsbruggen says of Carnival, "The ideological ambiguity gives the festival its dynamic political and social content, thereby preventing it from turning into a pure tourist attraction" (1997, 4).

Attempts to organize J'ouvert might channel or direct experience but they cannot completely determine it. In fact, under certain circumstances, attempts to organize lead to opposition. Whether it is the government or a private interest's attempt to use Carnival, the typical effort to harness it is to organize it by developing policies to control time, space, movement, or, in the case of censorship, the content of Carnival. Such policies extend only to limited spaces or limited groups of people. Outside of mas' bands and steel orchestras, the nature of Carnival participation is a rhythm of movement from place to place and from group to group. Outside the judging areas, in the early morning shadows of Port of Spain and other towns throughout Trinidad, J'ouvert is the part of Carnival that is traditionally the most antagonistic or oblivious to government efforts at control.

While the Carnival season lasts for weeks, Carnival officially starts with J'ouvert early Carnival Monday morning. For many, J'ouvert is

Carnival's climax—it is sometimes described as "the people's Carnival." It is the time of mud mas', when muddy and soiled bands parade with buckets of slime and goo, ready to spread their muddy loads on anyone willing to partake. The mud covers appearances of race and class, thereby forming an egalitarian mass in which the participants revel in the mud and their anonymity, their equality, and the resulting euphoria. J'ouvert is the time of individual masqueraders making political points. This involves people dressing up in idiosyncratic costumes, often carrying placards that make important social points. In addition, J'ouvert morning is the morning of the steelbands, before the musical celebration gives way to trucks carrying speaker columns. Despite being a time of individual expression, J'ouvert is also a time of experiencing Carnival as part of a social aggregate. Koningsbruggen captures this dimension of J'ouvert when he writes, "There is no room for individual manoeuvring in the darkened streets; everyone is forced to follow the collective, steady rhythm coming from the nearest source of music. Whether they like it or not, everyone is borne on the rhythmic wave which runs through the crowd, back to back and belly to belly" (1997, 234).

My friends prefer to "meet" J'ouvert on the streets of Port of Spain, then travel to Arima shortly after sunrise, and finally end the day in Sangre Grande. In Port of Spain, they encounter the mud mas' and the first mas' bands. In Arima they find many steelbands and often have breakfast at a fried chicken restaurant. In Sangre Grande, they meet friends and lime on their home turf.

For J'ouvert 1990, we left Anamat after the National Carnival Commission's Dimanche Gras show—the event at which the winner of the Calypso Monarch was determined that year. In the car, there was an ongoing debate about this competition. In the Calypso Monarch competition, performers are judged on the basis of their lyrics and presentation. Both the semifinals and finals of the event are televised, and many of the calypsos received extensive treatment in the newspapers. The National Carnival Commission appoints the judges who determine the winner, but the audience also acts as judge, and as is often the case with such competitions, there are discrepancies between how the formal panel judges and how the audiences judge. Among those watchers with whom I talked, there was a pervasive concern that, since the judges were government appointees, they would never award the prize to a calypsonian whose performance was too critical of the government. At the same time, it was felt that some calypsonians make it to the finals based on their ties to high-ranking government officials. Such was the case in 1990, when I heard the following comments: "What was Tambu doing in de finals?" "I hear he one of Robbie's [Prime Minister A.N.R. Robinson's] favorites—dat's why." "They thief Aloes, man, jus' because he like PNM and not NAR." "But Cro Cro come strong with his 'Political Dictionary.'" Tambu was known at that time for popular songs that competed for the Road March, but not for social commentary, a characteristic people look for in the songs of the Calypso Monarch. He was also thought to be supportive of the NAR. Sugar Aloes is still known for his "sweet" voice and incisive, often PNM-partisan, social commentary; he eventually did become Calypso Monarch in 2002. Cro Cro, like Sugar Aloes, is known for being a trenchant social critic. Some felt that the edge went to Cro Cro because he was less overtly in support of the PNM (then the party in opposition to the ruling NAR) than was Sugar Aloes. Despite differences of opinion between Cro Cro and Aloes supporters about who should have won, those who had both opinions shared the view that Tambu's songs were party tunes and did not contain content or commentary serious enough to justify his being included in the finals.

The conversation about the competition lasted the duration of picking up everyone in Anamat who was "riding out" in the car, and the length of the trip to Sangre Grande—about twenty-five minutes. In Sangre Grande, we picked up several relatives of the driver of the other car in our Carnival caravan. We then headed for Port of Spain, arriving at what was probably around 3:30 a.m.—in 1990, J'ouvert officially began at 4:00 a.m., but in 1991, it was changed to 2:00 a.m. At this time of morning, the streets were crowded. Disc jockeys lined the sidewalks, and people were moving about with some dancing in front of speaker columns. Soon afterward, the fete at Soca Village ended. Soca Village was a large party enclosure between the Holiday Inn and the docks in Port of Spain. It featured three stage areas on which performed the most popular soca artists and bands. When Soca Village closed in order to comply with the need to end fetes at 4:00 a.m., a wave of humanity spilled from the Soca Village fete complex and descended onto Independence Square (part of which is now called Brian Lara Promenade, named after the famous cricket batsman) in downtown Port of Spain. At this time, the first masquerade band passed in front of the viewing stands that had been constructed on the square between Frederick and Henry Streets. This band, like all subsequent bands, was followed by a large truck that was stacked high with speakers. As the band came to a stopping place in front of the stands, the truck blared out the song that was to be associated with the band, "No No We Ent Going Home," Tambu's contender, and the subsequent winner, of the Road March. As such trucks approached, the DJs on the sidewalks deferred to the trucks and turned down their own systems. The DJs gave the same respect to steelbands that passed.

Around daybreak, rain started to fall. At this time, fights also started to break out. As is the case at fetes, similar violence is expected during Carnival. The posse I was with did not wish to stick around and get caught in the violence, though. We headed for our car and left for Arima.

We reached Arima shortly after dawn. The driver happened to find a parking spot near Royal Castle, a fast-food fried chicken chain. During Carnival, Royal Castle and Kentucky Fried Chicken are open at all times, and even though the sun had just risen, everyone in the car decided to treat themselves to a hearty breakfast of fried chicken and chips (French fries). The streets were full of steelbands. Most of these bands were small neighborhood organizations, and not the large orchestras that compete in Panorama. The sidewalks were not as crowded as in Port of Spain, but the familiar faces were more numerous. Whereas in Port of Spain a member of our group saw someone they knew about every thirty to forty-five minutes, in Arima it was about every ten to fifteen minutes. Indeed, an important aspect of J'ouvert in Arima was seeing friends, although the posse did not really break up. After about two hours, we left Arima for Sangre Grande. Sangre Grande was dominated by DJs, with occasional appearances by the Cordettes, a steelband from the town. In Sangre Grande there were so many people that members of our group knew that the group disintegrated. That seemed to be an important part of the character of Carnival in Sangre Grande, namely, that enough of the crowd knew one another that individuals were much more likely to break away from their community posses and move about alone or in pairs.

The participation in J'ouvert for the residents of Anamat is typically a traversing of the Trinidadian landscape associated with particular times—a movement from Port of Spain for the opening of Carnival slowly back home. For many people with whom I worked, J'ouvert was the only time they were in Port of Spain during Carnival. In the context of the shared image of Carnival in Trinidad, the movement during J'ouvert also encompasses the differences between Carnival's celebration in different towns. Whereas the state and the state-sponsored media define judging areas with stands, bright lights, and television cameras, for many Trinidadians, their participation is outside of the bright lights and is definitely not defined by the space of a stage or a time limit for occupying any given space. The timing of movement for my friends followed a different rhythm from that imposed by the National Carnival Commission.

🐾 Carnival, Unity, and Dissent

One tradition of scholarly literature on the carnivalesque emphasizes the idea of how such festivals include role reversals and performances that represent egalitarianism but that ultimately reinforce the social order. Max Gluckman's analysis of "rituals of rebellion" implies that this function is due to the cathartic nature of such events and the reinforcement of social norms by their temporary violation (1969, 110–14). Daniel Linger rightly criticizes this model, saying that "The explanation is functional in form but the function itself is elusive; the argument seems circular" (1992, 11). Robert Dirks, in his description of Christmas in nineteenth-century Caribbean plantation societies, suggests a much more contentious model of carnivalesque reversals, arguing that they "disclaimed a lie by enacting reality" (1987, 190). In discussing role reversals in the context of preindustrial Europe, Natalie Zemon Davis (1978) portrays the carnivalesque as a mechanism of social change. Emmanuel Le Roy Ladurie, in his *Carnival in Romans* (1979), explores violent revolutionary and counter-revolutionary upheavals occurring in the context of a Carnival in a French town. William Jankowiak and Todd White demonstrate that any communitas in Mardi Gras is confined to small groups of friends and kin (1999). Dorothy Holland, William Skinner, Debra Lachicotte, and Carole Cain describe how women use music to criticize patriarchy (1998, 228–32) and to imagine possibilities other than patriarchally structured gender relations while they create new senses of self.

The temptation to constrain Carnival into oppositional categories is a conceptual prison, even when it is pointed out that the carnivalesque can challenge structure. Instead of opposition and inversion, exploring the play of forces over the duration of Carnival is important. The state's intervention, in terms of spatially determining judging areas, temporally limiting the time a band can perform in the judging area, and empowering a panel of judges, is just down the street from crowds that judge but do not award prizes and that wish for the more spectacular bands never to leave the space they occupy. Overlooking the judging area are covered stands into which one gains entry only by purchasing tickets, but to the sides of the stands are conglomerations of posses and individuals who are asserting their freedom for free. The group that I followed on J'ouvert moved from place to place in a deliberate manner. Carnival participation seeks social connections between old friends and new partners and at the same time can cultivate antagonisms between old enemies or new combatants. It is not opposition, but, once again, counterpoint that becomes a more useful metaphor—a temporal movement from dissonance to harmony between different themes. The clash with one person during Carnival can create a tie to another person, and the antagonist of the moment might have been a friendly fellow reveler previously. Even with regard to government competitions the movement of attitudes is important, since the praise of a competition and the qualifications of the judges can be followed by cursing the decisions of these same judges later in the evening.

Victor Turner's discussion of communitas (1974, 1977, 1987), which has been widely applied to carnivals and festivals, provides a different perspective, albeit one that developed in combination with Gluckman's model. *Communitas* is a feeling of unity that emerges in events such as carnivals. When combined with Gluckman's model, this feeling of unity implies a societal feeling that reinforces the social order and is thought to emerge from symbolic inversions. In other discussions, this is clearly not always the case (Davis 1978; Dirks 1987; Le Roy Ladurie 1979; Holland et al. 1998), although, from these perspectives, feelings of social connection do emerge within participating groups and form the basis for subsequent collective remembering. The same can be said for Trinidadian Carnival. Within steelbands and posses, feelings of connection emerge. At the same time, such connections within groups can foster conflict between groups, so the connections must be viewed contrapuntally and not constrained by the concepts of community and conflict. A communal action on the part of the posse at one point can give way to discord over the behavior of a posse member at another point—the flow of events in time matters in this counterpoint, and the counterpoint emerges only when one thinks of Carnival in terms of its unfolding, not its essence. Furthermore, within Turner's discussion of ritual is his idea of the orectic pole of meaning— the elements of ritual that involve physiology, emotion, and body processes (1967, 54; 1974, 55). Turner does not explore this pole much, but it is easily related to Bakhtin's (1984) examination of Rabelais and the folk culture of the Middle Ages that reveled in appetites, consumption, sensuality, sexuality, and body functions. The orectic pole also resonates with the power that Caribbean relational aesthetics gain from the creation of a holistic, contrapuntal nexus of body sensations, movements, conscious awareness of self in relationships to others within one's group, and larger issues of politics, economics, and identity.

In this light, the state's viewing Carnival as national theater and appropriating it for purposes of creating a national identity is ironic—the metaphor of theater itself suggests formally separating performers from an audience. Carnival competitions that in theory are unifying are, in practice, contentious. The national identity that the state imagined forging emphasizes diversity and unity, not underlying tension, although such a portrayal might be accurate. While the state focuses on discursive messages of unity, the revelers are immersed in body experience—heat, sweat, anxiety, euphoria, excitement, thirst, and hunger. They are pummeled with multiple sensory experiences constructed around music loud enough that it vibrates one's body as it monopolizes one's hearing, and the colorful clothes among the revelers, and, during Carnival proper, those playing mas'.

The musics and events appropriated by the state to generate national identity inherently compromise the state's project by including contexts of conflict and displaying the limits of the government's ability to organize and control. The state's use of folklore in the Best Village shows, and its appropriation of calypso and steelband music, all include state-sponsored competition in which political, community, ethnic, and personal conflicts are played out. Even the state's adoption of a national anthem, a seemingly innocuous badge of becoming independent, can create contention. The song claims equality of all groups, but many view its portrayal as a dream, rather than as a reality. Subtly, the anthem's own modulation from a minor to a major key punctuates a movement from colonial power to liberation. The veneer of unity highlights the existence of conflict. In a way, this is the strange twist on some theories of carnival and festival: rather than reinforce the fragmented social order through temporarily suspending social norms, the state appropriation attempts to threaten the social order through temporarily emphasizing unity.

The state's emphasis on using these contexts as vehicles for the distribution of messages makes its efforts look feeble next to the multisensory, overwhelmingly physical experience involved in participating in Carnival. Whereas the Best Village Competition is structured to create an audience for the performance of elements of nationalism, outside of the stage areas, Panorama, fetes, and J'ouvert engage the senses and the body in ways that reinforce kinship and friendship ties that already exist and potentially encourage antagonism between groups of strangers.

Forms of organization such as kinship, friendship, communities, congregations, and clubs are necessary conditions for Carnival's spontaneity. Because of its bureaucratic tendencies, the government is torn between using organization to foster Carnival's spontaneity and using organization to curb spontaneity. This conflict is found in James's writing about government involvement in Carnival through the Carnival Development Committee in 1959: "We have not seen the best of Carnival yet by a long way. It is only now that the Government is going to settle down seriously to organize that we are going to see the full possibilities of the extraordinary social and artistic form which has sprung from the depths of the people of Trinidad and which they have tenaciously pursued despite official discouragement against some of its most characteristic features" (1959, 5). James's vision was for the government's power to enhance that "which has sprung from the depths of the people"—an attempt to organize spontaneity that presages the contradictions that the government has experienced in relationship to Carnival since. While the government is conflicted, local practices are less so—social organization does foster spontaneity in ways that governmental organizing does not. The following chapters examine locally-based social organization in relationship to music.

chapter three 🐾 Parang: Christmas in Anamat

> What our culture needs desperately is not support from
> the top. We need the foundation and the push of our peo-
> ple from below.
>
> SAMUEL SELVON, "Three into One Can't Go"

A ppreciating the counterpoints generated by Trinidadian music
requires listening beyond Carnival and relating Trinidadian musics to one another. Such relationships do not require lyrical
statements but can instead consist of felt social dimensions of music. In
Anamat, the Christmas tradition of parang is an instance of embodied
social experiences overshadowing lyrical content.

Both Carnival and Christmas are embodied and multisensory, and
music is the force behind these features. Yet these two celebrations
differ in important ways. Carnival is a publicly celebrated event, whereas
Christmas is celebrated by families in their homes. Consequently, Christmas evokes intimacy and privacy, whereas Carnival does not. In Carnival,
people travel to the celebration, but in the Christmas tradition of parang,
the celebration comes to one's home. A last difference is the greater
attention paid to food. Daphne Taylor's book on parang (1977) devotes
an entire chapter to food, and the soca parangs that are sung in English
usually make reference to food, such as with Scrunter's popular 1989 soca
parang "Piece ah Pork" (*A Decade of Scrunter*, track 12).

Sentiments generated by practices of celebrating Christmas in Anamat
are episodic rather than enduring (Miller 1993, 144–46), but the frequency and rhythm of episodes and the frequency with which residents
discuss such episodes indicate that there are widespread instances of

social remembering that allow residents to discuss and affirm community when they wish. Furthermore, the seasonality of Christmas is part of the annual cyclical rhythm of celebration. This annual rhythm fosters antic-ipation of future Christmases based on remembering past ones. As one person told me, one year, in mid-January: "People know now is January month. You know sometime people get the feelings, the vibes of Christ-mas, you know sometimes it come into them, and you say, 'Well look, Christmas coming jus now,' and you have to do something for Christmas. Like Christmas and Carnival—sometimes people start to organize for these things for months, 'cause these are festival things." Likewise, com-munity disunity is episodic and has its own cultural patterns deployed in conversations or disputes (see Birth 1997, 1999). Disunity is more ar-rhythmic than rhythmic. It is based on irregular outbursts of animosity, or the cycle of elections—themselves irregular, since their date is set by parliament. Parliamentary elections are constitutionally required to be held at least every five years, but the ruling government can call early elections. A brief survey of when elections have occurred shows their irregularity since independence: 1966, 1971, 1976, 1981, 1986, 1991, 1995, 2000, 2001, and 2002.

Thus, in the unfolding of relation and fragmentation at the local level, there is a predictable rhythmic cycle of holidays and celebrations that relate the community's diverse groups to one another, and an irregular, unpredictable sequence of personal arguments, and arrhythmic govern-mental elections that fragment relationships. Holidays tend to bring relationships into the foreground. Holidays are celebrated by friends, neighbors, and kin, and yet some holidays—Divali and Christmas, in par-ticular—are occasions for community events and community pride. Musi-cal holiday celebrations connect kin, friends, neighbors, and ideas of eth-nic identity, interethnic relationships, and constructions of community.

The Christmas music of parang is a good example. In addition to the conceptual connections parang evokes of family, community, and Spanish identity, it has elements that make it psychologically powerful. In parang, the same practices are repeated year after year, and while Taylor docu-ments some changes to the parang tradition (1977), the basic features of house-to-house visitation and performance have remained central prac-tices. These practices engage all the senses: the music is heard; the move-ments of others are seen and often matched; the smells of food, drink, and sweat are palpably mingled; the refreshments in each house are tasted; and the strange combination of physical sensations of fatigue and elation are powerfully present. The synchronization, or pacing, of group activity through music is seen, heard, and felt. For musicians, there are added elements of pain: the soreness of one's throat from singing, the aches of muscles engaged in the repetitive motions of playing an instrument for hours on end, and blisters that impart a burning sensation on the fingers of the string players—an embodied, culturally marked, painful heat. The occasions can be emotionally powerful. When the sun rises on a parang, there is a sense of joy and accomplishment shared by the participants, most of whom are kin and neighbors. Multisensory experience and strong emotions lead to powerful experiences, and in parang they combine and enhance one another.

Parang music engages multiple senses to choreograph and coordinate body movement and emotional experiences. Interestingly, my participating in parang bands was a crucial moment in the development of rapport between those who lived in Anamat and me. Parang is also highly patterned. The messages conveyed in the parang tradition are the same every year: harmony, family, rural and Spanish identity. These messages are built into the context of parang, in terms of both the social organization of the participants and the spaces in which parang is performed. These messages are ideas that participants want to believe about the community—they want to imagine Anamat as a place where people of different races live in harmony. Such ideas combine in important ways in discussions about transracial kinship (Birth 1997) and ideas that "country people" are "cool and loving," in contrast to the violence and conflicts associated with town. Basically, at least the core of those who participate are predisposed to the messages communicated through the parang tradition. Some gain this predisposition from being members of kin groups that parang, but the house-to-house parang tradition of Anamat is contagious—many, once exposed, cannot resist participating. Particularly until midnight, the band grows with each house it visits, because some members of each household decide to join the band. The message of community and harmony becomes performed as dozens of people sing together. Since the lyrics are ostensibly in Spanish, few understand what they are singing, but instead imitate the pronunciations of the loudest singers. The communication of harmony is, thus, not lyrical, but participatory. It is not surprising that those who participate in parangs report heightened feelings of community belonging during Christmas time.

Parang is a form of traditional Trinidadian Christmas music that is also known in other parts of Latin America as *aguinaldos* (Roberts 1972, 118). Trinidadian oral tradition claims that parang came directly from Spain, but the music is primarily found in parts of the island where Venezuelans settled in the nineteenth century and where their descendants still live. Relying on Alan Lomax's cantometric analysis of parang (Lomax 1962), Elder emphatically declares that Latin folk music, which includes parang, is "absolutely contributed by Venezuelans" (1967, 69). There is no doubt that the persistence of parang has been due to contribution from Venezuelan immigrants, but that does not exclude the possibility that it was present before the British seized the island in 1797. In this debate using contemporary geopolitical divisions, though, it must be remembered that, at times during the Spanish colonial period, Trinidad was administratively tied to Venezuela. Venezuelans, also known as "Panyols" and "Spanish," contributed to the multiethnic composition of Trinidadian society.

Whereas most of Trinidad's population settled around the urban areas and sugar-producing regions of the island, the Venezuelans moved into the northern and central mountain ranges and settled in areas inhabited by the remnants of the indigenous population (Brereton 1993, 35) and maroons (Joseph 1838, 254; Carmichael 1834, 115). These same regions were also settled by Indians whose indenture contracts had expired (Brereton 1979, 130–31). One location in which the Venezuelans settled is Anamat. In Anamat, European elites were never resident and were always viewed as distant antagonists whose policies were carried out by local lackeys. The local, tangible divisions were between Hinduism, Islam, Catholicism, and Protestantism, as well as between Indians, Africans, and Venezuelans. The divisions were expressed through different traditions (Freilich 1960): religious rituals, endogamy, antagonistic labor relations, and, on occasion, arguments and fights that took on racial dimensions.

As played in Anamat, parang music consists of a vocalist and a chorus that are minimally accompanied by cuatro and *shak shaks* (maracas). The cuatro is a four-stringed guitar-like instrument that is very similar to baritone and tenor ukuleles (depending on the cuatro). The skilled cuatro players in Anamat use a strumming style that involves a downward strum of striking the strings with the fingers and then dragging the thumb followed by an upward strum of the thumb and fingers together. The shak shak player follows the rhythm the cuatro produces by the dragged thumb and upward motion, although skilled shak shak players often create additional rhythms that sound like they are engaged in a dialogue with the singers. During large parangs, the cuatros are augmented by guitars and a box bass. The box bass consists of a wooden box and broom handle with a string that runs from the center of the box to the far end of the handle. Different tones are produced by moving the handle to increase or decrease the tension on the string.

Most of the songs consist of a verse followed by a chorus. The lyrics are supposed to be sung in Spanish, but few in Anamat speak that language, so that there is little consistency even on most choruses. The greater the size of the group singing the chorus in a house-to-house parang, the more difficult it is to understand the chorus. It is important that "true" parang is sung in Spanish, even if most of those participating cannot understand it.

There is a national parang competition, and recordings are available of traditional parang music (as opposed to soca parang), but neither the competition nor the recordings drew much attention when I was in Anamat. The exception to this was the work of Daisy Voisin. Voisin was regarded as the greatest singer of parang music (*Daisy Voisin* contains some of her classic recordings), and her renditions of parang classics were viewed as examples of the reverence and skill that the music deserves. In Anamat, the performance and consumption of parang was intensely focused on local traditions.

This local focus implicated the ethnic diversity of Anamat. The relationship between members of different ethnic categories is highly variable. There has been limited intermarriage, and the recognition of the resulting transracial affinal ties is based on individual choices (Birth 1997). There is also some cooperation in working the land and hunting. Friendships form across these divisions, and some village activities are clearly multiethnic, such as the cricket team, wakes, and locally sponsored fetes. In Anamat, though, senses of identity and ethnically defined differences emerge contextually—a process that appears throughout Trinidad (Eriksen 1992; Yelvington 1993, 2001).

One context in which highly sentimental ideas that crosscut ethnic divisions emerge in Anamat is Christmas. One elderly Hindu Indian woman explained, "Christmas in the country is very nice. On Christmas morning, people prepare food and drink for the day. In the afternoon, they call on their neighbors. By night, the whole neighborhood is together." A middle-aged Hindu man said, "Christmas is when you go by people and just eat and drink and lime. It is also a good time to go by an enemy and make up—it is a day of peace."

It might seem odd that Christmas, a Christian holiday, could bring together Muslims, Hindus, and Christians. Miller argues that, despite the diversity and accompanying conflict found in Trinidad, with regard to Christmas, "The evidence suggests that for at least a chunk of the year tremendous effort is invested in creating a self-image of bounded society, nostalgic common culture, and sentimental roots" (1993, 146). Parang, in particular, seems to bring these different groups together. The evidence of parang bridging ethnic divisions is substantial. There are Indian paranderos (parang musicians), many of whom are Muslim or Hindu. During Christmas 1995, the most popular Christmas hit song in Trinidad was "Chukaipan" by Scrunter, a calypsonian from the same part of Trinidad as Anamat. "Chukaipan" fuses calypso, parang, and Indian music. Its opening lines are:

> This Christmas will be different—all of them can take it from me.
> This year I spending Christmas with my Indian family.
>
> (A Decade of Scrunter, track 8)

Moreover, the chorus of the song is actually the refrain of an Indian folk song. The representation of an Indian parang in the song derives its good-natured humor from the fact that in Scrunter's part of Trinidad, near Anamat, Muslims and Hindus play parang, and paranderos of all backgrounds incorporate elements of Indian music into parang music. One parandero told me of purposefully playing a "chutney serenal" at a Muslim home—a serenal is one of the standard types of parang song. In addition, Indians play in Indian, Spanish, and African homes, and, likewise, Spanish and African parang bands visit Indian homes.

Why is a Spanish Christmas tradition enjoyed by non-Christian, non-Spanish groups? What about the tradition brings together people of different backgrounds in the same space, and at the same time, to do the same thing?

✿ Why Spanish?

In much of Trinidad, "Spanish ethnicity" refers to those descended from Venezuelan immigrants (Khan 1993; Moodie-Kublalsingh 1993). That being the case, it still evokes a sense of Europeanness. Yet while it is linked to Europeans with the accouterments of hegemonic European superiority, it is also linked with ideas of hard work, and work alongside Africans and Indians in the rural areas. As Khan notes, there has been a change among Trinidadians from viewing "Spanish" as indicating a European, to "Spanish" as indicating a "'mixed' ethnicity," and, as she adds, "it is best to view this gradual transformation in identity as an accretive mosaic that gives rise to multivalence and ambiguity rather than as a linear falling away of *a* prior identity to *a* subsequent one" (1993, 193–94). In his research in a predominantly Indian area of Trinidad, Miller observed "it is at Christmas time that many Trinidadians manage to locate amongst their ancestry at least an element of Spanish. This provides them with a sense that they have a kind of natural affiliation with the associated music and food, but also has deeper consequences. To have an ethnicity that evokes a sense of Trinidad beyond the images of rupture such as slavery and indentured labor is to evoke a generic objectification of the land itself" (1993, 145). The Venezuelans who settled in Trinidad after 1797 were agricultural laborers. They pioneered the cultivation of cocoa in the northern and central mountain ranges of Trinidad and often served as wage laborers alongside African workers and indentured Indians. In some cases, they owned land and employed members of other groups, and in other cases they worked for members of other groups (Shephard 1935).

Not only were they linked to other ethnic groups through common work, but they also were tied through kinship links. As Khan points out (1993), Indians view Spanish as "diluted" Creoles who lack many of the stereotyped negative qualities of other Creoles. Indians and Spanish marry (Birth 1997). Likewise, since Spanish are classified as Creole, there are no obvious obstacles to marriage between Spanish and African Creoles. The result has been kinship links that transcend Indian and Creole ethnic groups, through ties generated by marrying Spanish individuals (Birth 1997).

Thus, "Spanish" is a mediating category between "African," "White," and "Indian." This makes the most notable Spanish tradition, parang, palatable to many non-Spanish.

Another factor is that parang's lyrics, while describing the Nativity story, are not comprehensible to most listeners. Many skilled paranderos sing the lyrics in Spanish, but the reality of most house-to-house parangs is that they contain few participants who speak or understand Spanish. In addition, the enunciation of those who sing in Spanish is drowned out by the volume of the chorus and the acoustic qualities of many houses (in which sound echoes off brick walls and concrete or tile floors). Indeed, many parangs involve instances of glossolalia. Felicitas Goodman defines *glossolalia* as "a vocalization pattern, a speech automatism, that is produced on the substratum of hyperarousal dissociation, reflecting directly, in its segmental and suprasegmental structure, neurophysiological processes present in this mental state" (1972, 124), and she relates pacing and synchronizing actions in a group to producing this phenomenon (1972, 75–76). Particularly from members of the chorus who are not from one of the recognized families of paranderos, what comes out of some singers' mouths is not Spanish. It is not English or Patois, either. When such outbursts are too outside what is acceptable, the established musicians shake their heads and attempt to curtail the singer's efforts. Some paranderos admit the divergence between spoken Spanish and the Spanish sung in parang. One informant said, "The Spanish in parang is not the same as Venezuelan Spanish." Since the lyrics are understandable to few, even when sung by someone who speaks Spanish, their Christian content is easily overlooked, which also makes the music acceptable to non-Christian audiences. Added to this is the incorporation of contemporary soca parang compositions, which incorporate secular lyrics in English into a parang musical style. Such songs include the previously mentioned "Chukaipan" and "Anita," both by Scrunter. Thus, there are two factors which make parang an ethnic tradition that is not confrontational, and that is potentially acceptable to non-Christians and non-Spanish: the respect that non-Spanish Trinidadians express toward the Spanish, and the lack of explicit Christian messages in the tradition for those who do not speak Spanish. In Khan's view, "*Parang* begs the question of the distinction between cultural traditions that are considered embodied in and exclusive to certain groups or collectivities, and cultural traditions that are not so contained" (1993, 194). These qualities are not enough to bridge ethnic divides, though. They simply facilitate the emergence of such bridges. These factors set the stage for participants to be sympathetic to cultural ideas of common kinship and unity, even at the same time that they recognize ethnic differences. In a sense, parang creates a context for relations to transcend fragmentations—to put aside differences momentarily for the duration of the parang. Furthermore, these ideas are presented in a nonconfrontational context that celebrates kinship, including transracial kin ties.

❄ Christmas 1989

Parang is a seasonal music having an annual cycle of growing anticipation and then catharsis. Parang events, or simply "parangs," also contain different cycles: cycles of songs at each home; and a cycle of the formation, peaking, and eventual dissipation of a parang. The unfolding of sensations linked to sentiments is a very important component of participating in a parang.

I arrived in Anamat in October of 1989, and almost from the beginning of my research, both men and women, Indians and Creoles, were telling me about the local tradition of parang. They said that it was a Christmas music sung in Spanish, and that the parang bands played throughout the night, moving from house to house.

With great anticipation, I looked forward to Christmas and parang. In early November, my first taste came when, one night, I heard a couple of men singing at the bottom of the hill. One of them was strumming a cuatro. I watched and listened, all the while mesmerized by the strumming patterns that produced a triplet while the hand seemed to be strumming eighth notes. In addition, either the first note of the triplet was dampened, or the accent fell on the last two notes of the triplet, depending on the choice of the musician (see figure 2).

Gradually, I learned that this strum was accomplished by striking the strings with one's fingers and then dragging one's thumb across the strings, thereby allowing the thumb to produce a chord separate from the fingers. This strum is magical to watch—literally creating a visual illusion as the downward and upward strums produce three notes, not two, as one would normally expect. This creates the illusion that more music is coming from the instrument and at a faster tempo than it looks like the musi-

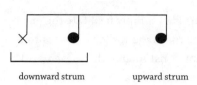

downward strum   upward strum

2   **Cuatro strumming pattern**

cian is playing. As I also learned, this strum was a matter of local pride—
literally, an embodied local tradition. Many cuatro players throughout
the island did not use it, but it was mandatory in Anamat. All of the
cuatro players attributed the strum to an old Panyol, long dead, who was a
noted local parandero. The informal commemoration included referring
to the house in which this man lived as if it still belonged to him, even
though its current residents are not related to him. At Christmastime,
when I rode with these paranderos or walked with them by the location of
this deceased cuatro player's house, they reverently pointed to the spot as
a monument to the man, to the local strumming style, and to parang.

By early December, I had started to accompany the Roman Catholic
and the Missionary Baptist Christmas caroling groups on guitar. My
village census was also progressing nicely. During the day, I conducted the
census, and during the evening, I visited the houses in a very different
role of guitar accompanist. Around this time, my census took me to the
house of a venerable man of Venezuelan ancestry who talked to me at
length about shak shaks (maracas). He explained, "When I was young, we
used to go all about. We parang from October right through to January. I
was the shak shak king! I could make them talk—you say a word, and I
make the shak shaks repeat you." As I would soon witness, a skilled shak
shak player does more than provide a driving percussive accompaniment
to parang; in the hands of a skilled musician, the shak shak engages in a
dialogue with the intricate strumming of the cuatro, and skilled shak
shak players create similar illusions of disjunction between movement
and sound.

Finally, around 9:00 p.m. on Christmas Eve, an Indian elder in a local
church who had organized some Christmas caroling invited me to come
with him on a parang. I grabbed my guitar and followed him to a house

belonging to a family with Venezuelan roots. On the front porch, the musicians rehearsed a few choruses around a kerosene lantern. Gathered there was the band: the leader, who played cuatro; two brothers, who played cuatro and were cousins of the leader; their brother, who played a box bass; and a more distant cousin who played shak shaks. Other family members and friends were there, as well, including the sisters of the cuatro-playing brothers and the box bass player. Before leaving, the band played through a few songs with me, and then we began to walk along the dark mountain road, over one mile from the last house with electrical service, instruments in hand, to a neighboring house. We climbed onto the front porch, and the parang band began to play. The song was known as a *serenal*, and the chorus was:

> Será serena, será serena,
> será serena serena será,
> será serena . . .

The last phrase varied considerably from singer to singer. Some said, "de la María," others "de la madrigal," while still others were incomprehensible. According to Moodie-Kublalsingh's Spanish-speaking informants, the correct wording is actually:

> Sereno, sereno, sereno será,
> esos son serenos de la madrugá.   (Moodie-Kublalsingh 1993, 69)

Admittedly, for many songs, I could not specify phonetic agreements between what many singers were singing.

Very quickly, the owner of the house, who was also Spanish, invited the band into his living room, which flickered with the light of kerosene lanterns. At the back of the room, on a table, were a bottle of rum and a bottle of scotch. After the first song, the paranderos all took a drink, and everyone wished one and all a merry Christmas, then broke into an impromptu and abbreviated rendition of the Christmas carol "We wish you a merry Christmas." After an indeterminate time and a few other songs, the lead singer/cuatro player announced it was time to go and began to strum the introduction to one of the standard songs for leaving a house, "Vamos, Vamos, Vamos." When we left, the owner of the house came with us to join the band.

After that first house, one of the cuatro players came to me to advise me on how to play. He praised the quickness with which I picked up the chords to the songs, but he then said, "Your strum is all wrong." He was right. I had a difficult time matching the strumming of the cuatros, but instead tended to produce a strum that waged violent rhythmic war on them. My teacher then used his cuatro to demonstrate the strum I should play. I tried to mimic him, and a frown crossed his face. I tried again, and he said, "Closer, but still not right." My training in classical music and my experience in rock music had ingrained in me a steady emphasis on the downbeat, but parang involved syncopated emphasis on the offbeats. Whenever I managed to finally get the correct rhythm, I would slowly evolve into its opposite and begin emphasizing the downbeat again. That night I slowly learned that to reduce the degree to which my tendencies clashed with the music, the safest strategy I could employ was to empha- size all beats equally.

The pattern of visitation continued through the night. The parang band had moved through the hamlet in which many of Venezuelan heritage lived, and by 11:00 p.m., we had begun climbing the hill into a hamlet populated by Hindu Indians, where houses were brightly lit by electricity. The leaders of the band, all members of the same Spanish kin group, had a sense as to which households would "take a parang." One of the musicians told me that he had never been in a situation where a household refused a parang. At each house, even at the Hindu and Mus- lim homes, the band gained new members.

At each house, the same pattern was repeated. The band would begin playing on the front porch, and then they would be invited inside, and all would drink. The lead singers, in particular, drank more heavily than the musicians. The beverages differed. At some houses there was only rum; at others, there was an impressive array of white rum, red rum, puncheon rum (150 proof), babash (a home-distilled, exceptionally potent, and oc- casionally lethal alcoholic drink), beer, Coca-Cola, and malta (an ex- tremely sweet nonalcoholic drink made from hops). While some members of the group drank only rum, many varied what they drank from house to house. Trying to keep a clear head, I limited myself to nonalcoholic drinks, such as Coca-Cola and malta. Soon, my head was buzzing from music, caffeine, and sugar.

On occasion, someone would sing a verse with Spanish words—such as an entire verse of chanting "uva, uva, uva, uva . . ." ("grape, grape, grape,

grape . . ."). Here and there, other phrases occurred, such as "de la playa" ("from the beach") or "de la vaca" ("of the cow"), but by and large the words were not recognizable. Many of the choruses that were sung by the large group continued to lack any clear enunciation. One song had a chorus that, for some singers, evolved into "I marry, I marry, I marry Maria." At around 3:00 a.m., the parang band had played at almost every house in the Indian hamlet, and the band broke up. The leader said that he wanted to go all night but admitted that some of the particularly drunk people who had joined the band were "spoiling" the parang. As we parted, he said, "Tomorrow we go 'til sunrise."

The next night, I joined the band again. This time, just as I was going to bed, I heard a crowd assembling on the front gallery (*veranda*) of the house in which I was staying. After a rousing serenal, I let the band into the house. They had come to ask me to play guitar again with them. The core of the band this night was around eight people, but with each household we visited, the band's number grew. By 11:00, the band had swelled to over fifty people. This time, the band struck to the main road, along which were strung several multiethnic hamlets. The musicians drank the least alcohol; the lead singers and "chorus" drank the most. Soon after midnight, the numbers began to dwindle again, but the leader of the band urged, "We goin' to mornin'; we parangin' 'til I see the sun come up." A decision was made to visit a particular Spanish household near the end of the village. There the band was served a meal consisting of dasheen (a large taro tuber) and smoked herring with coffee. Slightly rejuvenated, the band moved on. Still, the energy level of the band clearly dwindled. At every household from this point on, the alcohol was supplemented with coffee. By the next house, musicians started stumbling and swooning from exhaustion. Somehow the ensemble kept up the pace of the music, even though everyone was exhausted. I felt the odd sensation of losing consciousness only to find myself regaining it while still playing guitar. Looking around, I saw similar instances—shak shak players whose heads would drop to their chests for several moments only to be jerked back upright, but without missing a beat, and cuatro players whose eyes would roll up into their heads and their eyelids droop while they still kept playing.

Clearly, the continuous music and motion, the lack of sleep, the irregular eating, and the consumption of alcohol, sugar, and coffee were having an effect. While it was not practical to do the appropriate biochemical analyses of those involved in parang, many of those participating manifested characteristic behavioral features of trance: minor convulsive movements of the head and shoulders, particularly involving shaking of the head and shoulders, glazed facial expressions, and glossolalia. With regard to the latter, the singers were increasingly singing nonsense. Some of the singers were singing short snippets between songs that were clearly understandable, but hardly in the Christmas spirit, such as the evolution of "Feliz Navidad" to "Feliz, Mother Dead."

For myself, I felt no pain—just tiredness or nothingness. On several occasions, my parandero friends asked if I "burned," meaning if my blisters were bothering me. Thankfully, the calluses on my fingers were well developed, so I had few such problems; otherwise, I would have experienced the searing pain of sweat running into open blisters pressing on guitar strings. I had been keeping up a rapid strum on my guitar for over seven hours—something that normally would become painful, particularly with the rapid tempo of the music. Shortly after I finally stopped the next day, the pain came in a wave, and I discovered that, in a normal waking state, I could barely move the hands that, the previous two nights, had paranged for hours on end—a total of twenty-three hours of paranging in the previous forty-eight hours.

As the time of sunrise approached, the band obtained renewed energy. The leaders of the band deliberated and decided that they wanted to meet daybreak at the house of one of the Spanish matriarchs of the village, a woman whose offspring were known for their love of parang and their skill at playing the music. We arrived there shortly before daybreak. Her house faces east, so as the band played, it became bathed in the reddish-orange glow of the rising sun. When the sun was clearly visible over the horizon, the band finished, and exhausted, the members of the band went home.

The practice of parang indicates many additional dimensions of the music beyond its identification with the acceptability of a Spanish tradition to many ethnic groups: the reciprocal exchange of drinks for music, the altered state of consciousness, the penetration of the private, domestic sphere of activity with a public, communal activity, and the combination of all of these forming a culturally constructed setting that made those participating extremely receptive to the message of family and community

unity. These features of parang are related to the particular, multisensory way in which the ideas associated with parang are encoded and laden with sentiment; accompanying the discursive messages are strong physical experiences in domestic spaces in which one's presence normally indicates a close, intimate relationship with household members.

🐾 The Gift of Parang

Many households in Anamat look forward to "taking a parang" during the Christmas season. The anticipation includes having some extra drinks on hand. This is part of the yearly preparation for Christmas—a time when visits from family and friends are expected, in addition to the possibility of parang bands coming in the middle of the night. As a gift, parang manifests many of the qualities of gifts described by Marcel Mauss in his classic book *The Gift* (1967). He notes that gifts have several important qualities. First, gifts are "given and repaid under obligation" (1). Second, to refuse a gift is the basis for conflict (1967, 11). Third, the givers and the gift become conflated (1967, 18). Parang involves all of these qualities.

Mauss's treatment of gift giving emphasizes the relationship of exchange and identity. The sentimentality of exchange is, for Mauss, embedded in ideas of identity, and this dimension of exchange has received additional treatment, particularly with regard to exchanges of items in which the identity of the giver is embodied in the item (see Weiner 1992, Godelier 1999). A common pattern is that the more important the exchange, the more time-consuming the exchange. In the case of parang, the performance cannot be viewed outside of time but must be viewed in terms of its unfolding over time. The lived temporalities of parang in relationship to the movement of parang bands through space contribute to the sentimental significance of the practice. The temporalities include seasonal expectations and preparations for parangs, the challenge to biological cycles in the transcending of day and night, the cycles of songs performed at each house, and the rhythms of the songs.

Parang bands prioritize the houses they visit and do not play at every house in a community. Relatives of parang band musicians expect a parang, and since bands are often organized around a core group of related musicians, such expectations are recognized and usually met. For instance, one Christmas, a persistent member of the band kept saying, "If we don't go by my cousin, he vex." Prominent cuatro, guitar, shak shak, box bass, and, if they are locally available, violin or mandolin players also expect visits, and such visits serve as invitations to join the band. Certain households are also known for their love of parang, and performing at such homes is often a goal. Finally, parangs will visit all homes thought to be able to "take a parang" in a hamlet.

When Mauss argued that gifts are obligatory rather than voluntary, he made the point that not only must the giver give, but that the recipient cannot refuse the gift. The homes of kin, friends, and neighbors are given high priority, and there is a sense that the band should traverse the community. This becomes one of the temporal dimensions of parang—many households expect a visit from a band, and many band members understand which households are expecting them. As a consequence of this set of expectations, many households stock up on drinks, and even food, in preparation for a visit. All houses that the parang band visits invite the band inside. The expectation on both the part of the band and the hosts is that the band will be invited inside. This expectation holds, regardless of the religion or race of the hosts and the members of the band. The only exceptions to this are Seventh-Day Adventists, who reject the parang tradition, and Hindu households in which a family member has died within the past year, and the household is still in mourning. While these homes would be expected to turn away a parang, they were not visited by parang bands.

What if a household refused a parang? The answer to this question is related to Mauss's third point—that the gift and the giver become conflated. The core of musicians in a band is frequently from the same family, and they have almost always known one another since they were children. In many ways, the knowledge of parang music and the skills required to play the instruments are passed down from generation to generation, through the ties of kinship and friendship. This is yet another subtle temporal dimension to the tradition—parang represents a tie of contemporary performers to the past of their family. Thus, a parang band is more than an aggregate of musicians; it is the enactment of a kin group, and often of a hamlet within the village, as well. To turn away a parang band would imply turning away this kin group and hamlet group. Since I never heard of such an event, and nobody I asked could recall a house rejecting a parang, it is not possible for me to imagine the rancorous scandal such an event would probably cause. Just because it is unheard of does not mean it is not thought of, however. The possibility, however remote, was enough for one parandero to point this out as part of my education into the tradition. In retrospect, during that first night of parang in 1989, I learned far more than chords and rhythms. There was much more to parang than music, and the threat of rejection carried with it the threat of irreparable social divisions and conflict.

From another perspective, rejection seems a rational response, however. Visits from bands can occur at any time, even during the predawn early morning hours. Under such circumstances, it is remarkable that households greet bands with the joy they do as band members sing and dance their way onto the front gallery at, say, two in the morning. Such behavior is normally not welcome. Most nights of the year, being roused from slumber by song generates an irritable response. The Christmas season seems to grant special license to certain paranderos, and such license covers anyone who accompanies these musicians. In effect, parang allows for a violation of normal, diurnal temporalities in such a way that households welcome these musical interruptions of normally cherished nocturnal slumber. This license is also a product of a relationship between a time of year, a musical tradition, and individuals who, because of their musical and consanguinal genealogies, are viewed as bearers of the tradition.

The importance of the gift of parang and the inconceivable consequences of rejecting a parang can be related to some recent elaborations of Mauss's ideas emphasizing the idea of inalienability, or as Annette Weiner states it, keeping-while-giving (1992). Weiner and Maurice Godelier (1999) both emphasize possessions, but in the case of parang, a cultural tradition seems to manifest the same qualities as inalienable possessions: "Possessions that are imbued with the intrinsic and ineffable identities of their owners" (Wiener 1992, 6). Parang is not associated just with a specific ethnic group, but also with specific kin groups. Parang's authenticity is closely related to inheritance and kinship, as with the inalienable possessions that Weiner describes (1992, 33). Some individuals are so thoroughly imbued with parang that it is said that they live for Christmas and parang, and these individuals tend to be most closely tied by kinship to legendary paranderos. Parang thus connects a performer to the past by invoking the depth of connection between a kin group and a community. Since parang is Spanish music, its associations are to pre-British Trinidad.

The nature of inalienable gifts is that they are kept while being given away. Even when given, they retain the identity of the giver (Godelier 1999, 33). Weiner argues that they also present a tension between the necessity to give and the necessity to keep (1992, 150). Through the act of giving the inalienable, differences are displayed: "Such acts appear to disguise difference, but in reality they proclaim the variation between participants in status or rank authenticated by the inalienable possessions a person is able to retain" (Weiner 1992, 64).

One case was on the limits of what I am arguing, but as is often the case, the violation of expected patterns of behavior is instructive. A band that was paranging one afternoon visited a rum shop owned by a prominent Muslim Indian man in the community. As the parang continued, the owner did not ask the band into his home, which was connected to the shop. Instead, he had the band play in the bar area, which was hot from the afternoon sun beating down on the galvanized steel roof. Due to the heat, the band moved outside, with some grumbling about the owner's lack of hospitality. Soon after, a bottle of rum began to circulate around the band. One of the grumbling musicians shouted, "We don't want your fucking rum!" After a long tirade, he hurled the bottle toward the river across the street. This action provoked a debate within the band. Some argued that the rum should not have been discarded. Others took the stand that if the owner did not invite them into the house, then they were not going to drink his rum. The shouting began to escalate until one of the band leaders intervened: "Cool yourself. I bought the bottle—it was my rum you threw," he said. With this, the parang "spoiled," and everyone went home. Walking back up the road, a band member confided in me that the shop owner gave the bottle, and that everyone should have been grateful. He admitted that he and the shop owner had their differences and did not get along, but that Christmas time was a time to put those differences aside, not a time to "quarrel and be racial."

Why the connection between quarreling and "being racial"? The comment shows that parang is about ethnicity, and that the significance of a parang band at an Indian establishment is that the performance is about the relationship between people identified as Spanish and those identified as Indian.

My follow-up interviews corroborated what was hinted to me by my parandero friend as I walked home: this series of events unfolded against a backdrop of long-standing, racially tinged antagonisms between those involved. In effect, the conflict was not new, but a repetition of past grudges played out in a context that gave this fissure added significance. When the owner did not invite the band into his house, some members of the band interpreted this as a racial insult. This led to their truculent refusal of the gift of rum. Most of those there argued later that, whatever one's relationships the rest of the year, at Christmastime all hostility should be put aside, and the gift of rum should have been accepted. A couple of paranderos stated that the trouble came from people who were not core members of the band. This explanation refers to a fact of parang—sometimes people join a band "jus' to make trouble."

This instance pushes the limits of the cultural expectations of a parang with regard to time, space, and decorum, in many ways. First, it occurred during the late afternoon. Parangs are normally associated with night and early morning hours. Second, the shop owner invited the band into the shop connected to his house, but not into his house. Third, open hostility emerged in the context of the parang. Also, to complicate matters symbolically, in the give-and-take of inalienable traditions in the village, Muslims are the least visible—the exchanges primarily involve Hindu and Spanish traditions. Together, these anomalies can challenge the expectations associated with the practice of this tradition. Yet, even in the face of such a challenge, the emphasis on getting along still emerged in the post hoc interpretations of the event.

The acceptance of a parang, then, is loaded with implications about the relationship between one's family, ethnic group, and community, and that of the band. Joining the band allows one to possess parang while still being dependent on the core musicians who give the music authenticity. A household that accepts a parang without any member joining the band maintains the household as a member of a different ethnic or religious tradition. While this might imply inferiority, if there is a return gift of inalienable cultural traditions, such as the local Divali cultural show in late October or early November, which is organized and staged by Hindus, then there is a symbolic balance. Parang, then, allows either for unity based on claims of similar identity, or for unity based on balanced respectful displays of difference.

✙ Accessing Private Spaces

In Trinidad, almost all intergroup conflicts become cast in terms of ethnic conflict. So, to reject a parang band would imply not simply a rejection of the group, but a rejection of the group's ethnicity. Yet, as I was told, parangs are always accepted. This implies that the hosts accept the band as guests, regardless of their race and class. But the ethnicity of a band is evident—the musicians and their families are generally known to the host, and the various parang bands are identified by the families that dominate them. By inviting a band into the house, a host invites members of a specific family and a specific ethnic, class, and hamlet group, with the expectation that all will participate in a Spanish tradition.

In Anamat, the gift of parang occurs in a particular spatial and temporal context—the galleries and living rooms of people's homes at night. Indeed, it is often late at night, even after midnight—a time when a home is regarded as a particularly private, highly sentimental space. In contrasting Trinidadian Christmas and Carnival, Miller notes, "If Carnival is the festival of exterior display Christmas seems almost as exuberant in its passion for interiorisation" (1990, 70). Miller associates this emphasis on the interior with family, religion, and home—all crucial markers of ethnic differences in Trinidad.

Thus, in addition to generating the obligations associated with performing ethnic traditions across ethnic and religious boundaries, the tradition of parang involves members of different ethnic and class groups entering the private spaces, that is, houses, of one another. In Trinidad, the house becomes not only a living space, but also an ethnically and religiously defined space—a space that is typically entered only by kin, friends, and religious sympathizers. There are few occasions in which members of other ethnic groups enter one's home: the Hindu festival of Divali, the Muslim celebration of Eid, wakes, weddings, and parangs. While there are very few basic floor plans for houses in Anamat, it is often very easy to recognize the ethnic and religious affiliation of the owner of any particular house. Hindu houses usually have a cluster of colorful, triangular prayer flags planted near their driveways. These flags represent *pujahs* performed in the home—a pujah is a ritual offering dedicated to Hindu divinity. Each Hindu god and goddess is associated with a different color, so the flags also serve as a public message of the specific Hindu gods from whom the family has sought blessings. Catholic homes are adorned with crucifixes. Most homes contain calendars—gifts from local retailers—many of which have pictures based on religious iconography. Furthermore, Anamat consists of several hamlets, most of which are ethnically exclusive. Parang bands, despite their apparent ethnic, class, and kinship definitions, move between hamlets and, therefore, move between ethnically defined spaces. More important, for a parang band to access private spaces with clear ethnic and class definitions is an enactment of the bridging of ethnic and class differences. This bridge by no means dissipates difference, however. The metaphor of harmony, which people in Anamat so often apply to Christmas, is more appropriate in the sense that musical harmony requires two notes. What parang accomplishes through its transgressions of spatial boundaries between groups is harmony, not unison.

✿ Multiple Consciousnesses

Parang involves, then, a set of seasonal expectations that include transcending spatial and temporal boundaries that are not broached the rest of the year (weddings and wakes being exceptions). Because of the marathon movement throughout the community, and the physical demands of the music, successful parangs require overcoming pain and fatigue—body sensations are part of the experience of parang as much as senses of community. While this could be viewed as a victory of mind over matter, rather than as dividing body and mind in this way, it is more fruitful to view the experience of parang as revealing the multiple and contradictory physical and emotional sensations one feels. Paranderos sustain themselves through the love of the music and the love of its intimate performance. These sentiments provide the means to overcome the blisters, tendonitis, cramps, stiffness, sore throats, and fatigue that increase the more one parangs. One feels one's body providing the means of overcoming exhaustion and pain at the same time one feels a growing wave of soreness and throbbing tiredness. Parang distorts how one senses one's body, as well. As a guitar player, I shared with the other guitarist and the cuatro players the problems of pain on the tips of my fingers on my left hand, from pressing down on the strings, and pain from a growing blister on the edge of my thumb on my strumming hand. The day after a long parang, several people laughed at my right arm, in which the muscles had swelled up from the constant strumming—and, while I could laugh with them at my newly "pumped-up" appendage, the cramping and tendonitis in my right hand that caused it to contort slightly were less amusing. All parang instruments are asymmetrical to play—even the shak shaks are played asymmetrically, in order to achieve their distinctive rhythm and optical illusion. Consequently, parang creates a distinctive embodied consciousness as an important feature of its performance.

One could also say that parang generates altered states of consciousness, but the phrase "altered state of consciousness" oversimplifies and homogenizes the diversity of states of consciousness experienced during parang. The literature on altered states of consciousness focuses on the relationship between trance and spirit possession (see Bourguignon [1976] 1991), but the category of possession does not apply to parang, and there is no cultural marking of those playing parang as being in a trance state. "Altered states of consciousness" can imply distinct states of consciousness, rather than flows and ranges of experience. Without a nuanced view of the diversity of consciousness, the phrase "altered states of consciousness" combines multiple, and possibly quite different, experiences of consciousness under a rubric that implicitly contrasts them with "normal" consciousness, itself a concept left unexamined. The literature on circadian rhythms suggests important differences in neuroendocrine function throughout a "normal" daily cycle, and these differences have consequences for activity, awareness, behavior, and consequently consciousness (see McEachron and Schull 1993; Moore-Ede 1993; Moore-Ede, Sulzman, and Fuller 1982; Wehr 2001; Wever 1979). Thus, there is no consistent, stable, normal state of consciousness, even in normal cycles of activity. Rather than describe the parang experience as that of altered states of consciousness, it is preferable to discuss the multiple environmental factors that affect the experience: disrupted circadian cycles, consumption of alcohol or caffeine, driving rhythmic stimuli, multisensory experience, and pain. To do so moves one from claiming that all those who participate in parang have the same altered state of consciousness to emphasizing that the experience of one's body and consciousness qualitatively differs between an all-night parang and a normal diurnal cycle of work and leisure. This, then, leaves open the possibility of cultural discourses representing diverse, out-of-the-ordinary experiences as

the same, and thereby culturally creating an image of parang as an embodied collective experience, rather than as a collection of individual
experiences.

While cultural anthropology normally shies away from biology, a brief
examination of what is known about biological rhythms, in particular,
reveals that the fragmentary contradictory body awareness is, in fact, a
cognitive interpretation of fragmentary, contradictory, biological processes. Unusual physical sensations are culturally noted and biologically
encoded. There is also an interesting congruence between endocrino-
logical understandings of the hormone cortisol and Trinidadian ethnophysiological ideas about "heat."

There are important endocrine consequences of trying to stay awake
at night and engaging in physical exertion at this time. Under normal
circumstances, human circadian cycles are very stable (Czeisler et al.
1999). Attempting to change or reverse these has effects on many hormones, of which the effects on cortisol and melatonin cycles are best
documented. Cortisol is a hormone that encourages activity and the con-
version of sugars to energy. It plays a role in waking people up in the
morning, and its levels are typically lowest at the onset of nocturnal
sleep. Melatonin is a hormone that helps to trigger sleep. Among night-
shift workers, cortisol levels are much higher during daytime sleep than
during the nocturnal sleep of those who work during the day (Buxton et
al. 2003; Weibel and Brandenberger 1998; Weibel, Follénius, and Brandenberger 1999). At the same time, cortisol levels during nighttime work
hours are much lower than they are during work hours among day-shift
workers. Melatonin cycles are also altered by nighttime physical activity,
with the result that the secretion of this hormone is delayed (Baehr et al.
2003; Buxton et al. 2003; Mistlberger and Skene 2005; Monteleone et al.
1992; Mrosovsky 1996; Mrosovsky et al. 1989; Van Reeth et al. 1994).
This delay in secretion seems variable from individual to individual and
from day to day, however (Weibel, Follénius, and Brandenberger 1999).
For a minority of individuals, melatonin cycles seem to shift quite rapidly
when they work at night (Quera-Salva et al. 1997). Since these studies
indicate that there is a great deal of variability in endocrine function
among night-shift workers, there is probably similar variability among
those who parang. This undermines any case that could be made for a
consistent, uniform altered state of consciousness evoked by parang. The

studies of endocrine processes also show that wakefulness associated with the reversal of diurnal activities and sleep is physiologically different from diurnal wakefulness (United States Congress 1991; Bonnefond et al. 2004; Monk 2000). Consequently, even though there is not a uniform and consistent altered state of consciousness shared by all participants in a parang, for those who engage in all-night parangs, their wakefulness during the night is of a sort different than that of their normal, daily routines.

Cortisol is also sensitive to physical exertion. Daytime exercise results in greatly reduced cortisol levels at night. Nighttime exercise elevates nocturnal cortisol levels and decreases melatonin levels (Baehr et al. 2003; Buxton et al. 2003; Flinn 1999, 118; Monteleone et al. 1992; Van Reeth et al. 1994). What seem to be at work, physiologically, in parang are cultural expectations of behavior that result in physical exertion at night to help maintain wakefulness and that have biological consequences for awareness and experience. This is a wakefulness of a qualitatively different type than in normal daily activity, and a wakefulness that cannot be assumed to be uniform from one individual to the next.

Such a physiological perspective is not sufficient to understand what is going on. When viewed in the context of Trinidadian ethnophysiology of all-night parangs, there is an interesting congruence between the biomedical literature and Trinidadian cultural interpretations of physical states. Such congruence should not be taken lightly. Elevated cortisol levels accompanying disrupted sleep patterns are commonly associated with depression in the biomedical literature (Janssen and Nachreiner 2004; Knutsson 2003; Rajaratnam and Arendt 2001; van Dongen et al. 2003). It is interesting that Trinidadian notions of "heat" encompass both the elation of fetes, Christmas, and Carnival, and the dangers of forms of "madness" that result from "studying" and "tabanca" (Littlewood 1988). "Studying" refers to obsessively thinking about something, thereby making one's head "hot." "Tabanca" is a feeling of emotional loss often associated with one's lover or spouse terminating the relationship. Both of these types of madness are viewed as asocial and include the symptom of an inability to sleep.

The different experiences of consciousness associated with Carnival and parang are also encompassed in the idea of "heat." In the case of parang, heat is generated from rhythmic collective activity, and its social nature makes this heat a positive force when compared to the asocial, debilitating heat of certain Trinidadian categories of madness. The parallels between Trinidadian ethnophysiological ideas of heat and its consequences, and biomedical neuroendocrinological ideas of heightened cortisol levels and their consequences, are striking. The reason for the parallel is that both biomedicine and Trinidadian ethnophysiology identify emotional states using similar data: behavioral observation and individuals reporting their emotional states. Both biomedicine and Trinidadian ethnophysiology have arrived at the conclusion that a single agent, whether it be cortisol or heat, can produce opposite effects, and that these effects encompass depressive mental suffering and aroused physical activity, based on the duration of elevated levels and the social context of the elevated levels. A difference is that the idea of heat is part of everyday discourse in Trinidad and serves as a means of linking social, mental, and physical states in this discourse, whereas cortisol is part of a technical discourse in the biomedical tradition that has a potential for linking consciousness and biological processes. Another significant difference is that Trinidadian ethnophysiology links a humoral agent, heat, to both individual and collective states, whereas biology is often limited by paradigms that either split body and mind, or that seek to reduce mental function to biological function, and paradigms that see the body as a bounded entity, and consequently tend to think in terms of aggregates of individuals, rather than in terms of theorizing about social, collective states.

Trinidad's ethnophysiological discourse provides a means, then, for bridging body states and culturally defined categories of collective consciousness in ways that traditional biomedical discourse does not. In Trinidadian discussions of heat, the link between social behavior and physical state resembles the links found by George Lakoff and Mark Johnson (1980, 1999) in their study of metaphors, yet, for Trinidadians, the conceptual embodied links are more explicit than Lakoff and Johnson describe for American speakers of English. Taking Trinidadians' phenomenological description of heat seriously allows one to build bridges between their experience, conceptions of embodied minds, and intersubjectively shared experiences. Particularly when a parang is at its peak, it generates states of excitement, which are often indicated by paranderos with the chant of "heat, heat, heat, heat . . ." The times of the greatest heat during a parang are those times when the group is at its largest. At other times, particularly in the early hours of the morning, when paranging until dawn is an issue of pride, the paranderos are often fighting off sleep.

Both when the parang is large and in the early morning hours when it is not, the consumption of alcohol, sugar, and caffeine influence the experience of one's consciousness and one's body. Again, since different participants drink different beverages, it is not possible to argue that there is a consistent, uniform state of consciousness in a parang.

Parang is also marked by multiple sensations engaging senses of balance, touch, smell, taste, sight, and hearing. Multisensory experiences involve parts of the brain that are important to the generation of emotion, because these are the locations in which the different sensory areas of the brain are linked. Consequently, the combination of the focused attention required to sustain one's ability to play and sing the music with multisensory experience often has an emotional component that encourages the retention of the experience and its behavioral implications in memory. Here again, however, the sensory experiences of a singer whose throat is raw, versus a shak shak player whose arms are sore, versus a cuatro player with oozing blisters are very different.

So there are multiple factors to generate states of consciousness and body experiences that are unusual when compared to normal daily activity: the behaviors and physical states associated with heat; the consumption of alcohol, sugar, and caffeine; the disruption of sleep patterns; paced, choreographed activity associated with driving rhythms; the multisensory experiences; and the often-painful, prolonged physical exertion experienced by musicians that raises the likelihood of the release of endorphins, the body's self-generated painkillers. Without culture to guide behavior and to organize interpretations of sensations, these multiple factors and their complex relationships make it unlikely that every participant experiences the event in the same way, but the cultural ideas about how parang feels are shared by participants and are reinforced by culturally appropriate behaviors. How parang is supposed to feel brings together the ideas of mental, emotional, and physical states, as well as social relations. It is supposed to be a conquering of body limitations through the power of music. Parang is meant to sentimentalize ties between those in the band, such that there is a bond that lasts beyond the

Christmas season—after I started to play parang, there were several occasions when I met people with whom I paranged outside of the Christmas season and in a different part of the island from Anamat, and I was greeted with a warm "Mi parandero!" Parang is supposed to generate social, positive heat. All the possible experiences emerging from these physical factors and their combination to create parang states of consciousness, whatever their baseline physiological nature, are interpreted and discussed in the same way—as a cultural model for understanding body states that differ from normal states. This creates a powerful and important holistic nexus of physiology, body awareness, consciousness, and culture, aesthetically related to issues of family, friendship, and community.

Since experiences and states of consciousness change during the course of the night, thinking in terms of the temporality of consciousness during a parang is important. Parangs begin with unexceptional, nighttime states of consciousness, and during the course of the night there are changes. The drunken, euphoric state of the man who sang "uva, uva, uva, uva" was very different from the sober, serious state of another man who was dealing with an unruly member of the chorus. One evening, early in the parang, one cuatro player and a guitar player engaged in an exceptional display of virtuosity in playing an instrumental piece with interesting modulations from one key to another, but by the following morning, such performances had disappeared in favor of a tired but dogged performance of well-known standard songs. The wild dancing and singing associated with heat was very different from the drowsy, almost comatose states battled just before dawn. The points associated with heat clearly involved pacing and heightened awareness. Due to the intensity of the music, there was focused attention in some people. The predawn hours could not be described as encouraging focused attention. Still, over the course of a long parang, it is not necessary for everyone to be in the same state of consciousness all the time for the practice to have an intersubjectively consistent effect. One of the dimensions of parang's power is the constant pacing that the music encourages, and the constant emphasis on unity and community. As a result, people can waft in and out of a variety of states of consciousness, and, by the end of the parang, large numbers of those who participated will recall a feeling of euphoric community commonly associated with the tradition. In addition, even months after, when parang is discussed, the ideas of "everybody lovin'" and "we are a community" and "heat" remain connected in discussions with participants. The physicality of parang provides an experience of a common humanity that transcends ethnicity. As several Trinidadians told me, "If we get cut, we bleed the same color blood." Thus, in addition to seasonality and the use of space that pushes parang beyond just being Spanish and into being part of Trinidad's musical relational aesthetic, there is a shared discourse about abnormal body sensations that also relates the bodies of different ethnic groups to one another.

Parang must persuade musicians to keep performing; it must persuade sleeping households to rouse themselves from slumber and open the door to a band; it must persuade members of households to join the band to increase the chorus; it must persuade residents of Anamat that it is indicative of the "cool, quiet, and loving" qualities of the countryside, even though the music is avowedly hot and loud. For parang to persist and be welcomed, it must be very persuasive. Parang nurtures attitudes in its players and their audiences, and its messages of peace and harmony become tied to the physical exertion and struggle to keep playing. Many Trinidadians want to believe that ethnic harmony is possible, and residents of Anamat like to think of their community as "cool, quiet, and loving." Parang emphasizes fulfilling all these desires. Parang involves group pacing that creates a sense of mutual rapport coupled with fatigue. Tiredness—a state not often ethnographically examined—is important. When the idea of being tired creeps into the ethnographic literature in association with musical settings, it is usually related to affirming the culturally articulated meaning of an event. For instance, in Feld's powerful description of the transformation of men into birds during Kaluli ritual songs, he offers the following statement from a Kaluli man: "'In the middle of the night while the dancers continue, dancing and dancing . . . you get tired and lie down . . . and then, all of a sudden, something startles you, a sound, or something . . . you open your eyes and look at the dancer . . . it is a man in the form of a bird'" (1982, 235). Feld continues, "I was taken by this description of that hypnotic, tired, dreamy sensation promoted by a long evening of song, as well as the implication that one is emotionally prepared to experience the ceremony in this way" (1982, 235). Those who participate in parang associate it with harmony, and like the Kaluli, there is a link between the "hypnotic, tired, dreamy sensation promoted by a long evening of song" and the expectation to consciously and bodily experience the harmony parang is supposed to bring. Indeed, a parang that meets the culturally expressed goals of being hot and of lasting throughout an entire night into the following morning must generate both fatigue and sensations of social harmony. This constellation of factors encourages the internalization of parang's public message of family, community, peace, and love. The pacing inherent in the music is itself a powerful suggestion for a musician to continue to play. The rhythms and chord progressions give a structure to the immediate musical future that the parang musician, particularly with increasing fatigue, follows. In my own experience, it was far more difficult to stop paranging once I started, regardless of any physical pain and fatigue, than it was to decline to join a band for an evening in a feeble attempt to allow my body to recover.

These elements of parang—large groups, the multiple and changing states of consciousness, disruptions of circadian routines, trances, and tired/hypnotic awareness can all be linked to the concept of communitas. Discussions of communitas emphasize two features: the unusual circumstances under which communitas emerges, and the powerful sense of belonging that emerges from communitas (Falassi 1987, 2; Gluckman 1969, 123; Turner 1977, 96). The literature on altered states of consciousness (Wedenoja 1990; Bourguignon 1973, 1991) suggests that trance can play a significant role in the generation of communitas.

Parang falls into a category of unusual, liminal activities. It occurs during the night, it traverses normally private spaces, and it incorporates music and physical responses that include clapping, stomping, shifting from one foot to another in time with the music, and other ways of moving to the music. Through the elements of its practice, parang evokes a sense of belonging to the band, but also a sense of harmony that transcends family, kinship, religion, and ethnicity. Through the unusual elements of its practice, its physical bridging of ethnic/racial spaces, its bringing together of individuals from different backgrounds, and its doing so in a context which heightens suggestibility of an idea that those participating wish to believe, participation in parang generates the sense of unity Turner attributes to communitas. The residual effect of this communitas is a sense of community among Indians, Africans, and Spanish in Anamat, and Christmas serves as a symbol of such interconnectedness throughout the year.

Parang is part of how the residents of Anamat think about their local traditions and heritage. It creates a powerful counterpoint between recognized diversity and a sense of community. This is the forging not of unity, but of relationships. The awareness of such connections conceptually organizes other discussions. While parang is not overtly political, the association of ideas of community and diversity it spawns has clear implications for political discussions.

chapter four 🐾 Bakrnal: An Example of
Changing Opinions

> It is characteristic of the Trinidad sense of humour with its
> ability to turn grave international crises into private jokes that
> the unsavoury and dangerous night-club stretch of Wright-
> son Road in Port of Spain should be called the Gaza Strip.
>
> V. S. NAIPAUL, *The Middle Passage*

> Humor is no joke in Trinidad, because if you cannot appreci-
> ate it, you do not belong.
>
> JAMES M. JONES and HOLLIS LIVERPOOL (Mighty
> Chalkdust), "Calypso Humor in Trinidad"

The attempted coup d'état of July 1990 was enigmatic in Trinidad—an event of immense importance about which there were no
pervasive cultural ideas from which to develop easily a widely
shared interpretation. Such events provoke social processes in which
shared interpretations are negotiated (Black 1996, 253–54). The coup
was a violation of widely cherished ideas of peace and democracy. Also,
unlike parang, which is part of the annual rhythm of activity, the attempted coup disrupted the year and its social cycles.

From editorials and stories in the newspapers and the interpretations
embedded in the calypsos of the following Carnival, it was clear that there
was a society-wide desire to make sense of the attempted coup. I have a
sense, however, that my presence in Anamat led some to make an effort
not only to make sense of the coup for themselves, but to make sense of
the coup for me—they expressed sincere concern about my image of

Trinidad. Many wished to persuade me that the actions of the insurrectionists were not typical of Trinidadians.

The night of July 27, 1990, and the days that followed was a period
filled with anxiety that drove conversations, and while many encounters
were framed in terms of "this is not like Trinidad," the efforts to influence me were also, clearly, efforts on the parts of those with whom I
talked to comfort themselves. I was a sounding board for a dissonant
counterpoint between the events of the attempted coup and their cherished images of the peacefulness of the nation. This counterpoint desperately sought a harmonic resolution.

The strength of the effort to argue that the coup was "un-Trinidadian"
in late July and early August had, by Carnival, around six months later,
given way to a view, both tragic and comic in its sensibilities, that the
coup was profoundly Trinidadian, after all. The music of 1991's Carnival
is memorable, and it frames the remembering of the attempted coup. Yet
to understand this music and the offerings it made to address the enigma
of the coup requires insight into the intersubjective sentiments that
emerged and evolved starting the previous July. The music captures a
moment in the process of the development of ideas about the coup, not
the entire process. Interpretations metamorphosed between July and the
end of Carnival.

This change reflects the power of relational aesthetics to bring together that which seems incommensurable. In Trinidad, an event of the
magnitude of the attempted coup required a musical response in the
context of Carnival to interpret it. As Petrus Koningsbruggen says of
Carnival, it "animates social discourse" (1997, 4). This typical feature of
Carnival was overdetermined in 1991 because of calypsos that further
animated the already animated discourses about the attempted coup.

The importance of music to Trinidadians that I noted in San Diego,
before I left for Trinidad, was driven home to me in early 1991, when it
was clear that music was used to construct intersubjectively significant
views of the world. Thinking through the coup was not an act of individual cognition, but of people in relationships, with physical, emotional,
and cognitive experiences unfolding and evolving through discussions
about music.

For those who participate in Carnival, the experience can influence
their opinions by presenting a combination of cultural ideas about how
one participates in Carnival. Carnival involves social settings that encour-

age large crowds, and that, like parang, include pacing, multisensory experience, and psychophysiological factors involving a variety of states of consciousness. Carnival poses a dilemma, however: it does not transcend social boundaries but tends to recognize and to play with them. The play is one of subversive relationships, not of opposition. Again, the metaphor of counterpoint is useful—dissonance between notes can add to the aesthetic qualities of counterpoint. The decontextualized playing of notes too close together in tone creates a jarring dissonance, but when part of a play of consonance and dissonance over time, dissonance can become a moment of tension leading to a moment of resolution and harmony, with beauty emerging out of the transformation from dissonance/tension to harmony/resolution. In any contrapuntal chord, there can be both harmonic and dissonant elements, and such is Carnival—at any given moment it can simultaneously contain displays that affirm Trinidadian social organization and displays that jarringly contradict such social organization. For instance, Scher's discussion of the mas' band Poison shows that it reinforces the vision its women members have of themselves as middle-class and attractive (2002, 2003). These qualities are not reversed in Carnival but are linked by costumes to some theme, while at the same time the costumes themselves are designed to reveal the women's beauty and demonstrate their class status. Most of those with whom I work do not join mas' bands, but they also play with bacchanal and the blurred boundary of its double meanings of pleasure and violence. Some join in mud mas', others "crash" bands, and still others simply lime. Carnival play contrapuntally unfolds over time. It is relational, not oppositional, and the oppositions that occur in Carnival are often playful attempts at connecting and relating opposites, not at exchanging one for the other. For example, J'ouvert does not reverse day and night but connects night, dawn, and daylight in revelry. The calypsos that followed the 1990 attempted coup d'état dealt with that enigmatic event by creating associations, often comedic, between memories of the previous July and August and images of spirituality and music. Spirituality, violence, and music might seem to make an odd combination, but that reflects Carnival's tendency to bring together what would normally be conceptually separated, and, by making such relationships, to create new meanings.

This is not simply a play of images in a contrapuntal, relational aesthetic; it is a play that creates a holistic nexus of minds, senses, and

bodies. The anthropological study of carnival events emphasizes the social and the symbolic dimensions of the event but often neglects its
physical dimensions. Even when physical experience is recounted, as in
McKim Marriott's discussion of Holi (1966), it serves primarily as a rhe-
torical device for demonstrating the participation of the ethnographer in
the event, rather than as a conceptual framework for integrating the body
into Carnival (see Crapanzano 1986). In part, such ethnographic bias
descends from Émile Durkheim's emphasis on the separation of different
levels of experience that ontogenetically distinguishes between collectives, mind, and body, and that isolates each in different levels of analysis
(Durkheim 1966, xliii; Lukes 1985, 16–22).

Yet, Carnival confronts its participants, ethnographers included, with
some brute physiological issues: the need to stay awake, the stamina to
keep moving, the effects of alcohol, and the irregularity of eating habits
when participating in Carnival. As argued in chapter 3, the importance of
the symbolic fusing of day and night relies upon a culturally motivated
challenge to biological circadian rhythms that are very powerful. Such
basic biological processes are often overlooked, but the literature on circadian rhythms is unequivocal: humans have them; they involve multiple
neural and endocrine time-keeping devices; they are linked to cycles of
wakefulness and sleep, light and dark, and eating (see Aschoff 1981;
Czeisler et al. 1999; Lavie 2001; Moore-Ede, Sulzman, and Fuller 1982;
Wever 1979). Rather than divorce the physical from the cultural, in Carnival, as is also the case with parang, it is possible to demonstrate how biological processes are harnessed by cultural actors to achieve cultural goals.

These processes are examples of how public ideas become adopted by
individuals and groups, and how social and cultural processes can change
people's opinions. These dynamic processes include how social organization affects the distribution of cultural ideas and body states, and how
social activity affects the interpretation and internalization of cultural
ideas. The representation of the attempted coup during Carnival was a
powerful demonstration of such processes.

Messages, Pacing, and Suggestions

Musical events can play a role in changing interpretations and percep-
tions of social issues by aesthetically forming and manipulating relationships. The post-Carnival representations of the attempted coup emerged

from the interplay of physiology, social relationships, and the thoughts and feelings people had about Carnival and the coup. The parallels between the organization of parang and Carnival suggest why the shared interpretations changed among a specific group of people that attended "hot" events, rather than being uniformly distributed among all those exposed to Carnival music: such people became enmeshed in the holistic counterpoints of mind, body, and crowd created by such heat. Together, the factors of social organization and the embodied nature of Carnival thought/feeling account not only for the change, but also for the distribution of this change.

Carnival participation precipitated these changes. But what about Carnival precipitated them? More specifically, what about the events attended by these men changed their interpretations of the attempted coup? Mostly, these men attended fetes that involved large crowds of revelers and the performance of calypsos. Understanding this change and its distribution requires a close examination of the Carnival context, and also a close examination of the social relationships between these men that existed outside of Carnival. The latter issue was discussed in chapter 2. Those who attend do so depending on how hot the fete is considered to be. This affects the proportion of women in the posse; the particular composition of posses in relationship to ties of kinship, friendship, and residence; and the age composition of the revelers, with most of those at Carnival fetes being young adults.

In the case of Trinidad, musical events are powerful media for the dissemination of opinion. They are not the only means: politicians give speeches, journalists write articles for newspapers and magazines, and the television and radio stations broadcast programs. Participation in some musical events can lead to people changing their minds about important issues, though. When cultural ideas about music include expectations that music will coordinate and unify physical actions of large numbers of people (pacing) and will encourage physical activity and multisensory experiences of long duration (thereby increasing the likelihood of a variety of experiences of consciousness, including those encouraged by fatigue, caffeine, alcohol, and endocrine fluctuations), the odds that those participating will become susceptible to sharing the messages embedded in the music increases. These messages that are part of such a nexus of minds and bodies in a Carnival crowd are typically not novel ideas but, consistent with the idea of contrapuntally relational aesthetics,

Road Marches and Their Hook Lines

YEAR	SONG TITLE	ARTIST	HOOK LINE	ALBUM AND TRACK NUMBER
1989	"Free Up"	Tambu	I want to jump up jump up, free up free up	*Tambu... Once upon a Time,* track 4
1990	"No No We Ent Going Home"	Tambu	No, no, we ent going home, we ent leaving. I want to dance all day, dance all night, prance all day, prance all night.	*Tambu... Once upon a Time,* track 8
1991	"Get Something and Wave"	Super Blue	No curfew, no curfew . . . get something and wave	*King of the Road March Greatest Hits,* track 1
1992	"Wine on Something"	Super Blue	To hell with the clock, I done hear the cock, I feeling to wine on something	*King of the Road March Greatest Hits,* track 5
1993	"Bacchanal Time"	Super Blue	Are you ready to go home? NO! (4x) It's bacchanal time! Party can't done (4x). Start to wave (4x). Jump up (4x). Bacchanal Monday, bacchanal Tuesday . . . bacchanal Sunday, bacchanal every day!	*Bacchanal Time,* track 1
1994	"Jump and Wave"	Preacher	The party can't over; jump and wave, jump up and wave (2x)	*Soca Carnival '94,* track 1
1995	"Signal for Lara"	Super Blue	Signal everybody, Lara, start the Carnival, we ain't going home, bats in the air	*King of the Road March Greatest Hits,* track 15
1996	"Movin'"	Nigel Lewis	Movin' to the left, moving to the right	*Caribbean Dream,* track 8
1997	"Big Truck"	Machel Montano and Xtatik	Ride the big truck and jump up, follow the big truck and jump up	*Carnival Soca Hit Compilation,* track 2
1998	"Footsteps"	Wayne Rodriguez and Xtatik, composed by D. Henry and Machel Montano	Footsteps, stamp it harder	*Machel and Xtatik Charge,* track 5

Year	Title	Artist	Lyrics	Source
1999	"River"	Sanell Dempster	When the river come rushing by, if you want to be in the river raise your hand and put it in the sky. You better move out of the way. Jump up, water posse. Bottle in, bottle out, push your bottle all about, push it in, take it out.	*Soca Gold 1999*, track 3
2000 (tie)	"Pump Up" the official winner	Super Blue	Pump up! Wish I could wine on y'all	*Hot Carnival Hits*, track 4
2000 (tie)	"Carnival Come Back Again"	Iwer George	Show me your hand, wave your hand. Show me your flag, wave your rag. We need to nice up the session. Wave it, let me see it, jump up.	*Iwer and Family Soca Compilation I*, track 1
2001	"Stranger"	Shadow	Buy a little rag and put it in your pocket, Buy a little flag, that's the way they do it, Find yourself a band and find a good position, When the music blast, you'll find out how to play mas'. Shadow: When they say "rag," Chorus: Hold your rag, Shadow: When they say "flag," Chorus: Hold your flag, wave it, Shadow: Do your thing, Chorus: Jump up, Shadow: Do your thing, Chorus: Wine up, Shadow: Do your thing, Chorus: Dance up, Shadow: Do your thing, Chorus: Prance up, Shadow: When they say wine, Chorus: You got to wine, Shadow: When they say wine, Chorus: Hold your waist, roll it, All: Do your thing, jump up (2x), wine up (2x)	*Just for You*, track 1

are novel connections between existing, widely shared ideas. Such was the case in 1991, when many popular calypsos turned the coup into comedy by creating new associations for coup events and by leading audiences in physical affirmation of these connections. Indeed, in many popular socas, there are components of the songs that demonstrate whether the audience is suggestible, namely, the singer asks the audience to do something, and sometimes the audience collectively does it, for example, "Get something and wave." By obeying the singer in this way, the audience members' behavior suggests that they are amenable to the singer's other suggestions. Balliger describes these songs as responding to a "tremendous desire for a new form of sociality—one based on feeling and action, as the realm of words has become dominated by falseness and manipulation." Rohlehr identifies these songs as "command" songs (1998) and describes them: "The person on the mike, who in most cases is male, assumes an almost totalitarian power over the movement of female bodies in the Carnival fete" (1998, 89). In most cases, the gendered intent of such songs is made clear by their lyrical content, but the songs following the attempted coup were not as clearly gendered as command songs before and after 1991, and the power of the man at the mike extended to all those in the audience.

The choreography of physical action in these events is not overtly designed for participants to internalize public messages. Instead, it is the outcome of an attempt to meet another culturally defined goal, namely, achieving the party that never ends. Put more bluntly, the goal is to stay awake all night—a goal that is found in many rituals and festivals throughout the world. A popular theme in Carnival is revelry that defies day and night. This theme has also been the topic of many popular calypsos. For a stretch between 1989 (the year I began my fieldwork) and 1995, every song that was named Road March—the song most played during Carnival—juxtaposed ideas of body movement with ideas of revelry that never ends and transcends time. Between 1996 and 2001 the Road Marches have not highlighted issues of time, but have continued to emphasize body movement.

In many contexts, when the rhythms of day and night are reversed, such as in night-shift work, it has negative results on awareness and performance (American Psychiatric Association 2000, 622–29; Folkard 1997; McEachron and Schull 1993; Monk 2000; Moore-Ede 1993; United

States Congress 1991). Carnival is different; it involves a joyful, exuberant challenge to the body's biological rhythms using biological mechanisms in which vigorous physical activity at night suppresses melatonin levels and increases cortisol levels, helping revelers to fend off sleep. Carnival music is dance music. Attendance of a Carnival fete includes the expectation that one will dance most of the time one is present. Dancing is structured by the music, and in Trinidad's Carnival, many songs include cues on exactly how one should move. For example, in the chorus of Nigel Lewis's 1996 Road March "Movin'," he instructs the audience to start "Movin' to the left, movin' to the left, movin' to the right, movin' to the right" (*Caribbean Dream*, track 8). Consequently, the connections made by some songs between instructions meant to encourage widely shared and coordinated dance movements and political messages gives these messages both embodied and discursive qualities.

The case of the attempted coup d'état of 1990 and the following Carnival is interesting because it was an event that everybody talked about, and it was an event that was sung about during Carnival. It was also a Carnival season in which many of the most popular calypsos not only gave representations of the coup and the state of the country, but also had tests of audience suggestibility, such as "get something and wave." It provides an excellent case of the combination of political messages and orders for body movements in the nocturnal setting of Carnival fetes. Quite possibly, the need to intersubjectively make sense of the attempted coup and music's capacity to transform anxiety into a sense of comforting collective and cathartic social relationships revolutionized soca.

ꙮ The 1990 Attempted Coup

To fully appreciate the transformation of interpretations from coup to Carnival requires a discussion of the anxiety of the days following the coup. During those days, I culled my fieldnotes to craft a letter describing the events to my graduate program at the University of California, San Diego. Looking back, that letter captures the mood of the moment in a way that a new analysis of my notes, many years after the fact, could not do. I present a large, slightly edited, portion of the letter here.

> On July 27, 1990, Imam Yasin Abu Bakr led members of his organization, the Jamaat al-Muslimeen, in an attempt to overthrow the government. During

the early evening hours, one group bombed Police Headquarters and then seized the Red House, the building in which Parliament meets. This group disrupted a session of Parliament, and took the prime minister, A. N. R. Robinson, and many other members of Parliament, hostage. A second group, led by Abu Bakr, took over Trinidad's only television station at the time and broadcast the overthrow to the country.

During the early evening hours of July 27, 1990, I was liming near one of the rum shops in Anamat, a popular gathering place. I was sitting on the steps of the shop when I looked up the road and saw Sinclair, one of the young adult men of the village, walking quickly toward the shop, with a big grin on his face and a bounce in his step. He yelled to the group gathered along the road outside of the shop, "We all Muslim now! Abu Bakr take over!"

One of the men liming outside of the shop said loudly, "Nah, man."

Sinclair responded, "I ent kicksin' [kidding]! I jus' heard it on the radio. Abu Bakr take over the Red House!"

At this point, a taxi that worked the route between Anamat and the local market town pulled in front of the rum shop. Since the driver had not found any customers to "take down the road" (out of Anamat), he got out of the car to lime a bit. One of the men in front of the rum shop said to the driver, "Sinclair tellin' we that Abu Bakr is Prime Minister! Turn on the radio. Let we find out." The driver reached into his car, ejected a cassette he had been playing, and turned up the volume. The radio was silent. He turned the dial to the other radio stations, finally getting the National Broadcasting System (NBS), which was playing music. Those of us outside the shop had no evidence for or against Sinclair's claims. Since it was approaching seven o'clock, the time of the national news on television, I left the group at the rum shop for home, not knowing what to think.

When I got home, I suggested to my wife, Margaret, that we should go to a neighbor's house to watch the seven o'clock news on television. We did not have a television and had not watched the news on television in several months. In response to my wife's confused look, I said that I had heard a rumor that I wanted to check out. We arrived at our friends' house and waited for the news. At seven o'clock, the television station was playing videos of calypso and steelbands. This was not very unusual—the television station often used music videos to fill time between programs. Our hosts were slightly surprised that the news was not on promptly at seven o'clock, but on rare occasions, the news is late. At about ten past seven, everyone in the house started to get apprehensive, and shortly afterward, we saw the newsroom without hearing the usual theme music for the evening news. Sitting at the news desk was Abu Bakr, flanked by one of his men, and Jones P. Madeira, a local television personality who was not the usual news anchor. Behind them stood three men with rifles. Madeira introduced Abu Bakr, who began to read a statement: "As of six o'clock this afternoon, the government of Trinidad and Tobago has been overthrown. . . ." He then went on to announce that Prime Minister A. N. R. Robinson and other members of Parliament had been "arrested."

My wife and I returned home to pack just in case we needed to leave in a hurry. We then traveled to another neighbor's house. As soon as we arrived, we were asked, "What do you think?" We replied that we did not know what to think. We looked in the front room of the house, and everyone in the house was gathered around the television with a radio on at the same time. NBS (National Broadcasting System) was the only functioning radio station. The DJ, Dennis McCommie, made it clear that NBS had not been taken by Abu Bakr's organization, the Jamaat al-Muslimeen. The television station broadcast only calypso and steelband videos, particularly calypso videos critical of the elected government. Normally, the state-run television station would not play such videos. On the radio, NBS offered the commentary on a soccer game between Jamaica and Trinidad and Tobago at the national stadium. The family that my wife and I were with were starting to get worried—one of their adult daughters had not yet arrived home from Port of Spain. The few news reports given by NBS suggested that there was shooting and widespread fires in Port of Spain. Police headquarters had been bombed. No member of the government was known to be free.

Occasionally, NBS radio would break from the soccer game to announce that NBS was not controlled by Abu Bakr. The disc jockey, Dennis McCommie, told the nation that the security guards and staff had driven back the Muslimeen men, and then put out a fire that had been set on the first floor. McCommie announced, "The building has been secured, and we are locked inside." The owner of the house commented that, for whatever it was worth, NBS was not controlled, but that was not worth much to my wife and me, or to the family we were with.

By 9:00 p.m., McCommie announced that NBS had been contacted by the Protective Services (Police, Defense Force, and Coast Guard), and that they had requested that he ask everyone to clear the streets so that the "Protective

Services could come out and move freely." For all those in that house, NBS had become their government.

At this time, the missing daughter arrived home, asking, "What do you think?" She had been in Arima when the news of the takeover had hit. She said that, once people heard the news, transportation had been very difficult to find. The mother, relieved by her daughter's arrival, then turned to my wife and me to explain, "We Trinidadians don't like violence, and we love our freedom and democracy. You see those gunmen on the television—that is not our style." She was concerned that my wife and I would get the "wrong impression" about Trinidad.

As the evening wore on, Archbishop Anthony Pantin relayed a message, through NBS, that some members of the government were free, and that the military was loyal to the constitutional government. Abu Bakr came on television soon afterward and began to rant against the military and constitutional government, and he said that he would have free and fair elections within ninety days, and that Allah would prevail.

Just after this announcement, a man with a car arrived, and after asking, "What do you think?" he suggested that some of us go to Sangre Grande to find out what was going on. He suggested that Margaret and I go so that I could call my parents in the United States to let them know that we were safe.

On the way, the driver and passengers talked about Abu Bakr. Based on what I later learned was a widespread rumor, the driver said that most of Abu Bakr's men were ex-bandits that Abu Bakr had trained into a small army. He added that Abu Bakr supported his operation through theft and drug money—they would intercept drug shipments, steal them, and sell the drugs.

When we arrived in Sangre Grande, the streets were empty. The police station was shut and guarded by constables with automatic weapons. The police guard said he was under strict orders to defend the station, and that they were fearful of attack. He had nothing else to add.

We left the police yard and went to the home of a family that was originally from Anamat. We were greeted by two daughters; the rest of the family had traveled to southern Trinidad that day, and they were not home yet. Again, the greeting was, "What do you think?" I tried calling the United States, but could not get a line.

We climbed back into the car, and, on a whim, the driver went to a telephone booth and called 999, the emergency number. Someone answered and promptly hung up without a word.

As we drove about Sangre Grande looking for news, prayers started to be broadcast over NBS radio. Initially, leaders of the major religious groups in Trinidad called, but it soon turned into a free-for-all where it seemed that anybody who claimed any remotely religious office anywhere on the island called to offer a prayer. We returned home.

Back in Anamat, Margaret and I thanked the family we had visited, and returned to our house, where I turned on the radio. Heads of state from other Caribbean nations were now calling NBS to state their condemnation of the coup attempt. Long after midnight, Sahdeo Basdeo, the minister of external affairs (equivalent to the U.S. secretary of state), announced that the government had not fallen, and that there were several ministers that had not been captured, who were organizing to defend the constitutional government. With this, I went to sleep.

During these initial hours of the attempted coup, those I encountered were doing three things: expressing anxiety, particularly about the safety of loved ones who had not returned home; seeking information on what was happening; and beginning to develop interpretations of the events and predictions of what was going to happen. The pervasiveness of the question "What do you think?" was striking, as it became a mantra for the occasion and created, in retrospect, a form of oral poetic structure to my, and probably others', experience of the events. The question was asked in the climate of shared anxiety and often was juxtaposed with expressions of concern about loved ones. No shared interpretations had emerged to explain what was happening, but there was, seemingly, a powerfully felt need for such intersubjectively shared interpretations. It was as if emotionally driven thoughts were seeking some external organization. This was not simply individual minds engaged in the seeking behavior; it was groups of individuals collectively and repeatedly asking, "What do you think?" In thinking about my fieldnotes from that night, I noticed a bizarre parallel between the travels of my friends that night and how a parang begins: small groups of relatives traveled to the homes of kin and friends asking, "What do you think?" And with each home, someone new joined the group.

The search for order from which to develop an interpretation was also manifested in trying to contact those who impose order on chaos, or who symbolize order: stopping at a police station, and calling the emergency number even though there was no emergency. There were no immediate threats to me or to those with whom I spent time that night, but with the news that some members of the elected government were free and organizing, and that the defense forces were supporting the elected government, the group that had mobilized under the theme of "What do you think?" dissipated.

That night, the loved ones returned home, so, by the next morning, when the curfew and the state of emergency were announced, the activity turned toward building interpretations of what was going on. It was in this context that I ventured to the nearest rum shop at noon, the minute the curfew for my area was lifted. There, I found a group of adult men in a discussion in which the sole topic, not surprisingly, was the attempted coup. This, in itself, was unusual. Normally, at the rum shop, one would observe several small groups of men talking with one another, and each group would be discussing a different topic, but on the day after Abu Bakr's seizure of power, the men were standing in a single, large circle outside the shop. Some offered information; some recounted their harrowing escapes the night before; some bragged about the looting in which they had engaged; and all shared responses to the stories and information told. All present participated in building a shared representation of the events. The cultural interpretation that was emerging among these men was, therefore, collectively generated and public.

As the discussion unfolded during those brief hours when we were free from the curfew, the men offered reflections upon known events but soon began to produce intricate conspiracy theories and hypothetical musings about the future course of events.

The reactions to the insurrection were a mixture of analyses, wishes, fears, and storytelling.

Those who participated in the looting played a crucial role in the unfolding of these discussions. On the one hand, they were eyewitnesses to what went on in Port of Spain, but on the other hand, some listeners, generally the older members of the group, expressed mild condemnation of the looting. The narrators then began to craft stories that were partly humorous, partly apologetic, and partly defensive. One man, John, was at the soccer game. He said that he "came out" only to find chaos in the streets: "People runnin' everywhere." He went to the downtown area, quite a distance from the stadium, seeking some way to get home. There he met with young people looting on some streets and burning buildings on other streets. After displaying the shoes that he had acquired, he shifted his narrative to a third person, "The looters only looting Syrian stores—they pass black stores straight!" The news stories of burning, looting, and violence were merging with stories of class- and race-based looting told by eyewitnesses. This combination of humor, criticism, and bravado that accompanied the discussions of looting, in Anamat, seemed to have been true in other parts of Trinidad, as well (Ryan 1991, 201, 208).

The result was that the shared narratives that the men at the rum shop were building went far beyond what was stated on the radio. Their additions incorporated issues of conflict embedded in their representations of Trinidad and other Trinidadians. These conflicts focused on race and class but also, importantly, on age. Not only were the looters portrayed as young, but within the dynamics of those at the rum shop, it was young men who had looted, and older men who condemned the looting. Venturing away from the rum shop, the old heads, both men and women, resoundingly condemned the looting, claiming that it was irresponsible behavior, like it was looting that was destroying the country. The conceptual scaffolding that was emerging was built around the conflicts and tensions that receive public attention: ethnicity, class, gender, and age. It's not the case that the interpretations were borrowing from the clear opinions on other issues, but as Freud's theory of free association suggests, one set of ideas triggered the emergence of other ideas, and with discussion came increased elaborations—participants in the discussion generated connections for one another, resulting in a collectively created network of ideas. The search for interpretations evolved from the anxiety-driven "What do you think?" to a germ of an idea that grew by being connected to common opinions about the nation that predated the attempted coup.

As the events unfolded, the army and the police subdued the looting through powers granted under martial law, in particular the power to shoot on sight anyone found outside during the curfew hours. In fear of this order, the few men from Anamat who chose to loot stopped. In Anamat and nearby communities, the power to shoot on sight was rarely exercised. Instead, police used intimidation, with occasional beatings, to coerce people to obey it. People in Anamat found the curfew burdensome, although most obeyed it. Those who did not were primarily the young men.

These acts of disobedience were also grafted into the narrative of the coup. They included stories of police shaming local men by making them lie in the road. Another quickly disseminated story was of the police shooting the dogs of a man in a nearby town, rather than shooting the man. In general, though, the depiction of the enforcement of the curfew was playful—heroic tales of evading the police when they approached, or humorous tales of what the police did when they caught somebody. In this way, the police were not portrayed as a threat to people's well-being, but instead as a significant threat to freedom of movement and the freedom to lime at night.

After six days, Abu Bakr and his followers surrendered, after signing an amnesty agreement with the government, but the state of emergency and the curfew remained in place. Over the next several months, the government gradually shortened the curfew.

During subsequent days of August, groups of men congregated along the road for the six "free" hours allowed by the curfew. Their daily discussion of events led them to develop a shared set of topics, if not a shared outlook, on the attempted coup. It was on the first night riding in the car to Sangre Grande that I first heard the contrast of violence versus peace develop. It was during the first free period after the curfew that the issues of youth versus old heads emerged when discussing looting. It was also during those free hours that the issue of freedom versus restriction began to be discussed. Running through all these conversations were the major characters in the political drama: Abu Bakr versus Prime Minister A. N. R. Robinson, and the Jamaat al-Muslimeen versus the elected government. Gradually, out of the contrapuntal manipulation of the connections between these issues, a shared set of issues emerged. During the discussions, the men offered conjectures and narratives that experimented with connecting these paired elements. The only radio station that was broadcasting during the coup did not offer much information, which allowed imaginations to run wild.

One element of the emerging interpretation was an evaluation of Prime Minister A. N. R. Robinson's performance in office as a betrayal of the interests of the youth of the country. The young men asserted that Robinson's party, the NAR, won the elections in 1986 only because the country's young voters were dissatisfied with the previous thirty years of rule by the PNM. Under the NAR government, unemployment among young adult men rose tremendously. Since the government had been the primary employer of many young adults in the village before the NAR took over, the rising unemployment among youth was seen by them as Robinson betraying youth in favor of old heads, who often maintained jobs even if less physically fit than younger men to perform the work.

In contrast to Robinson, Abu Bakr was viewed as a self-proclaimed champion of youth and a critic of the status quo. Abu Bakr campaigned against the PNM in 1986 and was known for rehabilitating youth who were involved in crime. Yet there were nagging rumors about Abu Bakr and the potential that his organization, the Jamaat al-Muslimeen, was actually a front for a crime organization. While this rumor received a great deal of attention from middle-aged and elderly Trinidadians, the young adult men dismissed it.

In addition, Abu Bakr's use of guns was exciting to the young men, in the same way in which they found popular movies that featured Sylvester Stallone's character Rambo exciting. While the use of guns in movies was exhilarating to many, real bullets and real killing troubled them. Movie-goers are safe from bullets fired in the movie, but the attempted coup was a profoundly different experience for many, because it was not safe. Soon, the young men determined that the use of guns had the potential to restrict their freedom.

These men regarded freedom as the fundamental dimension of Trinidadian life and asserted that they were freer than "even the United States." The concepts of freedom and youth are connected. In contrast, the old heads are associated with imposing and desiring restrictions on freedom. Since Robinson had betrayed the youths' trust in him, he was labeled an old head. Consequently, the logic of the young men's opinions made him opposed to youthful freedom. Abu Bakr was not a likely champion of such freedom, however. The young men felt that the violence caused by his use of guns had (by the curfew) resulted in restricting freedom, as did the government's use of guns to suppress Abu Bakr. One said, "With general election a year away, what is the need to try to overthrow the government? I want to vote them out!" In a nationwide survey, Ryan discovered that even though the NAR was extremely unpopular, 75 percent of those he sampled thought the coup attempt was "unwarranted" (1996, 209). The difference was that Abu Bakr's rhetoric was about freedom and equality, whereas the rhetoric of the government

was that of a state of emergency and of granting power to law enforcement to restrict freedom.

Another perspective offered at the time was speculation that Abu Bakr
was merely acting as a pawn in a larger power struggle. These individuals
pointed out that he had supported Robinson in the previous election,
and rumor had it that Robinson, himself, had armed the Jamaat al-
Muslimeen, in case he lost the election. Several different scenarios were
proposed in which Robinson and Abu Bakr colluded to improve their
positions, or in which Abu Bakr suddenly felt betrayed by his former ally
and joined forces with someone else. Emerging amid such speculation was
the figure of Karl Hudson-Phillips, a former Attorney General who was
associated by the young men with an ideology of repressive law and order,
and the potential of turning Trinidad and Tobago into a police state.
Some wondered if Hudson-Phillips, who was deputy political leader in
Robinson's political party, had set up Robinson in order to assume the
mantle of power, himself. Such conspiracy theories grew from the play of
ideas, and a desire to seek conceptual connections. These connections
generated anxiety and concern among the young men. Due to the part
played by Abu Bakr in many of these theories, feelings toward him
evolved toward ambivalent or negative attitudes—part of what seemed to
be an islandwide trend (Ryan 1991, 219). These speculations did not
cohere but were part of the contrapuntal process to make sense of the
events through discussion.

Many of the young men wished that Robinson and select members of
his cabinet had been killed by Abu Bakr. They felt strongly that Robinson
had done enough wrong to the nation to deserve this fate, not only as a
punishment but also as a means of preventing his further ruining the
country. They articulated Robinson's failures as growing unemployment
and the implementation of a value added tax (VAT) of 15 percent, both of
which significantly affected the lives of the young adult men of Anamat.
Throughout Trinidad, rather than bolstering Robinson's support, the attempted coup further eroded it (Ryan 1991, 220).

As the coup attempt was resolved, the dissonant counterpoints of
opinion also resolved as the young men gradually worked out a position
in which, for all practical purposes, the attempt meant a threat to their
freedom and to youth. The state of emergency that resulted from the
attempted coup restricted freedom. The curfew ruined parties and dis-

rupted wakes. There were even rumors that Carnival, the annual condensation and expression of freedom, would be canceled by the government.

The first cultural interpretation of the young men, then, held that the insurrection had ruined Trinidad by introducing violence, by restricting freedom, and by investing a great deal of power and authority in the hands of the old heads in government, through the state of emergency. This contradicted the image of Trinidad as a place of freedom and peace.

❧ Carnival 1991: Moving from Dissonant to Consonant Images

The young men's interpretation of the attempted coup was reinforced in the subsequent months. When the government demolished the buildings on the Jamaat al-Muslimeen compound in the middle of the night soon after elected government regained complete control, the young men I talked to viewed this as supporting their position that Robinson was anti-youth. At the time of the demolition, the only members of the Jamaat al-Muslimeen using the compound were women and children, which made the act appear vindictive. The young men continued to complain about the curfew and how it restricted their movement. Much to the chagrin of many, the curfew resulted in the cancellation of a nearby harvest festival, as well as the curtailing of festivities of Anamat's own harvest festival. The topic of the attempted coup was gradually overshadowed by news out of the Persian Gulf, however. The growing confrontation between Iraq and the United States grabbed the headlines in news. By the time the state of emergency was lifted in early December, discussions had shifted almost entirely to "Saddam and Bush." Carnival in 1991 brought the coup events back into their minds through the medium of calypso.

The state of emergency was lifted on December 10, 1990, less than one month before the beginning of the Carnival season. Many people were apprehensive about Carnival: the disorder engendered by Carnival seemed too close to the disorder of the insurrection—both were examples of bacchanal. Many of the middle-aged and older Trinidadians feared that the segments of the population that looted would make Carnival like the attempted coup.

Among the young adult men who frequent Carnival fetes, the concern about violence was very real, as described in chapter 2. By coincidence, during 1991's Carnival, oil exploration work in Anamat provided these same men with large amounts of money to spend, far more than they were accustomed to having for Carnival. They attended the fetes, initially apprehensively; yet, with each fete, they became more and more convinced that Carnival would be "cool," in the sense that there would be little violence. In fact, the young men described this Carnival as a presentation and a performance of freedom: freedom from martial law, temporal freedom, freedom of expression, and freedom of movement.

While there were many calypsos that addressed the events of the insurrection (see Rohlehr 1992c), only a few received attention from the young men. This was due to several factors. First, calypsos that emphasize political commentary tend to be slower, making them unsuitable for dancing at Carnival fetes, the major context of Carnival participation for the young men. Second, political commentary calypsos tend not to receive airplay on Trinidadian radio stations. The major means to hear these calypsos was to attend the calypso tents, which the young men of Anamat did not do. The few political commentary calypsos that did receive attention from this group were performed in the competition for Calypso Monarch, a competition broadcast live on television and radio. The calypsos played at fetes, on the other hand, received a great deal of attention. Thus, even though the numbers of calypsos concerning the attempted coup were many, only a small number entered into the discourse of Anamat's young adult men.

The young men tended to remember only sections of the lyrics of these calypsos and responded to only certain parts of the songs during fetes. These parts tended to be the central themes of the songs around which the other lyrics were organized. As Robin Balliger (1998), Renu Juneja (1989), Rohlehr (1998), and Keith Warner (1982) have noted, audience participation is an important component of calypso. Calypsos elicit audience participation in many ways, ranging from calling for the audience to take specific actions (e.g., "Get Something and Wave"), to asking the audience to sing the chorus, or to echoing the calypsonian. Audiences tend to remember these lines but do not remember much of the other lyrics. Consequently, these few lines, performed in the context of Carnival activities, served as the basis for the reinterpretation of the events of the attempted coup. These reinterpretations were not widespread, general ones, however. The people from Anamat who attend soca fetes are pre-

dominantly young adult men. The discussions in which the reinterpretations emerged began with multigenerational groups of men at the height
of the crisis, but within a couple of weeks, these groups broke along
generational lines, with the young men carrying on their conversations at
the two places in Anamat where they limed, known as "the Junction" and
"Block 100," and the older men carrying on their conversations inside
rum shops or at their homes. Women continued to gather and talk, but
these conversations took place at home, rather than in a public place.
Long before Carnival, divisions of age and ethnicity had reemerged to
determine with whom people thought out loud. The reinterpretation
incorporated the coup attempt into the image of Trinidad as an island of
peace, humor, and freedom.

🌑 Soca Fetes

In 1990, the setting where most people with whom I talked heard popular
socas were on the radio, in taxis and maxi-taxis, and at fetes. Out of these
three contexts, the last involved young adult men participating in the
fetes in posses. Men from Anamat travel to these fetes as members of
posses. Consequently, these occasions involve groups of men defying
their circadian rhythms in a multisensory, paced environment. These
factors combine to encourage the adoption of any messages that are
associated with the fete occasion.

In this context, it is not surprising that calypso music, including soca,
is viewed by most Trinidadians with nationalist pride, but also as a genre
with historical significance. The key moments in Trinidadian history have
been marked by important calypsos and are treated by scholars of the art
form as important glimpses into particular periods (D. Hill 1993; Rohlehr
1990; Regis 1999). Thus, there is abundant evidence that the messages
conveyed by calypsos are often incorporated into Trinidadians' interpretations of current events. Importantly, however, it is not the case that
all calypsos have equal influence, nor is it the case that all Trinidadians
are equally influenced. As with the specifics of the case of the 1990
attempted coup, the general issue with calypso has to do with why some
messages become topics of conversation, and why these messages are not
evenly distributed throughout the population.

While audience response is crucial in answering these questions, the way in which artists and disc jockeys structure Carnival contexts is also important. The playlist for a soca band or a disc jockey is not a randomly ordered and selected collection of the latest tunes but instead a carefully crafted presentation of the music. The most popular song, the most likely contender for Road March honors, is likely to be played often, but not likely to begin a band's or a disc jockey's set. The revelers know they will hear the song eventually, and they await their favorite songs with anticipation. Performers encourage and gauge audience response by using these popular songs. The songs discussed here were those that were popular among the young adult men studied. The treatment of each song emphasizes where it was heard, the issues with which it was associated, and, in some cases, how performers used the song. It should also be noted that while each song is associated with a particular performer, all soca bands at all fetes performed all the popular songs.

The popular coup calypsos of 1991 contained messages that mixed images of destruction with hope in an elaborate lyrical counterpoint. For example, the popular calypso "Get on Radical" (by the Mighty Duke) used somber lyrics such as:

> I hear you let go so much of lead
> Over fifty wounded, as many dead.   (lyrics in L. Williams 1991, 17)

The song began with shouts of "doi," an onomatopoeic expression used by Trinidadians to represent a gunshot, in this case, the gunshots of the coup attempt. The portrayals of violence and disorder in the calypso were juxtaposed with the phrase "get on radical"—a phrase serving as a call to bacchic freedom. For the young men of Anamat, the details of the violence portrayed by this song were lost, and "doi" and the "get on radical" hook lines were remembered. Among young adult male Trinidadians, the use of "doi" can signal joking and equality, and is similar to a particular greeting used when an individual surprises a friend, "Bao shot—you dead." In this way, the lyrics of the song were connected to informal relationships between young adult men.

"Get on" is a phrase with many uses. In some contexts, it refers to angry confrontations and fights. In other cases, such as Carnival, it refers to behaving with reckless abandon. In the context of fetes, informants said that to "get on" involved excessive drinking and dancing, and to "get on radical" was interpreted as doing so superlatively. The selection by fete-goers of "doi" and "get on radical" from a long song with somber lyrics, and their response to and interpretation of these phrases, suggests that the song served as a call for solidarity, peace, and freedom. The song did not exist in isolation from current events, either. It was performed, and in one performance that many of Anamat's young men attended, "doi" also received a special use by a popular soca band. In reference to growing tensions generated by Iraq's occupation of Kuwait, the lead singer suggested that everyone send "soca shots to the Gulf, to bring peace to the Middle East." He then raised his hand in the air, pointed his finger to the sky, and began chanting "Doi, doi, doi, doi," urging the crowd to join him. The large crowd (announced ticket sales were around 22,000) responded by "sending soca shots" and screaming "doi." His ability to get the crowd to do this suggests several things: first, that he was able to unify the actions of the crowd; and second, that he was able to get the crowd to do what he asked, which suggests that he had some power over them. An interpretation of the texts of "sending soca shots to bring peace to the Middle East" and "doi" in the context of the somber lyrics of the song would be misleading in this case. The "gunshots" in the context of festival-driven revelry gave a sense of a shared collective message in favor of global peace and freedom. These shots were guided by a performer, and the audience's physical response was, from my vantage point of being in the middle of the fete, unanimous and enthusiastic.

The juxtaposition of embodied unanimity, enthusiasm, freedom, peace, celebration, and onomatopoeic gunshots seems strange, at first glance. Yet when taken in the context of Turner's discussion of liminality (1967, 1974, 1977), it parallels what he stated about ritual transitions: "Such rites characteristically begin with ritual metaphors of killing or death marking the separation of the subject from ordinary secular rela-tionships (in which status-role behavior tends to prevail even in informal situations) and conclude with the symbolic rebirth or reincorporation into society as shaped by the law and moral code" (1974, 273). The use of "Get on Radical" by both performers and the audience in the Carnival setting seemed to be marking a conceptual transition from one view of the coup and nation to another—a transition based on linking the disor-der of the attempted coup to Carnival in a nonthreatening way. Impor-tantly, this transition was marked by physical, choreographed action. Indeed, its power emerged from physical, collectively coordinated action.

This power came, on the one hand, from the perception of consensus—
after all, *everyone* around was chanting "doi" with their hands thrusting
into the air. The power also came, on the other hand, from the power of
pacing, as it linked the event to memories of the coup and the seemingly
contradictory image of Trinidad as a peaceful, nonviolent nation. After
the party, revelers remembered sending soca shots and they, importantly,
remembered everyone around them sending the same soca shots. The
result was the generation of a feeling of unity in attitude, encouraged by
unity in physical action toward the tensions in the Persian Gulf. In this
way, the song addressed many of the components of the already existing
cultural interpretations about the coup. The shared ideas of the coup had
settled on concerns about freedom being threatened, mass destruction,
and the future of the country. The uses of "doi" and "Get on radical"
carried clear double meanings in this regard. It was the double meanings
that were conducive to changing cultural ideas about the coup—signs
with double meanings entail connections to two different interpretations
and readily play transformative roles. This possibility is not sufficient to
explain the transformation, and a single song was not convincing. "Get
on Radical" was often one of the songs that signaled the "hot" portion of
the set, however. While Trinidadians did not use the term, it could be
described as a "warm up" for the even more popular soca songs that
addressed the coup, which also played upon double meanings to transform the cultural interpretations of the coup from being an event of
anomalous destruction to being an event that manifested humor, unpre-
dictability, and hope.

Another popular song, "Calypso Coup" by Bally, depicted a coup attempt by calypsonians who seize Port of Spain. The chorus of the song,
which attracted the attention of fete-goers, was:

> Fire, we comin' to take over
> Fire, we combat them with soca
> We wining, we grinding, we running, people tumble down
> Fire, fire, oh, oh, fire, fire, oh, oh, fire, fire all over town.
>
> (*The Best of Rootsman and Bally*, track 9)

Fire was associated with the widespread arson during the attempted
coup. Fire is also associated with being hot and, as noted earlier, a good
fete is a hot fete. As discussed in previous chapters, such heat is not only

metaphorical but is also linked to Trinidadian ideas of the body and its functions (Littlewood 1988).

In this context, it is worth exploring the implications of soca fire. Like the use of "doi," fire was an aspect of the attempted coup taken out of the context of the coup and applied to the Carnival setting, which thereby created a contrapuntal contrast and connection between coup and Carnival. In the discussions during and immediately after the attempted coup, the topic of the fire that ravaged Port of Spain after the looting was prevalent. Indeed, many of those from Anamat who sold their agricultural produce in Port of Spain worked on Charlotte Street, an area hit hard by the fires. Their daily sojourn to "town" to make a living was a daily reminder of the fires. Yet Bally's song juxtaposed fire with dancing and soca, which again evokes the concept of heat that has played such an important role in understanding the relationship of music to cultural images of Trinidad. Soca fire is a good fire, although, as the title of the song suggests, it is a powerful weapon that can take over the city. Just as the streets filled during the coup, during Carnival they filled because of bacchanal or, as sung in "Calypso Coup," "bakrnal"—a clever pun that highlighted bacchanal as a crucial concept for tying together violent disorder and euphoric revelry. It played with the possibility of the two meanings of bacchanal being fundamentally related to one another. Two people yelling at one another in a heated dispute is as much bacchanal as is dancing to the Road March, caked with mud during the early hours of Carnival. While both instances seem quite different, both are examples of "heat," as well. Thus, the double meaning of Bally's "fire" is coupled with the pun on the coup leader's name. "Bakrnal" became a memorable pun that endured the hazy memories of late-night feting to become part of the discussion of the calypsos and coup on the ride home and the morning after. It was widely regarded as one of the best puns of the Carnival season. The looting, fire, and disorder associated with the attempted coup and its leader became material for how to define the postcoup Carnival: Abu Bakr and the government were replaced by calypsonians, and the violent disorder was replaced by "bakrnal."

The most popular calypso of the season, "Get Something and Wave" (Super Blue, *King of the Road March: Greatest Hits*, track 1), contained three hook lines which were frequently repeated: "Get something and wave," "No curfew," and "Ding-a-ling-a-ling." The lines leading into "no curfew" portray several different authority figures proclaiming that there is no curfew because it is Carnival. As mentioned, according to the young adult men, the curfew was the single most onerous aspect of the state of emergency, so the song's emphasis on there being no curfew, thus allowing one to fete day and night, was a declaration of freedom. During Carnival fetes, the audience joined in this declaration by chanting "no curfew" with performers. This drew the audience's attention to this hook line, and because of the frequent performances of the song, gradually revelers also began to pay attention to the figures in the song who declared "no curfew." These characters are, themselves, symbols with multiple, interacting meanings.

One is Mother Muriel, who represents a leader of a Spiritual Baptist church. A defining feature of the Spiritual Baptists is that they practice an extended period of sensory deprivation known as "mourning," during which participants get visions (see Glazier 1983; Simpson 1966; Herskovits 1966; Herskovits and Herskovits 1947). Sometimes, these visions call for a group of Spiritual Baptists to go to a particular place and deliver a message to passers-by. This consists of bell ringing, hymn singing, and preaching. Often, the Spiritual Baptists dress in long robes and tie their heads, giving them a distinctive appearance, adding to their conspicuously clamorous presence. In every Spiritual Baptist congregation, there is a leadership position known as the "mother." According to Glazier, the office of mother in the Spiritual Baptist church is in charge of all of the logistical arrangements for the mourning ceremony (1983, 63).

The lines "ding-a-ling-a-ling" from "Get Something and Wave" were connected to Mother Muriel's bell. With Mother Muriel being a Spiritual Baptist, the reference was, by implication, to a Spiritual Baptist bell, and even to a vision. Indeed, at one point the song describes Mother Muriel as having a vision, although this was not acknowledged much in discussions by many of the young men of Anamat.

The metaphor of mother is based on the powerful roles played by women in religious groups and within the family. Trinidad, like other West Indian societies, is associated with matrifocal household units— households in which "women *in their role as mothers* are the *focus* of relationships" (R. T. Smith 1996, 42, emphasis original). Matrifocality is not a household with no father as a member, but is more appropriately seen as a household with a particular constellation of roles in which fathers are physically absent for much of the time. The absence of the father makes the mother an especially powerful figure in the life of the child. This was manifested by adult men who frequently referred to their mothers as their "queens"—a metaphor depicting complete and absolute power that must be obeyed. Taking this into account, the figure Mother Muriel ringing a bell is imbued with maternal and supernatural powers, with which she declares, "No curfew."

The song also depicts Abu Bakr as prime minister declaring, "No curfew, no curfew." This particular line drew a great deal of attention and hilarity from listeners. Abu Bakr was at no time prime minister—that title was reserved for A. N. R. Robinson. For some, this line evoked a feeling of getting back at Robinson by making Abu Bakr the prime minister and having him make a popular, emancipating decree. For others, it reminded them that Abu Bakr had made many popular decrees during the coup attempt, but while his decrees were met with popular approval, they produced no results. Therefore, the line "Prime Minister Abu Bakr" evoked an interpretation of Robinson as powerless on the one hand, or of Abu Bakr as powerless on the other. The ambiguity of the line allowed for a semblance of consensus, even if there was actual disagreement in interpretation, and even when the different interpretations were driven by different evaluations of the characters of these two men. Yet, the ambiguity affirms a link between Robinson and Abu Bakr. This consensus was punctuated by the obedience to the command of "no curfew." The fact that revelers were hearing this line at fetes long after midnight provided one demonstration of consensus, and the physical response to this line— a response that consisted of revelers jumping into the air or raising hands when the fete was hot—provided another demonstration of pacing, indicating consensus. Again, with heat serving as an indicator of arousal, focused attention, and emotional intensity, the coincidence of unanimous paced action to punctuate a literally amplified message led to powerful sentiments of consensus among partygoers.

Finally, fete-goers responded to the imperative "get something and wave" by waving towels and articles of clothing. More than any other activity during the Carnival season, this evoked a sense of connection through unison—so much so that it continues to be an important element of Carnival and many popular socas. Waving things provided an immediately visible expression of simultaneous, unitary action. In addition, like the previous example of "sending soca shots to the Gulf," it was also a means of demonstrating the singer's power over the audience—they obeyed his commands. This generated a feeling of oneness among those participating. But it also put in place a modified hierarchy in which the calypsonians were given power. Bally organized a calypso coup; Duke and Super Blue ordered the audience to perform certain actions, and the audience obeyed. As Rohlehr wrote of the calypsos of 1991: "Interactive Soca empowered the person with the microphone to instruct assemblies of hundreds of thousands to perform together whatever command was shouted to them" (2004b, 420).

One of the few political commentary calypsos popular with the young men was "Attack with Full Force" (by the Watchman), which documented the events of the attempted coup while poking fun at the leadership of the major political parties. Its title is a quote from the prime minister who, while held hostage, instructed the police and army to "attack with full force." Most people did not hear this song until it was performed on the televised Calypso Monarch semifinals. By this time, those who attended Carnival fetes had been to several such events before hearing "Attack with Full Force." Moreover, the weekly tabloids had reported on the song's increasing popularity at the Calypso Spektakula tent. The song is an open challenge to censorship and restrictions on freedom of expression, beginning:

> I've been accused of being a traitor.
> They say is I who cause Abu Bakr
> To hijack the parliament
> And shake up them rich boys in government,
> 'Cause the first thing them fellows do
> After they stage the coup
> Is to play all them calypso
> That was ban from the radio.
> But the ink ain't dry on the amnesty;
> The ruler talkin' censorship already;
> Either he bounce he head in the brawl,
> Or they didn't have no sense to start with at all.
>
> (*Plenty to Be Sorry For*, track 6)

At the end of every verse, Watchman sings: "Boy, watch your mouth, and don't say a thing," and he continues by saying that one or another political leader might be listening, as in: "Robbie [for Robinson] and he boys might be listening." The chorus of the song—phrases that elicited gleeful repetition by Anamat's young men—was: "Who vex can vex; tell de boss he loss, cuz when they maintain that course, I attackin' them with full force." "That course" referred to in the song was open to wide-ranging interpretation. In the shared interpretations of young men, "that course" was connected to Robinson, his government's policies, and his government's restrictions on freedom. By implication, it was also associated with old heads. It was those who advocated restricting freedom who were to be attacked with full force, and attacking with full force meant taking advantage of freedom of expression to make incisive criticisms. Watchman's calypso turned out to be very effective at coordinating audience actions, as well. Very quickly, the audience began to sing with him when he sang "Boy, watch your mouth, and don't say a thing" and "who vex can vex." During the car ride to a fete, after Watchman's performance at the semifinals, my fellow passengers discussed his song and spontaneously broke out into the chorus. The topic of the attempted coup was increasingly being linked with revelry and challenges to authority. The transition from a view of the events as tragic to a view of the events as comic was well under way with several weeks of the Carnival season left.

The shared interpretations of the attempted coup initially developed by the young adult men of Anamat were built on a counterpoint of several contrasts through which they represented the coup as a threat to their freedom. Furthermore, they maintained that any threat to freedom was anomalous in terms of Trinidadian culture and undermined Trinidad's national image. Through participation in calypsos at fetes, a new interpretation emerged from the associations created by the counterpoints of the songs. The Robinson-Bakr and the government-Jamaat contrasts were eliminated. Abu Bakr, Robinson, the government, and the Jamaat were all similarly viewed as those with authority who threatened freedom. The calypsos portrayed calypsonians and their audiences as having the real source of power in Trinidad. The calypsonians proclaimed freedom supreme and made it the most potent weapon against restrictions and violent disorder. Such messages were conveyed through the participatory nature of calypso, and in a context of pacing and heat, were frequently topics of discussion during the ride home and on the day after. This indicates the influence the combination of context, participation, and message had on audiences' imaginations.

Most of the audiences at fetes were young adults. Calypsonians are regarded as ageless, in large part because it is the popularity of the calypso with youth that determines its power, and the youthful enthusiasms behind the calypso then, in turn, reflect upon the calypsonian, no matter how old he or she is. Indeed, calypsonians such as Sparrow and Kitchener remained extremely popular in 1991, even though their careers respectively had begun about thirty-five and fifty years before 1991. Calypsonians habitually ridicule the government and public figures. Since the government and restrictions on freedom were associated with old heads, by the young men of Anamat, calypsos involved undermining the authority of all old heads and, in so doing, undermining the ability to carry out the desire, attributed to them, to restrict freedom.

Through the calypsos, the victory of freedom and youth was not only proclaimed but performed by the thousands of young people who participated in the fetes and eventually celebrated in the streets of Port of Spain. The young men in Anamat articulated the significance of Abu Bakr taking over the streets during the coup, the government taking over the streets during the state of emergency, and the youth of Trinidad taking over the streets during Carnival. Consequently, just as some of parang's power to create a sense of community involves its ability to enact relationships in a holistic nexus of physical experience, cultural interpretations, and collective action, so, too, did some of the power of 1991's Carnival to change ideas about the attempted coup d'état. Out of the reaction to the interpretation of, and embodied participation in, the calypsos, the image of the attempted coup was rearranged, with freedom, peace, and youth contrasting with old heads, Robinson, the government, Abu Bakr, the Jamaat al-Muslimeen, and restrictions.

Most importantly, the attempted coup became incorporated into a teleological cultural image of Trinidadian history. Prior to Carnival, the attempted coup was seen as anomalous—a dissonant counterpoint with the image of Trinidadian character as loving freedom and peace. The calypsos of Carnival 1991 made the coup and its resolution in favor of youth and freedom all seem predestined. Following a device important to all counterpoint, the dissonance between coup and Carnival was transformed into harmony. In this regard, the calypso "La Trinity" (by Denyse Plummer) is worth mentioning. This song was not heard at fetes but was frequently played on the radio. The song maternalizes and deifies Trinidad, suggesting that she survives the threat of violence and political repression by divine power:

> Don't cry for me my children, for all the fire that falls upon me.
> Don't cry for me my children; it was given to me to test me.
> But I will not be shaken; I am La Trinity.
> And there is no destruction; if you look, then you'll see
> There is a mountain top;
> There is a sea and sand;
> Child, I am your rock;
> I am your island.   (*Carnival Killer*, track 3)

This version of the chorus (there are two in the song) made a profound impact on listeners, along with another portion of the song:

> Look in the mirror. Tell me what you see:
> A beautiful child of La Trinity.

In this calypso, the attempted coup and its aftermath were portrayed as a challenge that the Trinidadian people successfully met. The youth of the island proved, through Carnival, that they were defenders of freedom. Through hearing and interpreting the calypsos of 1991, and through participation in the fetes, the youth of the country redefined the events of the coup as predestined, and as an example of Trinidadians being unable to carry out or to support a plan involving violence and political repression.

The same young adult men who had wished for the prime minister's death during the coup, and who had expressed support for Abu Bakr, now viewed the events of the coup through the lens of Carnival. The coup became a comedy, although one tinged with tragedy, in which the country was given reason to laugh at Abu Bakr, and even more so at the government. It also became an instance in which freedom, youth, and humor triumphed over restriction, age, and authority through the performance of calypsonians.

This change in interpretation depended on physical participation in Carnival. The cultural expectations of behavior during Carnival that were organized and punctuated by performers' uses of hook lines created shared physical action. This shared physical action also made the fetes "hot." The messages to reinterpret the attempted coup were inexorably

linked to consensual, paced, widely shared, focused attention and heightened emotion.

⚜ Carnival and Contrapuntal Connections

In examining the influence of participation in Carnival on cultural interpretations of the coup, two processes have emerged as particularly important: (1) the influence on interpretations by the fragments of calypso
lyrics remembered by audiences, and (2) the development of consensus
from participation with crowds at Carnival fetes in unitary physical action. The processes are closely related. Song phrases remembered were
often those associated with participation at fetes. Indeed, Carnival involves choreographing differing cultural ideas. As Balliger suggests, "For
soca audiences, the music generates truth in the rhythm, trust in face to
face encounter, solidarity among peers, and security in an insecure world"
(1998, 62).

To some extent, the processes of manipulation and consensus building
parallel the concepts of symbolic inversion and communitas, concepts
that have been prominent in the anthropological study of festivals and
ritual. Turner's use of these concepts (1974, 1977, 1987) is not as rigid as
the term *antistructure* implies. Instead, Turner emphasizes antistructure's
generative qualities, rather than conceptualizing a situation without any
structure—antistructure is closely associated with liminality and communitas, which are ideas linked with embodied, concrete, experientially
dense relationships between the people involved (1974, 271–75). In such
contexts, the symbols associated with individuals could be readily manipulated. It is not a significant leap, then, to suggest that contrapuntal
connections within and between cultural ideas are also manipulated in
these settings. Or, as Glissant has argued, the poetics of the Caribbean are
poetics of relation (1997). It is important to keep in mind that not all of
the ideas and symbols presented in Carnival are manipulated, however—
only those elements that are selected, remembered, and discussed by
participants. Consequently, manipulation emphasizes the agency of participants over the abstract relationships between symbols. Related to
consensus building are the actions and processes leading to feelings of
communitas. Not everyone who participates in festivals experiences communitas, but many do. In Trinidad, at least, one source of communitas,

BAKRNAL   181

and consequently a feeling of consensus, is active participation in the choreographic embodiment of interpretations. The cultural goals are related to cultural expectations for behavior that have physiological consequences with cognitive and emotional implications.

This case shows that the young men of Anamat used the presentation of ideas in popular calypsos to manipulate, and to reinterpret their ideas about the attempted coup—or were their ideas manipulated? In some ways, this involved establishing new connections between common topics of discussion, and in other cases it involved reinterpreting events so that they could be connected to a cherished image of Trinidad.

The coordination of dance and discourse through music has become common in Carnival, and it is crucial for overcoming the human body's diurnal tendencies. In 1991, the choreography of movement in relationship to messages encouraged by the songs also encouraged sensations and sentiments of consensus about interpretations of the attempted coup. Through the participation in 1991's Carnival, the ideas and evaluations of a specific event changed in the minds of the group of young Creole men from Anamat. It is not the case that all Trinidadians participated in these fetes, however. Many did not. Consequently, the images and interpretations that the young adult men adopted were not distributed much beyond their segment of society and formed only one contrapuntal voice among many perspectives. The centripetal aspects of Carnival participation remained, and the opinions of the young adult men continued to contrast with the opinions of old heads and women, who both remained profoundly troubled by the coup events. Despite calypso's and Carnival's power, in the wake of the attempted coup d'état, they were able to forge images of the nation that were distributed only among a small segment of Anamat's population, the young adult men.

chapter five ❧ "Chukaipan," "Lootala," and the Counterpoint of "Mix Up"

ELECTIONS AND BOUNDARIES COMMISSION NOTICE
Election Offences
The Elections and Boundaries Commission wishes to remind the public of offences on polling day as stipulated in the Representation of the People Act, Chap. 2, 01.
SECTION 88—Prohibition of employment of bands of music.
(1) No person shall hire or make use of any band of music on polling day within an electoral district for which an election is being held until two hours after the closing of the poll.
(2) No person shall play in any band of music at any meeting or in any procession held on polling day within an electoral district for which an election is being held until two hours after the closing of the poll.
(3) Any person who contravenes this section is liable on summary conviction to a fine of seven thousand, five hundred dollars or to imprisonment for six months.

Full-page announcement in the
TnT Mirror, October 4, 2002

In Trinidad, music is so politically significant that not only are there laws restricting its use in relationship to elections, but of all the election laws, the ones pertaining to music are the ones the government ensures are published and disseminated in newspapers.

All elections in Trinidad are, to some extent, enigmatic events, but the parliamentary elections of 1995 that produced a tie were particularly so.

Just as the attempted coup of 1990 generated discussion and debate, the parliamentary elections of 1995 did so, as well. As before, references to music played a prominent part in discussions of the course of events, and music played an important role to frame how the events of the time were remembered.

Music is important in parliamentary elections. It galvanizes popular support and is a campaign tool. Its significance is such that the use of music on election day is restricted and regulated, as the above announcement, placed in one of the weekly newspapers, attests.

The connection between calypso and politics has been well studied, but all Trinidadian music stands at the ready to be made politically relevant. Elections are times of great musical and political significance in Trinidad. This has been the case ever since Trinidad and Tobago gained internal self-rule in 1956. One of the elements of calypso music that allows it to be viewed as the "voice of the people" is the extent to which the music engages political consciousness and eludes political control. Calypso is not alone in that. Indo-Trinidadian music also plays an important political role, and since the 1980s, this role has been increasingly publicly noted.

Many traditional forms of Indian music are associated with Hindu rituals. Tassa drumming was originally associated with the Muslim tradition celebrating the martyrdom of Mohammed's grandson, Hosein, and known in Trinidad as Hosay. For a long time, it has also been associated with Hindu weddings in Trinidad. Myers notes that the nineteenth-century Presbyterian missionaries to the Indians, the Mortons, described drumming in association with weddings (1998, 116). Pujahs, ritual offerings to Hindu divinities, often involve a harmonium player who accompanies the singing of devotional songs called *bhajans*. Often, the bhajans are accompanied by a variety of percussion instruments: the *dholak*, a double-headed barrel drum; tabla drums, an upright pair of drums; and the *dhantal*, a metal rod struck rhythmically with a u-shaped piece of metal.

Politics and religion have been closely related within the Indian community. As Trinidad and Tobago moved toward independence in the 1950s, Bhadase Maraj, the leader of the largest Hindu organization in Trinidad, the Sanatan Dharma Maha Sabha, formed the People's Democratic Party (PDP). After the PNM won the 1956 elections, the PDP united with other opposition political parties to form the Democratic Labour Party (DLP), although in this coalition, the Hindu voting block led by Maraj was the largest. The closeness of Hindu religious organizations to the DLP and to the political parties that followed the DLP after its demise in the 1970s waxed and waned, although the Sanatan Dharma Maha Sabha is still the largest Hindu organization in Trinidad and Tobago, and is therefore an important political voice. Even though the formal ties between Hinduism and the opposition political party changed, Indian music continued to be related to both, and the Sanatan Dharma Maha Sabha has continued to advocate for traditional Indian music to be given recognition equal to that the government gives to calypso and pan music (Ryan 1999).

The parliamentary elections of 1995 were probably when the political significance of Indian music burst into the national consciousness. This had not happened before because most Indian music is either sung in Hindi or Bhojpuri, languages that most Trinidadians do not understand, or, unlike political calypsos, does not contain lyrics that openly and explicitly comment on the politics of the moment. The political significance of Trinidadian Indian music is not explicit in its lyrics.

In the 1995 election campaign, the PNM used Indian music, specifically the song "Lootala" (Rohlehr 2004b, 433). Unlike the calypso tradition, where the political commentary is closely tied to the lyrics, the use of Indian music to make political points has relied more heavily on sound styles and the context of performance. The aftermath of the 1995 parliamentary elections showed that it is not necessarily the words sung that serve as the catalyst for discussions of politics in relationship to ethnicity, but the ways in which music genres interact and are combined: The counterpoint of "Chukaipan," "Lootala," and the elections in 1995 demonstrates this.

"Chukaipan" (A Decade of Scrunter, track 8) was a soca parang popular during Christmas of 1995 and performed by Scrunter, a calypsonian from Sangre Grande, the market town nearest Anamat. The song describes Scrunter going on a parang with his "Indian family," thereby invoking transracial kinship ties, but doing so, interestingly, without mentioning interracial marriage. Scrunter uses Hindi kin terms that refer to one's mother's side of the family to describe his fellow paranderos and paranderas, and the chorus is taken from an Indian folk song.

At the same time, a remixed version of "Loota La" released under the title "Lootala" (*Soca Gold 1997*, track 12) was extremely popular through-out Trinidad. The original version was a chutney performed by the artist Sonny Mann, but the remixed version featured not only the Bhojpuri lyrics and chutney style of Sonny Mann, but also English lyrical additions by the calypsonian Denise Belfon, and lyrical reggae dancehall stylistic additions by the artist General Grant. The setting for the song is a wed-ding, and in the remixed version, Denise Belfon sings of dancing with Sonny Mann, and General Grant flirts with the female (and presumably Indian) wedding guests. In addition, General Grant chants that everyone at the wedding refers to him as "mamoo," the Trinidadian Hindi term for "mother's brother." Like "Chukaipan," the remixed version of "Lootala" plays with images of transracial kin ties.

The simultaneous popularity of these two songs by themselves forms a very interesting counterpoint, but their popularity took place in the con-text of a parliamentary election that resulted in the first Indian prime minister of Trinidad and Tobago.

Like the attempted coup d'état of 1991, the parliamentary elections of 1995 demanded explanation. These elections resulted in a tie in parlia-ment that, when broken, resulted in the first Indian prime minister in the history of Trinidad and Tobago. This was reflected not only in the concep-tual struggles of the residents of Anamat, but also in the efforts of analysts of Trinidad's politics to understand the elections (see La Guerre 1997; Premdas 1998; Premdas and Ragoonath 1998; Ryan 1996; Wells 1999), and the fact that the calypsonian Cro Cro won the 1996 Calypso Monarch title with a song that analyzed the elections called "All Yuh Look for Dat," in which he criticized African Trinidadians for not voting in sufficient numbers to win the election for the PNM.

Anamat's residents note that the village reflects the nation's ethnic diversity. In practice, this complicates the usual association of ethnicity and political party representation. Popular consciousness and scholarly analysis both associated the PNM with people of African descent and the UNC with people of South Asian descent. In Anamat, these associations are both acknowledged and subverted at the same time. Anamat is part of an electoral district that, for many years, was represented by a Hindu Indian member of the PNM. In 1995, the local PNM candidate was a prominent local Indian businessman. These facts serve as fodder for impassioned discussions that emphasize political leaders as making racially motivated choices, rather than as simply blaming a party's behavior on its ethnic associations. In Anamat, the association of each political party with a racial identity exists in counterpoint to the PNM often putting forth Indian candidates, and the Democratic Labour Party (DLP), a party associated with Indians until its demise in the 1970s, putting forth Victor Bryan as a candidate, a Creole of mixed European and African descent who had served on the Legislative Council. In addition, the longtime Indian member of parliament for the PNM once complained about anti-Indian racism within the PNM, and some Indians perceived anti-Indian sentiments in Bryan. Consequently, in recent years, when the PNM has had Indian candidates locally, discussions have split over whether this is an honest attempt by the PNM to broaden its base, or a calculated, cynical move to obtain some Indian votes.

In 1995, music, politics, and ideas about ethnic relations were temporally merged as the parliamentary election coincided with the Christmas season. While elections are memorable events, 1995 was particularly noteworthy. First, it ended in a tie. As is the case with parliamentary systems, the political party that secures the most elected seats in parliament determines the prime minister—the chief executive of the government. A tie between two parties in parliament creates a governance crisis that was avoided in 1995 by a third party, the NAR, with its two elected seats, breaking the tie (although when a tie occurred again in 2001, a constitutional crisis did follow until elections were held again in 2002). Second, when the NAR broke the tie, it was in favor of the UNC, and resulted in Basdeo Panday being chosen as prime minister. These unusual events prompted much conversation and were enmeshed in webs of association.

1 The November 1995 parliamentary elections resulted in a tie between the People's National Movement (PNM) and the United National Congress (UNC), with the National Alliance of Reconstruction (NAR) coming in a distant third. With the tie between the PNM and UNC, the balance of power was determined when the UNC formed a coalition government with the NAR. This resulted in the selection of the first Indian prime minister, Basdeo Panday, in the history of the nation. Panday was also the first prime minister who had not previously served in a PNM-led government.

2 There was a newly elected village council that had quickly succeeded in some major local accomplishments, in contrast to the previous inactive village

council. These accomplishments included the renovation of the community center.

3 The remixed version of Sonny Mann's chutney "Loota La" became widely popular—this remixed version was released under the title "Lootala" and involved the collaboration of reggae dancehall artist General Grant, calypsonian Denise Belfon, and Sonny Mann to produce what can best be described as a chutney-dancehall-soca fusion. Some people in Anamat attributed the success of the UNC, a party dominated by Indians, to the popularity of "Lootala." Others attributed the success of the chutney to the UNC.

4 Scrunter's soca parang "Chukaipan," which discusses an interracial parang band, was also released. "Chukaipan," which stands for chutney-kaiso-parang, is a song sung by a calypsonian about visiting his Indian family at Christmas. The title represents the fusion of musical forms in the song. The success of "Chukaipan" can be attributed mostly to its singer, Scrunter, whom many view as master of the soca parang art form. Yet this chutney-soca-parang inspired local paranderos to mimic its mixed style for several songs during their house-to-house parangs during the Christmas season of 1995.

These are different events, but those I talked with in Anamat saw them as conceptually connected and linked to an image of themselves and the nation as "mix up." The increasing popularity of chutney music with many groups in Anamat played an important role in the development of a relational aesthetic connecting cultural ideas concerning music, politics, the community, and the nation. Such sentiments seem to have been widespread in Trinidad. Prime Minister Basdeo Panday wrote in the Sunday edition of the *Guardian*, one of Trinidad's daily newspapers: "The level at which chutney music has entered the Carnival celebration this year (1995) is indeed symbolic of the times in which we now live—the time of awakening and of coming together of our people as never happened before" (quoted in Ryan 1996, xxx).

Such sentiments were part of a complex counterpoint of opinions. Again, these divergent views of the election were articulated through music. Rohlehr writes:

Calypsonians' immediate reactions in 1996 to the new régime were ambivalent, ranging from bitter rejection and feelings of having been betrayed by the black ethnic electorate (Cro Cro, *Black Man All Yuh Look for Dat*; Sugar Aloes,

The Facts) to joyful approval (Valentino, *Time to Love Again*). Brother Marvin (*Jahaji Bhai, Unity*) and Delamo (*Stay Together, Trinbago*) both felt that patriotism should transcend ethnic rivalry and separation. . . . Watchman saw in the new government a tendency to avoid responsibility by blaming previous governments for everything that needed to be set right. . . . Chalkdust in *National Unity* (1996) dismissed UNC claims that that party had brought unity to the nation.   (2004a, 365)

The cognitive entangling of political events and songs involved public processes of musical consumption coupled with group discussions in public settings. Shared cultural models of Trinidad evolved out of these discussions that mingled politics, music, and issues of identity. The concept of the cultural model that I employ here emphasizes learned and shared cognitive *and* emotional processes that are used to think about the world and experience (see D'Andrade 1992, 1995; Quinn 1996; and Strauss and Quinn 1997). One of the important features of cultural models is that many of the processes that produce the models remain unarticulated. The connections that form the basis of the models, then, are not connections that people are necessarily aware of when speaking but are manifest in the transition of topics, attitudes, and behaviors. Indeed, if an individual pounds the table when making a point, I would consider the motor behavior of pounding to be as much a product of the cultural model as of the speech. The evolved cultural models of Trinidad that emerged in 1995 were intertwined connections of ideas—often sites of counterpoint. Indeed, by the time 1996's Carnival had ended, the hope of overcoming ethnic differences through politics and music had dissipated (Reddock 1999; Manuel 2000, 193–94). The idea of transcending ethnicity through music was tarnished by the incident in which Sonny Mann, a chutney artist, was pelted with bottles and stones as he tried to perform "Lootala," a song from 1995, at the 1996 Soca Monarch Finals. So, Carnival did not end up reinforcing the messages that were prevalent at the beginning of 1996. The messages of late 1995 did not become persuasive due to participation in Carnival fetes—the power of these messages emerged before the large fetes and in the context of the Christmas season.

As will be seen, a theory based on conceptual connections and counterpoints actually portrays a situation of great conceptual fluidity. New connections added to any cultural model can substantially alter how the model is used to interpret events, and group discussions often have this effect. This is because the application of cultural models to interpret the world is a hermeneutic and often collective enterprise, each new interpretation can change the model, and, as events unfold, they pose interpretive challenges to cultural models. This chapter, then, looks at the process of the formation of connections in a cultural model of the Trinidadian nation that unfolded in a particular place, at a particular moment in time, when the counterpoint of national identity and diversity seemed especially salient.

✿ Definition of Chutney

An important component of understanding the complex, contrapuntal connections that emerged in late 1995 and early 1996 is the emergence of chutney music as a national, as opposed to an ethnic, art form. Tina Ramnarine reveals another important dimension of this counterpoint: "'chutney' actually means different things to different people" (2001, 15). Throughout the history of calypso, Indian musical forms had been experimentally incorporated into various songs. Beginning in the 1970s, some Indian artists began to incorporate elements of calypso and soca into Indian music. This was the same period in which a new form of calypso, soca, was emerging. Traditional Indian music also contained layered rhythms between either the drums and cymbal in tassa, or between the drums and dhantal in bhajans and folk songs. The fusion of Indian music and soca, then, often consisted of complementing Indian harmonium and percussion parts with guitar and bass guitar playing in soca-style rhythms. By the 1980s, some Indian performers were achieving success with their fusion of Indian and soca music, although it was still associated with Indian cultural shows at this time. By the early to mid-1990s, the market for this music included the large Carnival fetes, and some songs were explicitly marketed to national and transnational audiences, rather than just to Indian audiences, although the music retained its distinctive Indian identity. The receptiveness of non-Indian audiences to chutney, the burgeoning experimentation with Indian music in all forms of popular music in Trinidad, and an Indian prime minister taking office are three events that from the perspective of a non-Trinidadian anthropologist seem too closely related to be completely coincidental. From the talk of Trinidadians, all seem to be cognitively linked, as well.

I have asked many Trinidadians the question "What is chutney?" They all provide a seemingly paradoxical definition: it is Indian music that is distinctively Trinidadian. Regardless of race or background, the residents of Anamat share a prototypical image of chutney music, but the boundaries are blurred and contested.

Chutney music is thought of as a music that is Indian in derivation and that incorporates contemporary Trinidadian and West Indian musical elements, particularly soca and reggae. The Indian influences include sacred bhajans, folk songs, and what has come to be known as "Indian classical" music. The first two are associated with the Indian traditions brought to Trinidad by the Indian indentured laborers (Jha 1985; Manuel 2000; Myers 1998; Vertovec 1992). The category of Indian classical music, as distinct from sacred music, actually refers to several different musics that include folk songs, the nonbhangra music commonly found in Indian films, and secular songs composed using Indian ragas—modal scales and structures of themes and variations that are developed according to South Asian music theory. From the Trinidadian perspective, bhangra is a mixture of Indian classical music and disco music, and it has not received much attention in Trinidad because of chutney's greater popularity as a dance music. The soca influence in chutney is primarily twofold. First, chutney adds a standard soca rhythm section (drums, guitar, and bass) to traditional percussion instruments and synthesizers programmed to sound like harmoniums. Often, traditional Indian rhythms played on traditional instruments (or percussion machines imitating those instruments) are combined with soca drumbeats, to create an intense and captivating set of polyrhythmic relationships. Second, chutney has emerged as a dance/party music and shares themes and parallels styles of presentation with soca party music, often including what some call "winer girls," albeit dressed in Indian garb, whose dancing accompanies the artists' performances.

While this prototype of chutney is widely shared, the edges of the category are blurred. Some suggest that all locally produced and performed Indian classical music is really chutney. The explanation given for this emphasizes the distinctiveness of Trinidadian Indians from Indians still living in south Asia. As one man of Indian, Creole, and Spanish descent said, "We'll know if an Indian come from India and play a tune here for we, and an Indian from Trinidad play the same song. You will know when it's the Trinidadian Indian that play it, and [when it] look like the Indian Indian play, because it get a different [sound]. As I tell you, we born with that." In effect, this person argued that Trinidadians, Indian Trinidadians included, could not play Indian music the same as it was played in India—they would put a Trinidadian "style" on it. This genre blurring is between chutney and traditional Indian music, as well as between chutney and soca—and it seems endemic in Trinidad (Myers 1998, 368–97; Manuel 2000, 172–83, 188–95).

As one of my informants rhetorically asked, "What is this chutney?" As he then answered this question, he said, "Chutney sweet! Chutney hot!" Several individuals described chutney as "hot like pepper." This indicates that the metaphor of taste, as applied to chutney, is important. The name "chutney" is derived from a food. As a food, chutney, particularly mango chutney, is both sweet and peppery. This metaphor is applied to the music, which is described as both "sweet" and "hot like pepper." These two metaphors extend into other domains.

A number of things can be sweet, but the underlying characteristic of the Trinidadian metaphor of sweetness is that it makes people feel good, even euphoric. In this use, it parallels some of the potential of "heat." Indeed, the juxtaposition of the metaphors of sweetness and heat is something Trinidadians commonly apply to their music: soca, parang, pan music, and chutney can all be both hot and sweet.

From the perspective of men, women can be sweet. According to Trinidadian men, a sweet woman is very attractive and pleasant to be with. The metaphor in this case links women with fruit. A sweet fruit is one that is at the peak of ripeness, and Trinidadian men apply such views to women. Sweetness implies "fullness." A sweet woman is not "magre" (meager/thin), nor does she have "size" (obesity). Instead, she is full-figured. As Sobo points out with regard to Jamaican standards of beauty, an attractive woman is not soft like an overripe fruit, but not hard like a green fruit (1993, 33). In another strand of associations with sweetness, certain singers are labeled by Trinidadian women as having a "sweet" voice, implying that the voice has romantic qualities. The calypsonian Baron is probably the most notable of these.

Based on how Trinidadian men define sweetness in women, and Trinidadian women's definition of a sweet voice, it seems that there is a seductive side to sweetness. This implies that chutney's sweetness not only makes its audience feel good, but that it also seduces the audience.

Chutney is not only sweet but is also hot. Heat is a theme that runs through many musical contexts, and represents a cultural model of bodily experience in these settings. The combination of sweet and hot in chutney is very important in how it is viewed. Being both a hot and a sweet music, chutney also implies dancing and the erotic. Some of the debates over chutney music have focused on the wining that accompanies it. In particular, some Indians are concerned about how the wining compromises the virtue of the Indian women who participate. Throughout the Indian diaspora, there is a concern with women's virtue as being foundational in the maintenance of ethnic distinctiveness and religious purity. Consequently, by threatening women's virtue, wining threatens Indians' purity. Furthermore, wining is associated with Creoles and African-derived music and dance traditions. Consequently, not only does wining compromise virtue, but it is also interpreted as a sign of creolization (see also Manuel 2000, 188–92).

Thus, chutney is viewed as an Indo-Caribbean music that is hot and sweet: beautiful, seductive, and potentially dangerous. Some calypso is viewed as sweet and hot, as is some pan music and parang. Indeed, it is parang that is probably most commonly referred to as also combining these elements. Yet the combination of these elements is part of the definition of chutney music. Indeed, the combination is implied in the name. There is yet another dimension to the linkage with food: the development of Trinidadian cuisine. Indian-derived dishes, such as curries and roti, are now regarded as Trinidadian foods, not simply as Indian foods. Indians are proud of this contribution to Trinidadian culture, and non-Indians are grateful and complimentary of this contribution. The parallelism between the food and the music, then, suggests that since the food is now seen as Trinidadian, and not simply as Indo-Trinidadian, the music is seen as such, too. This structural logic has not entirely come to fruition: both Creoles and Indians see chutney as uniquely Indo-Caribbean, but the degree to which chutney is seen as representative of Trinidad is contested and discussed.

✿ The Contested History of Chutney

What is even more contested than whether chutney represents Trinidad is the history of chutney. Ramnarine notes that there are different histories told of chutney, and that these differences are related to different images of Trinidadian culture (2001, 11). Scholars who have interviewed chutney performers and audiences about the origins of chutney find the music attributed to several sources. Some suggest that chutney came from folk songs (Rohlehr 2004b, 428; Ramnarine 2001, 23–25). Others, referring to the bawdy lyrics about relationships and the female dancing styles that accompany chutney, suggest that the tradition of the *lawa* ceremony at weddings contributed to the emergence of the musical style (Rohlehr 2004b, 428; Ryan 1999, 175; Ramnarine 2001, 23–25). The lawa ceremony is a time at a Hindu wedding when the women break away from the other guests and go to a location that is kept secret from the male guests. *Lawa* means "popped rice," a component of the ritual, but from reports that I heard of these events, the highlight of the time away from the house where the wedding is held is the exuberant, sometimes suggestive dancing and singing, which often has humorous content that is abusive of men.

In Anamat, there are divergent Creole and Indian accounts of the emergence of chutney. These different accounts are interesting not as a window into the actual history of chutney, but in terms of contemporary interpretations of the music. One account sees a Creole-inspired genesis, and the other emphasizes Indian origins. These divergent histories do share an emphasis on the distinctive West Indian contributions to the music, although the Creoles tend to downplay the role of Guyanese influence, and Indians tend to include Guyanese influence. These different narratives do not stand in simple opposition, however: following a contrapuntal pattern, they move between consonance and dissonance.

According to Indians, chutney was the product of innovation by Indian musicians. "We always have we music," one man explained, "but some take a little from here and take a little from there, and make it mix up, and so chutney is." As the Indian narrative tells it, starting as long ago as the 1960s, Indian musicians were experimenting with singing English lyrics with Indian classical styles and incorporating guitars and electronic keyboards into their music. The story is that artists who sang Indian classical music, such as Sundar Popo, began to sing more and more in English, and more and more with the mixed accompaniment of traditional Indian instruments and instruments associated with soca. In the mid-1980s, artists such as Drupatee emerged, promoting a new art form known as Indian soca. Drupatee was soon followed by Rikki Jai, and bands such as Second Imij and Triveni Brass. At the same time, artists who were also incorporating soca elements but not catering to Carnival audiences were gaining in popularity—such as Sundar Popo, Anand Yankaran, and Ramrajee. The term *chutney* came to be applied to the music of this last group, and then came to include the Carnival-oriented music of Drupatee and Rikki Jai.

According to Hindu Indians, in particular, some of the Creole calypsonians' use of Indian music has been inappropriate, such as Ras Shorty I's "Shanti Om" (*Shorty's Greatest Hits*, track 7). Many Hindus' complaint about "Shanti Om" was that it contained sacred Hindu text, which ended up being performed in the context of licentious Carnival behavior. Indians see other songs, such as Black Stalin's "Sundar" (*Message to Sundar*, track 4) as long-overdue recognition of the Indian contribution to Trinidadian public culture.

The Creoles provide a different history of chutney. They say that the Indians were "keeping to themselves" musically, but that Creole musicians began to experiment with the Indian music that they had heard. The most important artist to do so was Ras Shorty I. He began with his songs "Indrani" and "Shanti Om," but other artists also incorporated Indian music into their songs, such as Crazy's heavy reliance on tassa drums in his popular song "Nani Wine" (*Soca Anthems*, track 8). As the Creoles tell it, when the Indians heard the mixing of soca and Indian music, they "outburst" with their own version of the mixing, and that is the origin of chutney.

The Creole version sees Indian artists such as Drupatee and Rikki Jai as derivative from the experimentation of Creole soca artists. The Indian version sees Creole soca artists' appropriation of Indian music as sometimes denigrating and completely derivative from the pioneering efforts of early chutney musicians, such as Sundar Popo. These two different versions of the history of chutney have important ideological implications. The claim of Creoles that something that is identified with Indians has a Creole origin is very different from the more common claims throughout Trinidad's history of Indians' "alienness" (Rubin 1962, 441–42; Singh 1985, 33; Segal 1993, 97; Munasinghe 2001, 67–96). The recognition on the part of Indians of the adoption of soca and calypso styles into their music is tacitly a claim of a form of creolization. While the different histories still indicate significant divisions between Indians and Creoles, the implication of both of these histories is acceptance, even appropriation, of the other group's musical tradition.

Furthermore, despite these two versions of chutney's history, there is agreement that chutney is a sign that Trinidad is "mix up." This concern with "mix up" is powerful and persistent and has been noted several times in the ethnographic literature on Trinidad (Crowley 1957, 819–20; Khan 2004; Munasinghe 2001, 82–87; Segal 1989, 80, 143). The metaphor of "mix up" is often related to the metaphor of callaloo (Khan 2004; Munasinghe 2001). Callaloo is a stew that combines dasheen leaves (*Colocasia esculenta*) with crab and other ingredients. As Khan demonstrates in her *Callaloo Nation* (2001), the metaphor of "mixing" has many dimensions, including cultural traditions, music, food, and even "blood." Blood refers to ethnophysiological ideas about racial purity. Certain groups, such as the Spanish, French, and Chinese, are described as "dissolving" or "melting out." Others, such as the Creoles and Indians, are seen as mixing, which leads to both figurative and literal "douglarization"—a concept derived from *dougla*, a term applied to children with one Indian and one Creole parent. Trinidadian music is viewed as mixed. As one informant said, "They mix up together. They put a little bit of zouk; they put a little bit of soca; they put a little bit of chutney; they put a little bit of samba; they put all in one."

The recognition of social and musical mixing was particularly evident during the Carnival of 1995, when Black Stalin released his song "Message to Sundar," and a year later when "Lootala" (the soca-dancehall-chutney remix of Sonny Mann's "Loota La"), Chris Garcia's "Chutney Bacchanal," and Brother Marvin's "Jahaji Bhai" were huge hits. The video for "Chutney Bacchanal" elicited very interesting responses from audiences. It featured Chris Garcia stripped to the waist and singing with Indian women garbed in saris dancing around him. In many ways, the video parallels a story about Krishna's youth when he was a cowherd: one night, he played his flute, and all the women in the village were overcome by a desire to be with him, and they rushed into the forest to dance with him. Some young Indian women who watched the video debated whether Garcia was Spanish or Indian or mixed, and generally they reached the last conclusion. Basically, Garcia's race is phenotypically unclear, and his surname indicates some Spanish ancestry, but the theme of the song, the theme of the video, and the Indianness of the characters represented in both the song and the video made Indian women assume that he had Indian ancestors (Reddock 1999).

❧ The Counterpoint of State Cultural Policies and Chutney

In Anamat, the growing commercial significance of chutney within Trinidad is frequently included in discussions of the nation. It is also frequently asserted that chutney has emerged separate from state sponsorship and was not part of the PNM-dominated state's project from internal self-rule in 1956 to the election of the NAR in 1986. Nor was chutney adopted by the NAR or the PNM subsequent to 1986. A case can and must be made that emergent ideas about the nation associated with chutney, and conceptually connected to chutney, have emerged institutionally separate from the state's efforts. In some ways, this parallels the argument I made in chapters 1 and 2 that the state's concerted and coordinated effort not did create in the minds of the residents of Anamat the image and sentiments of the nation that the state intended. Since Indian music and chutney were not promoted by the government's policies on expressive culture as much as calypso and steelband music were, one might think that this created a zone of independence for Indian music to develop. Institutional separation does not entail isolation but instead emphasizes the counterpoint taking place at parties, in homes, and wherever else music is consumed when identity is represented. As the state promoted calypso and steelband music, Indian music emerged into national consciousness in counterpoint to the state policies and in a fashion that demanded attention.

In Anamat, despite forty years of state effort and foreign support, an image of the nation based on the state's model of the nation has not been internalized. Coincident with the state's efforts, but not determined by them, a cultural model of the nation momentarily coalesced in Anamat in late 1995 and early 1996, based on the similarities and contrasts residents of Anamat drew between one another, and between their conceptions of Trinidad and the United States. First, the global connections of this emergent image are very different from the global connections of the state-promoted image. Second, the cognitive connections made by informants in their cultural model of the nation do not mimic, or even parallel,

the connections made by the state in its public efforts to construct national identity. These substantial differences suggest that the emergent
images of the nation in Anamat are not determined by the state's model
of the nation. Most important for my argument, the locally emergent
cultural model was based on a relational aesthetic that connected events,
politics, and music, whereas the government projects involved the creation of competitions and institutions to convey messages.

As discussed in chapter 1, after 1956, the state produced a model of
the nation that included connections between several key elements, such
as racial harmony, cultural performances, and economic development,
which was conveyed, in part, by state sponsorship of Carnival and folklore competitions. My informants have been bombarded by these ideas
for decades, but these are not the only ideas to which they have been
exposed. They have heard critics of the state, political calypsos, ideas
about Trinidad from relatives who have moved abroad, and a wide range
of other views. Each individual's past has its own set of experiences that
has generated its own network of associations. On the other hand, most
of these experiences have taken place in a public domain and have entered
into discussions carried on in public spaces, such as rum shops, taxis, or
along the road. As a result, other individuals share elements of these
experiences, and this generates cultural and social counterpoint of ideas.
Among these public experiences have been the persistent, long-term attempts by the state to define the nation.

While I was not in Trinidad for the 1995 elections, and I arrived
shortly after Christmas, what struck me on my arrival was the consistency with which the topics of the elections, the new village council, and
the popularity of "Lootala" and "Chukaipan" were linked in conversations seeking to represent recent events to me, and in the process, to
make sense of the unusual outcome of the election. Usually, they were
also linked to four other topics, specifically, the idea of "mix up," the evils
of racism, the increase in interracial cooperation, and the existence of
transracial kinship links—many of my Indian informants were suddenly
talking about their Creole family, and many of my Creole informants were
suddenly talking about their Indian family.

Admittedly, my initial field techniques at this time are best described
as haphazard, but then again, serendipity may be an important means to
stumble upon analyzable examples of what Edwin Hutchins calls "cogni-

tion in the wild" (1995). Indeed, Naomi Quinn has endeavored to make interviews similar to conversations for methodological reasons (1982). Charles Frake takes this a step further: "Perhaps instead of trying to devise provocative questions and other instruments to persuade people to talk about things they do not ordinarily talk about in that way, we should take as a serious topic of investigation what people in fact talk about, or, better, what they are in fact doing when they talk. When we look at talk, we find that people do not so much ask and answer inquiries; they propose, defend, and negotiate interpretations of what is happening" (1997, 37). My serendipitous research style at this time began with conversations that gradually evolved into interviews. My friends wanted to talk about the election, and I encouraged them. Upon my arrival in Anamat in January of 1996, I visited as many people as I could to say hello, and to get their impressions of what had happened since I had last been in Trinidad. Not surprisingly, the main topic of discussion was the recent election, which resulted in an Indian, Basdeo Panday, becoming prime minister. Informants moved from this topic to the evils of racially mobilized politics, or to the importance of interracial cooperation as evidenced by the new village council, and these topics commonly led to discussions of transracial kinship or to the related topic of "mix up" (meaning that racial distinctions are now blurred). This topic, in turn, prompted discussions of "Chukaipan" and the new chutney hit "Lootala" as examples of how Trinidadians are "mix up." Granted, there were variations on this progression of topics. When radios were on, it was almost inevitable that "Lootala" would be played, and this would suddenly shift conversation to a progression from chutney, to "Chukaipan," and then to the other topics. Whatever the order of topics, their association persisted with a wide variety of people: the old and young, men and women, Indians and Creoles. Contiguity of topics is an important indication of cognitive connections (Strauss 1992, 211).

The phrase "mix up" seemed to be the central node in the cognitive network connecting these various topics. The progression of topics was not identical among different people, but the phrase "mix up" was ubiquitous. In talking about chutney, one Creole man said, "It mix up. [We] like to mix: take a piece here, take a piece there, take a piece and mix it up. So this chutney thing, this thing, through the cause of the nation from where the Indian come out from Indian [and] come in the West Indies and the Caribbean. They have to speak English, so this chutney, that is the word they put for the break-up music from Indian music. It ain't come from India. It originate here, right here in the Caribbean, mostly Trinidad." But, for this man, the metaphor "mix up" also applies to races mixing:

> Here real mix up now, you know. Real mix up now. . . . If you see my mother, you wouldn't say this [I] is her child. . . . You see my father, you'll put him before me. He a real nigger man, real, real, real, black, hard, hard hair, and I come out like this. Through he case, hear thing, my grandmother is a French and Spanish, and she take an Indian man and she bring forth my mother, so you see what kind of breed my mother is, so my mother come, and she get French, and she get Spanish, and she get Indian. And my mother go and take a nigger man and bring forth me, and all my mother rest of children are from a Chinee man from China.

Another man made the same connections through the metaphor "mix up." When he discussed the different people who live in Trinidad, he said, "We have basically African and Indian and Creole people, which are French, Spanish, Portuguese, well mix, eh. What we call 'mix' some people call the French Creole, and the Spanish Spaniard mix, we call them Panyol, and then you have some people of Asian, Chinese, and so on." With regard to chutney, he said,

> [Calypso and chutney] are similar, especially right now with the soca calypso. You find it kind of mix up with the chutney. [In] this year's calypsos [1996], you find many of them use these Indian phrase and so on, right, in lyrics to compose to make a mix. They trying to integrate the culture in such a way, so normally the other music, like pan, steel—we have all the different people mix right now, because of the best pannists you'll find are from Spanish descent or Indian.

This individual was a fan of pan music more than of soca or chutney, but even in his own favorite music he found "mixing," despite pan music's long identification with an African Trinidadian heritage (see Stuempfle 1995, 221).

An elderly Indian again used the metaphor of "mixing" in describing both music and race relations. Indeed, in his discourse, the discussion of the mixing of music flowed seamlessly into the mixing of the groups: "If you go to a party, you'll get it because they have the Indian style, and then they have the, you know what I mean, the different group mix—Spanish, Creole, all kind of thing—their music, and it is nearly the same."

A woman who had an Indian mother and an African father described herself as a mix of "both cultures" and then described chutney as a "mixed music." She concluded by saying that people like her and music like chutney were the "future" of the country. One day in a rum shop, I met an Indian and a Creole man talking about the songs playing on the radio in the shop. The two men agreed that the fetes until then (late January) during the Carnival season were "real nice" because, when people went, they discovered that the music was "all mix up." By this, they meant that the disc jockeys were playing a mixture of reggae, chutney, and soca. The Creole man said that the music brought everyone together by mixing the cultures, but that in the day-to-day life of Indians and Creoles, the mixing "lagged behind." He then said that, with an Indian prime minister, he thought the mixing in day-to-day life would catch up to the mixing in the music. Then the two men started to share how their own ancestries were "mix up." At this point, their discussion was more to inform me, the anthropologist, than to inform one another—they knew one another very well. The Indian admitted to having a Spanish ancestor. The Creole said that he had Indian and Creole grandparents. Then the Creole referred to a recent wake: "Last night at the wake, two Creole and two Indian sit down to play cards. They did not want the game to become racial, so they divided up so that each team in the game [All Fours] had one Creole and one Indian."

These are just some examples of the way in which the metaphor "mix up" was used to link music, politics, and race mixing during discussions in early 1996. This metaphor came to serve as a key component of cultural models about the nation. In a sense, it also seems to have become a major means for accounting for contemporary events, whether they be musical events or political events. As the core of a fluid, evolving model to interpret national events and to build an idea of the Trinidadian nation, it stands in contrast to the structured government policy model that drove state attempts to define the nation.

🐾 Making the Connections

The topics of the election of Panday, the new village council, and the popularity of "Lootala" and "Chukaipan" are linked to one another to support the idea of "mix up." This idea was the core of the assertion of a new image of Trinidadian identity and racial harmony in Anamat during late 1995 and early 1996. Those I encountered used art forms, such as chutney, and transracial kinship ties to represent mixing. These representations changed since my first visit to Anamat in 1989–91. Then, chutney was seen as Indian music performed for Indian audiences, but now it is popular among Creoles, and it has been incorporated into parang. Then, transracial kinship was not often discussed, even though census and genealogical data I collected at that time demonstrate such links (Birth 1997). In effect, interracial cooperation and sentiments of interracial unity seemed to be increasingly linked to the idea of "mix up."

As described on the previous pages, the links between topics were clearly patterned, and it is not the case that each topic was linked directly to all the others. In fact, it is because the idea of "mix up" was linked to the most topics that I view it as the idea that connects the other issues in this cultural model. What is described below is the transition of topics. For instance, when I say that "Lootala" was linked with "Panday," I mean that, in conversation, "Panday" would often follow "Lootala," but not necessarily that "Lootala" would follow "Panday."

1 "Mix up" was linked with "Lootala," "Chukaipan," interracial cooperation, the evils of racism, and transracial kinship.
2 "Lootala" was linked with "mix up," "Chukaipan," and Panday.
3 "Chukaipan" was linked with "mix up," "Lootala," and transracial kinship.
4 Interracial cooperation was linked with "mix up," the evils of racism, transracial kinship, and Panday.
5 The evils of racism were linked with "mix up," interracial cooperation, transracial kinship, and Panday.
6 Transracial kinship was linked with "mix up," interracial cooperation, and the evils of racism.
7 Basdeo Panday was linked with "Lootala," interracial cooperation, and the evils of racism.

These connections have several implications, among which I shall highlight two. First, while it was not possible to predict which one of the range of topics "mix up" led to in conversation, it is clear that the topics of "Lootala," "Chukaipan," interracial cooperation, the evils of racism, and transracial kinship all led to "mix up," eventually. Second, Prime Minister Panday, and by implication his government, was not automatically linked to the idea of "mix up." This suggests that this indirect link was still negotiable. Furthermore, since Panday was linked with both positively valued interracial cooperation and negatively valued evils of racism, it suggests that his place in these connections was still fluid in 1996.

By 1998, the links between "mix up" and politics had changed. Creoles in Anamat complained that the local village council had disintegrated, and that a faction controlled by a single Indian family had taken over. Consequently, members of this family got the vast majority of government work available, and this sometimes even led to men thought to have few or no qualifications serving as foremen over public works projects. These local events, which even many of the Indians felt were "too racial," led to an erosion of support for the UNC and Panday among Creoles in the community. The Creoles who were willing to give Panday and the UNC a "chance" in 1996 now felt that the UNC had a poor record at controlling favoritism toward Indians in employment. The metaphor "mix up" was still present but was much more hotly contested with regard to daily interactions and politics. Such was the case with the arguments that emerged over Iwer George's soca hit "Bottom in de Road," in which he complained that he had not "had" an Indian woman yet (*Soca Gold 1998*, track 9). Many Indians were publicly and privately outraged, and many Creoles were outraged at the Indians' outrage.

Some of the links of 1996 are easy to understand and interpret. For instance, the association of "Lootala" and "Chukaipan" ties two songs that share the features of mixed Trinidadian music. It is easy to understand the links of such musical styles to "mix up," as well. Other links that seem obvious are the conversational movement between the evils of racism and the benefits of interracial cooperation—they are contrasting issues. In turn, "mix up" is often tied to transracial kinship to show interracial cooperation and the sinister and immoral qualities of racism. Using these simple inferences, the links between "mix up," transracial kinship, interracial cooperation, the evil of racism, "Lootala," and "Chukaipan" are easily seen, especially when "mix up" is seen as the key node tying together the rest.

The ideological importance of the connections between "mix up" and kinship must receive proper emphasis, though. West Indian cultural ideas of kinship include assertions that kin are equals and that kin cooperate

(Sobo 1993). Using kinship to bridge racial barriers was an important ideological step toward images of national unity and racial harmony. On the other hand, increased racial harmony does not necessarily follow from the existence of transracial kinship ties; sometimes the opposite is true (Birth 1997). Because of ideas about kinship and cooperation, knowledge of transracial kinship ties is a moral resource in representing relationships between Indians and Creoles. Sometimes, despite publicly known kinship ties, disputes between Indians and Creoles lead to public division, rather than to racial harmony, which thereby suggests that racial difference takes precedence over kinship. At other times, such kin ties are used to break down racial barriers. To be "mix up" is a double-edged sword that can be used culturally and strategically, either to challenge or to affirm the naturalness of racial categories.

The explanation of other connections, while not immediately obvious, is still readily available. The association of "Chukaipan" and kinship is the most notable of these. Kinship and "Chukaipan" are related through the practice of parang. "Chukaipan," whatever its "mix up" origins, was performed in the context of parang.

While parang is associated with those who claim Spanish heritage, parang bands often become multiracial over the course of a night. In Anamat, the bands typically begin with members of Spanish Creole kin groups—these form the core of musicians—but as the band, and particularly the chorus, expands, it takes in non-Spanish Creoles and Indians. The people of Anamat are proud of their parang. Moreover, there are Indians who have learned to play parang. These Indians sometimes form their own bands, and sometimes they join with Creoles.

When viewed from the perspective of "Chukaipan," the link between music and kinship is expected. In addition, "Chukaipan"'s lyrics explicitly mention transracial kinship by describing a Creole going to his Indian family to parang. At the same time, parang itself evokes ideas of kinship, since the core of most parang bands is based on kin ties, and since the visitation patterns of parang bands tend to follow kinship links.

The nascent cultural models of the nation that emerged in 1995–96 among diverse people in Anamat, then, are built on a notion of "mixing," which is tied to kinship and music, and tangentially to politics, although the latter tie is indirect and presumably weak. Due to the importance of kinship in many societies, and the importance of metaphorical kinship in the formation of nationalist ideologies, it should come as no surprise that kinship and "mixing" are important, but that the local model stands in contrast to the carefully crafted policy model generated by the People's National Movement and Dr. Eric Williams. The state's model integrated economic development, local government, national festivals, and cultural competitions. The only area of overlap concerns that of race relations, yet the local view emphasizes mixing and relationships, rather than attempting to establish equality and harmony through competitions. This should not be confused with a local advocacy of interracial unions, but with the understanding that such unions occur, as is clear from the discussions and interpretations of their existence. An additional dimension that diverges from typical discussions of creolization, where Indians lose their identity, is that the mixing involves the adoption of Indian traditions into Trinidadian identity, rather than a loss of Indianness.

The conversational connections between the topics of Panday, "Lootala," "Chukaipan," kinship, interracial cooperation, and "mix up" is not the product of public policy but exists in the context of forty-year-old policies and long-standing local relationships. The contrast between the ease and quickness with which the emergent model was internalized and distributed, and the inability of the state with its resources, the resources of the United States, and the resources of transnational corporations to inculcate and to disseminate a convincing model of national identity clearly demonstrates that there is more to internalization than exposure, and that there is more to the acceptance of public discourse and ideologies than the wielding of power.

Why did these connections emerge at this time in Anamat, and separate from the state's efforts, though?

The question is actually more complicated than "What caused the change?" Not everyone in Anamat has expressed feelings of racial harmony, and this harmony was not reflected in all of Trinidad, such as at the stone- and bottle-throwing incident during the finals of the 1996 Soca Monarch Competition, where some of those in the crowd angrily said that "Lootala" was not a soca but Indian music, and consequently it did not belong in the Soca Monarch Competition. As Rohlehr notes, chutney soca with its unifying rhetoric was part of a counterpoint in 1996, which included divisive rhetoric in music, as well (Rohlehr 2004b, 434–35). In commenting on the audience at the Soca Monarch competition throwing stones at Sonny Mann, Rohlehr adds that this showed "that beneath the masks of unity and tolerance lay the bitter reality of antagonism, which had not disappeared" (2004b, 436), although I am not sure that the metaphor placing antagonism beneath tolerance is accurate—antagonism and tolerance coexist, and there is a movement between them. Creole residents of Anamat could both approve of "Lootala" as a song and as a unifying force, and disapprove of it as a soca, and they could see Sonny Mann's attempt to translate his popularity into a Soca Monarch title as divisive and a form of racial hubris.

Thus, not only must the growing racial harmony of 1996 be explained, but its uneven distribution in Trinidad must also be explained, as must my perception of a decrease in the discourse about racial harmony by 1998. Complicating any explanation of the distribution of these ideas is the fact that they were distributed across men and women, Indians and Creoles, young and old, rural and urban, and wealthy and poor. In effect, analytic models that appeal to race, class, gender, or generation are unable to account for this distribution. This fact demands that, in this case, one break away from these old categories, and the notions of power and resistance that are often associated with them, to look at other possible sources of explanation, and at other groupings of people that are relevant to social practice, rather than at disembodied and abstracted ideologies.

An adequate explanation would have several features. It would include mechanisms for the internalization of ideologies, and mechanisms explaining the distribution of the ideologies that are consistent with the actual distribution witnessed in Trinidad.

"Loota La" was sung in Bhojpuri, a language that very few Trinidadians understand and that many conflate with Hindi (Ramnarine 2001, 60), another South Asian language used in Indian music. The remixed version of the song, known as "Lootala," contained some English lyrics, but these lyrics were mostly mixed into the older Bhojpuri version. Consequently, neither "Loota La" nor "Lootala" can be treated simply as a text or a discourse but must be treated as a sonic, nonlinguistic symbol. In dealing with these songs, the fact that the vast majority of Trinidadians do not speak Hindi or Bhojpuri and do not understand the lyrics suggests that the power of the song to generate feelings is not linked to the persuasiveness of words, but to other factors related to sound and style. Thus, the relational aesthetics that connect the representation of these songs and issues of identity involve aspects of thought beyond the use of language. In a sense, one must ascertain the web of connections between the experience and the memory of the experience of the song in particular contexts with statements such as "mix up," and with feelings of belonging and unity attached, again, to particular issues—a complicated counterpoint of sound and identification.

Thus, what needs to be explained is not the notion of "we all mixed up," but the number, strength, and interactions over time of the associations between this idea and other ideas in multiple contexts. Another element that needs to be explained is the interaction of "mix up" with ideas of ethnic and racial distinctiveness. In effect, what needs to be examined is how the associations emerge and how their strength changes— again an issue of how Trinidadian aesthetics create conceptual relationships tied to how a holistic counterpoint forms the strength of the connections. In the case of the ideology of "mix up," the strength of the connections between this idea and other ideas is reflected in the degree to which specific topics, such as "Lootala," lead to "mix up" in conversation. A rough gauge of this is the frequency with which a subject leads to "mix up," and the frequency with which "mix up" leads to a particular subject.

When I applied this logic to the example of "Lootala," I obtained the following results: the association of "Lootala" with Panday and interethnic solidarity and national identity is not automatic but is frequent; and the connective strengths between each one of these is dependent on the connective strengths between the others. In other words, when the topics of Panday and interethnic solidarity appear together, they also tend to appear with the topic of "Lootala." It does not work the other way around, however. "Lootala" does not always entail Panday or interethnic solidarity. The most frequent connections to the metaphor "mix up" are mixed ancestry and music that draws from Indian and Creole traditions, that is, family and music are most commonly linked to one another and to the metaphor of mixing.

Whereas one can outline the connections between cultural models of family, mixing, and music, then describe, in a relative way, their strength, the existence of the connections still needs to be explained. Here, I make the assumption that, for the connections to be widely shared, as they appear to be, they need to have emerged in a social context in which many people participate. The rapidity with which the ideas spread in Anamat, and the indication that they grew during the period between October and January and then began to wane, indicates that the ideas emerged in a context of a specific part of the year in which many participated. Assuming that this is the case, then there are relatively few occasions in the months before Carnival in which this occurs. These occasions include wakes, Divali, All Saints' Night, All Souls' Night, and parang. The connections that I am exploring most likely emerged during the period from Divali to the following year. The Hindu holiday of Divali focuses on the goddess Lakshmi. Above all, Lakshmi is associated with light and is identified as the mother goddess. Beyond these widely shared ideas, there is a great deal of variation in what individuals associate with Lakshmi. These associations include Lakshmi as the goddess of family, marriage, motherhood, education, wisdom, and wealth. The ideas that Lakshmi is associated with family, marriage, and motherhood are most prevalent, but the ideas of education, wisdom, and wealth are often associated with the goddess Saraswati by many Hindus.

While Divali is the subject of theological discussions among some Hindus, the most important public dimensions of the holiday are the pageants and lighting displays sponsored by Hindus. In Anamat, the local Hindus stage an elaborate pageant consisting of music (bhajans, chutney, and Indian classical music), traditional dancing, and plays based on sections of the *Ramayana*. Such performances are attended by people of all the ethnic groups represented in Anamat. Some religious groups publicly condemn the performances, such as the Pentecostals, the Seventh-Day Adventists, and the Missionary Baptists, but despite such public pronouncements of disapproval, it is common to find members of all of these groups in attendance. The pageant usually takes place on a night shortly before the actual night of Divali.

On Divali, the women in Hindu households prepare large amounts of food, while the men, in particular the young adult men, construct elaborate frames of bamboo for holding the hundreds of small clay lamps called *deyas*. At sundown, a *pujah*—a ritual of devotion in which food is sacrificed to a divinity—is performed, and then people begin to light the deyas and visit one another. The visits are made by both Hindus and non-Hindus, although only Hindu households are visited. Upon arrival, a guest is given a plate full of food.

Often, either a few days before Divali or a few days after, the Roman

Catholic holidays of All Saints' Night and All Souls' Night occur. On All Saints' Night (November 1), candles are lit outside of Roman Catholic homes in memory of the dead. While the displays of candles do not rival the spectacular arrangement of deyas for Divali, there are obvious parallels between the two holidays—parallels that many residents of Anamat were quick to point out when they met on All Souls' Night (November 2). On this second night, the candles are lit in the cemetery on the graves of family members. While the holiday is a Roman Catholic one, many Muslims and Hindus also go to the cemetery to see the lights. The more theologically oriented members of the community discuss the parallels between Divali and these Catholic holidays, focusing, in particular, on the victory of light over darkness, an important part of the symbolism of all three holidays.

The concurrence of Divali, All Saints' Night, and All Souls' Night every year creates a predictable, periodic harmonic counterpoint of symbolism: a flame signifying the victory of light over darkness connected to an emphasis on family. So in this context, a few months before Christmas, there is a set of events that ends up emphasizing the similarity of Hindus and Catholics, and it is a context in which Muslims and Protestant Christians also participate. Within weeks of this event, people start to prepare for Christmas and parang.

As described in the previous chapter, the parang tradition involves traveling from house to house during the Christmas season. At each house, the parang band begins to play on the front gallery (porch), and by the end of the first song, the owner of the house has opened the front door and allowed the band to come inside. Once inside, the band mixes with the household members, who provide drinks and occasionally food, and the band plays several more songs. It is quite common for many of the members of the household to join the band as it moves to the next house. Sometimes, house-to-house parang bands can grow in size to include as many as fifty people.

Parang is a musical context in which family is emphasized. Parang also creates a context in which a harmonic counterpoint of diversity and community emerges. Hindus and Muslims join the choruses of parang bands. Since the band begins as a literal kin group, its expansion creates a metaphorical kin group. Music and family become linked with ideas of mixing in this context. This context is one of "sweetness" and "heat," as well—this implies collective action and altered states of consciousness, which enhance the persuasiveness of messages.

Coincident with Christmas in 1995 was the growing popularity of Sonny Mann's "Lootala," a remixed version of his song "Loota La." "Lootala" added English contributions by Denise Belfon and General Grant to Sonny Mann's Bhojpuri lyrics in the original "Loota La." The new remix prominently features English lyrics sung by a female calypsonian about dancing with Sonny Mann, and less interpretable dancehall lyrics by General Grant expressing his desire to dance with Indian women. The song's reference to recounting the events of a "big wedding," and the implication that it is an Indian wedding, had a major influence on people's interpretations. Indian weddings, like weddings in general, emphasize the bringing together of two families. In addition, Indian weddings symbolize Indian traditions. It is a context in which social change, family, kinship, and identity are closely linked (Birth 1995). "Lootala" emphasized the presence of non-Indian musicians at an Indian wedding. The non-Indian female calypsonian sings about dancing with Sonny Mann, the male chutney artist, and the non-Indian dancehall artist sings about dancing with Indian women. Within this immensely popular song is the bridging of racial boundaries in terms of social relations, spatial relations, ritual relations, and potentially sexual relations.

Elections

Relative to the 1995 elections, Divali, All Saints' Night, and All Souls' Night occurred before the elections, and the parang season started soon after. The descriptions that I obtained of the elections suggested a great deal of contention. The favored candidate in Anamat was the PNM candidate. He was an Indian from a family with many friends in Anamat. While he was widely liked, the PNM government made a major blunder just before the election, which destroyed their chances of winning the majority of votes around Anamat.

The scandal involved the condition of the road. On the major road leading into Anamat, there was a large "land slip" where the road had sunk about thirty yards down the side of a hill, toward a river. In the months before an election, it was typical for the party in power to pledge to fix this part of the road, to begin a project, and then to leave the project

partially completed after the election. By the next election, the land slip
was usually worse than it was before. Before the election, the PNM government began a project to fix the road. The people of Anamat saw this
for what it was, a shallow attempt to win votes, but such projects were
typical of election years.

At the beginning of the project, the PNM-led government appointed a
local man to be in charge of hiring workers. According to the story told by
both PNM supporters and critics, the party's instructions were that only
PNM supporters should be hired. In Anamat, this would have meant the
hiring of only Creoles. This raised the ire of almost everyone in Anamat,
including Creole PNM supporters. The PNM man put in charge of hiring
resisted this policy; the Creole PNM members of the Village Council were
among the loudest critics of the policy. Everyone in the village described
the PNM's heavy-handedness on hiring as "stupidness" and an example of
"racialism." In the wake of the election, many reported that they voted
against the PNM because of this incident. Others, who had voted for the
PNM candidate, made it very clear that they did so because they personally liked the candidate and voted for him "despite" what the PNM-led
government did.

During and after this incident, then, there was a strong sense of community as distinct from the state. Indeed, evidence of this has already
emerged from the nature of participation in Carnival and the local pride
taken in parang. Admittedly, my only knowledge that the nascent cultural
models of the nation I found in Anamat in early 1996 were in place before
or after the election was based on information gathered after the fact, but
these nationalist ideas were related to a constellation of pre- and post-
election events. What emerged out of my conversations was that the
cultural model that created all the connections emerged in the context of
parang and the Christmastime conversations that reflected on parang,
the remixed version of "Lootala," and national events.

The Strength of Associations

These cultural connections are widely shared in Anamat. Parang's importance in this case is that it creates a social context that brings together all
age groups, all race groups, and both men and women in common, coordinated action. As a result of Scrunter's song "Chukaipan," chutney was

injected into the context of parang. Chutney evokes ideas of Indianness, and in the wake of the elections, Indianness suggested the UNC and Panday. In parang, kinship is linked with equality and cooperation. And, of course, "Chukaipan" is "mix up." In the performance of "Chukaipan" during house-to-house parangs, and because of the local innovations with incorporating chutney into parang, these disparate topics of Panday, Indianness, Spanish culture, equality, cooperation, kinship and "mix up" were tied together in song and in action, in a context of sleep and food deprivation, consumption of alcohol or caffeine or both, paced physical exertion, rhythmic music, and, in the case of the host, being suddenly awakened from sleep. In this way, a relational aesthetic linked issues to "mix up," and the holistic counterpoints of the season strengthened these links and encouraged both the subjective internalization and the intersubjective distribution of the shared images of the nation.

Since the house-to-house parang tradition is found in only a few places in Trinidad, parang did not develop and distribute these cultural cognitive connections throughout the island. On the other hand, while I could not do systematic, islandwide research during my short visit in January 1996, my impressions, based on what little traveling I did do throughout the island, and the tone set in the newspapers, is that these cultural models were limited to Anamat. They had not emerged and been distributed throughout Trinidad by means of Carnival, Phagwa, and fetes throughout the year.

In the moment I ethnographically encountered the counterpoint of elections, "mix up," and music in 1996, two factors seem significant: (1) widespread exposure and interest in ideas and images of racial harmony and "mixing," and (2) the holidays and the election that occurred between October and January, which served as topics that focused and structured informal discussions about racial harmony and "mixing." This is a case where the interaction of timing and counterpoint shaped the ongoing, intersubjective interpretation of events that I observed.

chapter six ❧ Concluding Relations

> Break a vase, and the love that reassembles the fragments is
> stronger than that love which took its symmetry for granted
> when it was whole. The glue that fits the pieces is the sealing of
> its original shape. It is such a love that reassembles our African
> and Asiatic fragments, the cracked heirloom whose restoration
> shows its white scars. This gathering of broken pieces is the
> care and pain of the Antilles, and if the pieces are disparate, ill-
> fitting, they contain more pain than their original sculpture,
> those icons and sacred vessels taken for granted in their an-
> cestral places. Antillean art is this restoration of our shattered
> histories, our shards of vocabulary, our archipelago becoming a
> synonym for pieces broken off from the original continent.
>
> DEREK WALCOTT, 1992 Nobel lecture

> Only the poetic spirit links and reunites.
>
> AIMÉ CÉSAIRE, "Calling the Magician"

The attention I have given to audiences' engagement with music leads to five themes that I want to develop in conclusion: (1) the problems of an atemporal representation of Trinidadian music and the tendency of the state to adopt such representations; (2) the annual rhythms of Trinidadian musical experiences; (3) the fashion in which enigmatic and anomalous events, such as the 1995 elections or the 1990 attempted coup, become absorbed into the annual rhythms; (4) the idea of social, psychological, and biological fragmentation; and (5) the contrapuntal engagement of Trinidadian music with these myriad fragmentations. These themes then will allow me to address my final concerns about the divisions and limitations in much of social theory when it addresses Trinidadian music.

⚜ Atemporal Music

The association of music and identity often lifts both music and identity out of the flow of social processes over time. This creates an image of enduring cohesiveness within groups, and even between groups within the nation. Consequently, such atemporal representations are important, and the desire for such enduring representations has consistently been a concern of government policies.

The government promotes such representations by making music iconic of the nation. From this perspective, the relationship between the national anthem or steelband music and the nation are unchanging. In the effort to craft such a transcendent concept of music and identity, state policy creates structures, looks at function, defines, classifies, plans, and is met with agreement or opposition. Chapter 1 documented part of this process.

The significance given to music by the government is a result of the importance of music to Trinidadians. As I learned from Trinidadian friends before going to Trinidad, music is a matter of national pride, but aside from the national anthem, few specific songs are associated with this pride. Instead, the pride is grounded in the annual production of new songs that are stylistically Trinidadian in an annual ritual of innovation melding with tradition.

It is easy to think of music in terms of its contribution to defining national identity. But such identity is often cast as transcendent and enduring—in effect, atemporal. This atemporality can affect how music is viewed, and as a result, an art form that exists through its unfolding over time is objectified. Fanon warns that "the man of culture . . . will let himself be hypnotized by these mummified fragments which because they are static are in fact symbols of negation and outworn contrivances" (1963, 224).

Philip Scher has documented how the government's policies toward Carnival practices have encountered trouble because of administrators' atemporal assumptions. For instance, he describes how scheduling the

Carnival King and Queen of the World Contest in September—well out-side of Carnival season—diminished the interest in the event because the administrators ignored "the very basic fact that Carnival is seasonal" (2003, 136). The cultural objectification that Scher documents in Trin-idad is an example of the sort of objectification that Richard Handler sees as tempting social scientists (1988). The recognition of this issue should not lead to ignoring atemporal, objectified presentations of identity, but instead, such representations should be related to the temporality of the change and dynamism of social life.

Trinidadians' atemporal sentiments toward their music are, then, one theme in the counterpoint of issues associated with Trinidadian musics' centripetal powers. Alone, however, atemporal representation has no contrapuntal sensibility. In fact, sometimes those who promote it conceal multiple voices in their drive for imagining coherence. Rarely is this suc-cessful—every time the government has chosen to celebrate music as de-fining national identity, there have been Trinidadians who have opposed such initiatives on the grounds that the selected music is not their music.

✸ The Rhythmicity of Trinidadian Music

Trinidadian music is temporal in two ways: it is very seasonal, with antici-pated cycles of musical styles; and with regard to soca, calypso, chutney, and pan music, new songs are expected from artists every year. Conse-quently, there is a temporally unfolding annual rhythm of musical repeti-tion and change.

This cycle is actually a polyrhythm. Trinidadians expect new material every year from steelbands, and from soca, chutney, and calypso singers. Certain songs become inextricably linked to the year in which they were sung, as with "Jean and Dinah" and 1956, "Get Something and Wave" and 1991, and "Lootala" and 1995–96. In contrast, the core repertoire of parang songs is the same year after year. The same is true of Hindu bhajans (sacred songs) and the tassa drumming associated both with weddings and the Muslim solemnity of Hosay (the martyrdom of Hosein, the grandson of the Prophet Mohammed). Consequently, there is a subtle difference between the annual pulse of some musics that produce new songs each year, and the rhythm of other musics in which the same songs are performed every year. A representation of identity in relationship to music without attention to the question of time and timing hides such subtle differences of the rhythms of repetition and change.

Even in the genres where there is an expectation of annual innovation, the audience responses tend to be reproduced year after year. Chapters 2 and 3 described the community-based nature of participation in Carnival and Christmas that seems to repeat every year regardless of what musical innovations are made.

These genre-specific cycles of change and repetition are further syncopated by their association with different calendars. There are multiple rhythms to Christmas, Carnival/Lent/Easter, Hindu holidays, Muslim holidays, and Trinidadian politics. These cycles of holidays are not temporally segregated—the first Carnival fete almost always occurs before the last parang of the Christmas season. Christmas is fixed at December 25. The date of Easter determines the date of Carnival, and both change according to the interaction of lunar and solar cycles. The timing of the Hindu holiday of Phagwa is determined by the Hindu calendar, and it is often close to Carnival. In the Muslim calendar, each year consists of twelve lunar months, and totals around 354 days. This eleven-day difference between the lunar year and solar year results in Muslim observances such as Ramadan/Eid and Hosay moving eleven days earlier in relationship to the solar year each year. Parliamentary elections can be called at any time by a government.

Consequently, the seasonality of Trinidadian music is not a simple rhythm that repeats itself without variation, but it is a dynamic polyrhythm that changes from year to year due to the differing calendars and cycles. This polyrhythm interacts with the cycles of repetition and change associated with different musics, and the repetition of participation styles.

Such annual, social polyrhythm affirms Wilson Harris's observation that West Indian aesthetics chooses to focus on the "human" through rhythm (1967). In Trinidad, music plays an important role in defining those rhythms, punctuating them, and relating them. Whereas Trinidadians have a profound appreciation of the seasonality of their musics, this seasonality is not emphasized either in government policies for representing Trinidadian identity or in some social scientific representations of Trinidadian music—social science and governmental bureaucracy are challenged by rhythm and sometimes choose to ignore it.

Since music is associated with moments of time during the year, it has a now-for-now quality. The now-for-now quality of music gives it power in the moment to which it is applied, and, importantly, it also influences the ways in which that moment is remembered. This gives Trinidadian music a dual quality—it is both ephemeral and enduring. This is a facet of the important contrast that Daniel Miller describes in Trinidadian culture between transience and transcendence (1994). A particular song can be tied to its time, and then captures its time for all time. This now-for-now quality embedded in the polyrhythmic annual cycle of the musical participation moves in counterpoint with the often atemporal manner in which the government has promoted Trinidadian identity through the appropriation of music.

✿ Enigmatic Events

The attempted coup of 1990 and the parliamentary elections of 1995 discussed in chapters 4 and 5 are not musical events, yet the annual cycle of Trinidadian music established powerful relations between these events and music. In some ways, this is true of every Carnival when calypsonians use the previous year's scandals and public enigmas as subject matter for their songs. The more enigmatic and socially significant the event, the more memorable the calypsos tend to be. The great calypsonians earn their reputations from their ability to make sense of what has attracted the public's attention as nonsensical or disturbing. Whatever happens that is of widespread concern, Trinidadian music draws into its counterpoint and polyrhythmic cycle.

Trinidadian music is about the poetic, aesthetic spirit drawing connections and putting together fragments of memory, history, identity, and subjectivity. Trinidadian music embraces this fragmentation of history, memory, and subjectivity, and within its aesthetic sense, the concern is less about whether the fragments naturally go together, and more about the effort to put them together. In 1991, soca brought together wide-ranging ideas and themes to rework conceptions of the attempted coup d'état—soca fire, Saddam Hussein, and Mother Muriel, among other images, became tied to the burned-out shell of the Police Headquarters and the devastation along Charlotte Street in Port of Spain. Chutney and parang in 1995 and 1996 linked kinship, music, race, and parliamentary elections. Through music, Trinidad's complex social counterpoints become manifest.

☙ Fragmentation

Fragmentation is a catalytic force for Trinidadian music, then. This is not a stable fragmentation, but one that is dynamic and changing over time. It is possibly the desire to overcome fragmentation—the desire to reassemble the vase Walcott describes as broken—that drives the strong attachment to music as a force for momentary feelings of harmony, if not unity. Maybe this is why, when there is an enigmatic event—such as an electoral tie or an attempt to overthrow the government—Trinidadians turn to music as a means of interpreting their world.

The complicated history of the West Indies that has brought together so many different immigrant groups, indigenous populations, political perspectives, and economic interests has fostered an open, often raw, fragmentation. Such fragmentation defies attempts to impose a structure on it. In a phrase laden with multivocal multidimensionality, Holger Henke describes a comment from Jamaican musician Lee "Scratch" Perry as "polyvalent, heteroclitic, hyperhybrid, Chagallian Caribbean cosmological and epistemological heterotopia" (2004, 37). This is part of Henke's argument that the categories of thought derived from European-derived social theories do not move quickly enough in all the necessary ways to catch Caribbean praxis.

Many recent ethnographies on Trinidad have addressed the issues of fragmentation and relationships through the lens of the coexisting, dual processes of creolization and ethnic exclusivity. Yelvington (1993, 1995a, 2001) emphasizes a contextual and processual approach to these issues; Segal (1993) documents how racial categories and color distinctions are two different principles of classification that interact in historically contingent ways; Miller (1994) points to the dualisms of heterogeneity and homogeneity articulating with temporal transience and transcendence; Munasinghe (2001) documents processes of creolization and ethnic exclusivity with regard to the relationship of Indian identity to Trinidadian political and social history; Khan (2004) focuses on the complicated articulations between different metaphors of mixing as applied to religion and identity. All of these authors start with investigations of ethnicity in

relationship to social heterogeneity, an important dimension of Trinidadian life, and then move into other domains of Trinidadian social life,
showing how the complicated coexistence of opposed ways of thinking
about self in relationship to others pervades many social contexts.

I have chosen to look at aesthetics—a complementary approach to the
ethnographic work that takes ethnicity as a starting point in understanding Trinidadian social life. This has precedent. In reflecting on his initial
work in Trinidad that challenged representing daily life in terms of cultural pluralism and ethnic exclusivity, John O. Stewart writes that in the
beginning of his research he focused on pragmatic concerns that drove
people to transcend their "pluralist heritage," but that over time he came
to understand that the choices Trinidadians make in these circumstances
"are dominated not only by pragmatic exigencies, but by aesthetic imper-
atives as well" (1989, 219). Yet, in looking at aesthetics, it is clear that
identity politics is not the only realm in which opposing images of the
world collide. For instance, the attempted coup d'état of 1990 instigated
discussions of contrasts based on young versus old, freedom versus restriction, and peace versus violence, and at points related them to ethnicity. Trinidadian musical aesthetics seem energized by addressing all
domains of colluding, competing, and conflicting images and ideas. The
metaphor of counterpoint that I have chosen to adopt—itself a form of
mixing metaphor—emphasizes movement over time, and also the experience of relief when dissonance resolves into harmony or unison. Through
music and aesthetics, I have tried to capture the experience of moments
of tension transforming into moments of relief, or moments of compla-
cency shifting into moments of anxiety. Trinidadians experience their
nation in terms of contrasts and similarities, and this profoundly influences the modulation of sentiments over time. Interestingly, the sentiments of both angry fear and euphoric joy are encompassed by the same
concept of bacchanal.

Caribbean fragmentation inspires aesthetically constructed relations
between fragments, and such relations are often broad enough to link
discourse and biology. The Caribbean was forged by terrible labor exploitation where people were literally worked to death (see John 1988)—
where bodies' forced actions were pitted against biological needs. The
very real biology of suffering, sickness, and death was related to fictive
biologies underpinning racism and exploitation. The relationship be-

tween racism and mortality is a relationship of ideological, false biologies and tangible biological processes.

Presently, many Trinidadian musical contexts fragment biological processes that are otherwise coordinated. The link between physical action and the ability to stay up all night pits some hormonal cycles against others that are more firmly entrenched in the cycle of day and night. The experience of one's body during Carnival or a parang is often an experience of simultaneous dissonant physical sensations, like excitement and fatigue, or pain and pleasure. The drive to keep playing cuatro or to keep dancing has social, mental, and physical components that are in conflict with the simultaneous desire to stop and rest. This is not a monistic unity of mind and body, but is, instead, a counterpoint of multiple biological, psychological, and cultural processes—it is a movement away from the dualism of body and mind to a myriadism of physiological and mental processes.

The aesthetics of relations can, thus, have positive, negative, or ambiguous effects. The concept of bacchanal implies this in how it relates festive euphoria with tragic violence.

✨ Reassembling the Fragments

As part of the annual cycle, the activity of playing traditional musics, such as parang, and the distribution of new songs associated with Carnival addresses the fragments that are at the forefront of public consciousness. Since fragmentation is constantly shifting, the musical reassemblages are momentary. "Get Something and Wave" was the right salve for the wounds of the attempted coup, but its power peaked at that moment, and its present performance brings back memories of that time. "Jahaji Bhai," "Lootala," and "Chukaipan" were also songs that captured a moment of political sentiments that had the potential to bridge ethnically based divisions, but they were unable to overcome suspicions and doubts. Consequently, songs that evoked a sense of cohesiveness at one moment were sources of division a few months later.

A particular song can say much about Trinidad at a particular point in time. It can reveal the sentiments of fragmentation of that moment, and the attempts to relate the disparate issues, challenges, and triumphs. Yet, because of the counterpoint between music as an enduring symbol of

Trinidadian pride, the recurring concern with certain themes such as ethnicity and politics, and the now-for-now relationship of music to specific fragmentations, there is often a sense that the sentiments evoked by particular songs at particular moments do not endure but transform over time. For instance, with regard to the issue of ethnicity, in the case of songs such as "Lootala" and "Jahaji Bhai," the sentiments they evoked changed within a single Carnival season, in a radical shift from these songs inspiring discussions of interethnic unity within the Trinidadian nation to these same songs instigating discussions of ethnic conflict and national fragmentation.

⚘ Ethnographic Counterpoints to Social Theory

With the exception of the discussion of government policies, the different ethnographic moments in this book have emphasized issues other than national identity. Indeed, the idea of the moment importantly contrasts with the often implicit association of identity as transcending time. The different cases reveal the processes through which these multisensory musical settings allow for the intersubjective crafting of sentiments and ideas. By looking at such process, the movement of experience from moment to moment is acknowledged. In pursuing the unfolding of conceptual connections, it is clear that the way in which music is used is to relate biology to the body, the body to the self, and the self to neighbors, friends, and family, and then to tie this intersubjective community to political, national, and even global concerns. In Carnival, parang, the period after the elections of 1995, and the events of the 1991 attempted coup, all invoke deeply personal ties and sentiments of kin and community. When national or global events command attention, they are refracted through the conceptual connections that already influence a great deal of intersubjective relationships—such was clearly the case in 1995, when the prime ministership of Basdeo Panday was refracted through a locally based, intersubjective web of associations with the phrase "mix up." In the case of the attempted coup, such intersubjective frameworks had to emerge over time for people to make sense of the coup—the evolution from the mantralike "What do you think?" to the placing of the coup event in the context of Trinidadian history shows this process.

Fragmentation in motion involves the flow of divisions and relations within society, the counterpoints of cognition, the complicated and often conflicted relationship between different biological processes, and the links between society, cognition, and biology. Such relations challenge the deep divisions that are maintained in social scientific discourse between biology, psychology, and culture. Such divisions can be attributed to the formation of an academic discipline, a process documented by Michel Foucault in *The Order of Things* (1994). Through its fears of reductionism, contemporary social science seems to manifest a conflicted relationship to psychology, and even to biology. At the same time, psychological and biological language and metaphors abound in social science—without much reflection, we talk of structures of feeling, cognitive mapping, and hybridity (a biologically derived metaphor). Such terminologies often serve as black boxes that keep agents from being automatons, and, at the same time, maintain their inscrutability. Some of these psychologisms become key terms in academic discourse, such as Benedict Anderson's "imagined" communities (1983), a term that invokes imagination without addressing cognition, or Jameson's "cognitive mapping" (1988), a term that combines "cognitive," an unexplored psychologism, with "mapping," an unexamined metaphor. One of the most notable of these psychologisms is Raymond Williams's "structures of feelings." In this case, Williams discusses this concept by referring to other psychologisms: "We are talking about characteristic elements of *impulse, restraint*, and tone; specifically *affective elements of consciousness* and relationships: not *feeling* against *thought*, but *thought* as *felt* and *feeling* as *thought*: practical *consciousness* of a present kind, in a living and interrelating continuity" (1977, 132, emphasis added). It is not that Anderson, Jameson, and Williams are representative of all scholarship that has occurred in the last several decades, but in providing important insights that have spurred a great deal of discussion, their works contain prominent examples of anti-reductionist perspectives containing psychological terminology.

In reflection upon the evolution of her thoughts about the relationship of political economy and psychology, Ann Stoler notes: "As a cultural anthropologist trained in political economy and ethnographic history, I was schooled to be wary not only of psychological and cognitive assessments of human behavior, but to treat them as analytic strategies that deftly circumvent questions of power and thus represent pernicious substitutes for political analysis" (1997, 101). Her point is cogent for students of both politics and psychology—the reference to psychologisms in political analysis can be construed as "pernicious substitutes" for both political analysis and psychological theory.

Politics, psychology, and physiology can be connected, but in a contrapuntal and polyrhythmic way rather than in a reductionist and essentializing way. It is hard to imagine anyone suggesting that Fanon's psychiatric knowledge provided him with a substitute for political analysis. His letter about his resignation from the Psychiatric Hospital of Blida-Joinville in Algeria demonstrates otherwise:

> If psychiatry is the medical technique that aims to enable man no longer to be a stranger to his environment, I owe it to myself to affirm that the Arab, permanently an alien in his own country, lives in a state of absolute depersonalization . . .
>
> Monsieur le Ministre, the present-day events that are steeping Algeria in blood do not constitute a scandal for the observer. What is happening is the result neither of an accident nor of a breakdown in the mechanism.
>
> The events in Algeria are the logical consequence of an abortive attempt to decerebralize a people.   (1967, 53)

As Fanon's work *Black Skin, White Masks* shows, the burdens of past and present racist ideologies and labor exploitation continue to influence West Indian life in ways that resist views of the body as merely discursive. This is powerfully manifest in his haunting, provocative ending to *Black Skin, White Masks*: "My final prayer: O my body, make of me always a man who questions!" (1967, 232). This is neither a Cartesian separation of mind and body nor a rejection of this dualism that ends up treating the body as discourse. Instead, the body and its multiple processes can inspire discourse, and discourse can influence the experience of the body.

The close ties between some Caribbean intellectuals and the surrealist movement (Richardson and Fijałkowski 1996) also suggest ways of thinking about consciousness more akin to Freud's free association than to Kant's analytic judgments. Instead of placing Caribbean societies into a category such as "creole" or "culturally plural," associationist logic emphasizes the movement of divisions to relations in fragmentation—this allows a counterpoint of pluralism and creolization. A social setting can feel creole at one moment—such as reveling in the chutney-calypso-dancehall version of "Lootala" in 1995–96—and can feel plural at a subsequent time—such as the pelting of Sonny Mann with stones when he attempted to sing "Lootala" in the Soca Monarch Competition in 1996. Creolization and pluralism are part of the counterpoint of Trinidadian social and political discourse, and they form part of the rhythm of society that is punctuated and coordinated by holidays and festivals.

Creolization versus pluralism is too simple a contrast, however. The concern with fragmentation that runs through the work of many Caribbean thinkers (e.g., Glissant 1989, 1997; Brathwaite 1977; Walcott 1992) explodes any simple dualistic formulations into fragments. Creolization/pluralism, hegemony/counter-hegemony, and domination/resistance all become broken into multiple relations. In the wake of the attempted coup of 1990, the people with whom I talked had a difficult time sorting out who was resisting whom, and the conspiracy theories that proliferated served to confound cultural interpretations of power relations. Trinidadians use music as a means of coming together to sort out these relations and to make sense of nonsense, but such sense is temporary, and there is a recognition that whatever conclusions are made during one Carnival will have to be reevaluated the following year as part of the ongoing temporally unfolding dissonances and resonances between multiple physical, biological, subjective, and intersubjective positionings.

Incorporating a dualistic view of culture and body into one's approach to such problems widens the gulf between individual and collective, since biological states are associated with individual organisms, and culture is associated with collectives. The adoption of a monistic perspective leads to either reducing culture to psychology or biology, or reducing biological and psychological processes to culture, or even denying the importance of culture, psychology, or biology. But what if culture included visceral encodings in embodied, biological ways (Worthman 1999)? What if collectives had some shared biologies, not in the sense of shared genes, but in the sense of shared and learned body chemistries that respond to environmental changes? Is it possible to complicate the divisions of culture and biology in relationship to individual and collective? Can we connect biology, psychology, culture, and politics in a way that does not reduce one to the others or make them into a monistic whole, but that allows us to think in terms of multiple contrapuntal and polyrhythmic connections of biology, mind, and society moving and transforming between dissonances, harmonies, and unities? If so, then processes of defining collectives include relationships between cultural and biological encodings—the stuff of culture *includes* shared body-states that are linked to shared ideas, just as autonomic nervous system processes, emotions, memory, and reason are all physically connected through neural networks and chemical processes.

In Carnival and Christmas, there is no fear of relating the global to the body. Events with ideological significance are marked by challenges to normal biological processes. There is no purging of the grotesque. Bakhtin (1984) argues that such a purge is the trend in consciousness after Rabelais and even more so since the Enlightenment. Trinidadian musics create intersubjective, embodied, holistic counterpoints and poly-rhythms. They continue to do so even as political conditions change. Consciousness of change and repetition is punctuated, and possibly mag-nified, by moments of physical action and involvement in response to music.

This change and repetition and these bodies do not march forward. The marching metaphor is one that is manifest in Foucault's discussion of discipline in relationship to prisoners, students, and soldiers (1979). This belies a tendency of social theory to privilege structure over motion. Marching is a metaphor of an aggregate of individuals moving in unison. If the march becomes the model, then there are only the possibilities of marching in time, or not marching—structure or resistance. In marching, the subject is dead because there is attempt to kill the subject. Trinida-dian music is not marching music; even steelbands do not march down the street during Carnival—with their audiences, they dance, chip, and wine. When everyone does engage in the same movement, such as in response to Super Blue's call to "Get Something and Wave," the unitary action is momentary—in every context in which I saw this song per-formed, by the time the verse was sung, many in the crowd had stopped waving—the unison had already broken down into parallel individual actions. This suggests that the coordinated movements evoked by Trin-idadian music are not aimed at creating conformity or inculcating disci-pline, but at creating experiences of relation and permitting spontaneity.

Trinidadian music is imbued with spontaneity and change, and the Caribbean produces intellectuals who provide insight into the relation-ship of aesthetics, fragmentation, spontaneity, and change. In his work outlining Caribbean philosophy, Paget Henry (2000) draws a contrast between the historicist approach and the poetic approach. The historicist approach emphasizes how West Indians have strived for their own political and social fulfillment. In contrast, the poetic school is less concerned with the march of history and more concerned with drawing relationships out of experience. It emphasizes consciousness as contrapuntal and evolving. Henry sees the value of bringing together these two philosophical approaches. In many ways, Trinidadian music does this. The now-for-now character of musical experience is multisensory and multidimensional. It engages consciousness and the body at the same time it can fragment both. Yet, Trinidadian music is also historicist. It involves the creation of memories of the present for the future. The memory of a particular event at a particular time is mediated and socially coordinated by musical experiences. Returning to a quote from C. L. R. James that I discussed in the first chapter, James remembers the night he was in a calypso tent when Sparrow first sang his song "Federation." The dissolution of the Federation of the West Indies and Sparrow's song were linked in James's memory.

The Caribbean is often described as having fragmented histories, identities, and subjectivities—Walcott's metaphor of the broken vase being only one very poetic example of this. As Walcott mentions, however, the fragmentation instills efforts at assembly. Such assembly cannot produce a homogenous identity in the Caribbean. Instead, these efforts occur with multiple participants engaged in multiple rhythms of action and involved in the unfolding of multiple themes, with both the themes and the rhythms moving in dissonance and consonance over time. In the future, present counterpoints will be remembered in fragmented ways that are shaped by musical experiences that captured the counterpoints for consciousness and memory.

appendix

🌼 **Given names of performers whose stage names are used in this book:**

Atilla the Hun . . . . Raymond Quevedo
Bally . . . . Errol Ballytine
Baron . . . . Timothy Watkins Jr.
Black Stalin . . . . Leroy Calliste
Brother Marvin . . . . . . Selwyn Demming
Crazy . . . . Edwin Ayong
Cro Cro . . . . Weston Rawlins
Delamo . . . . Franz Lamkin
Drupatee . . . . Drupatee Ramgoonai
General Grant . . . . Curtis Grant
Iwer George . . . . Neil George
Lord Invader . . . . Rupert Grant
Lord Kitchener . . . . Aldwyn Roberts
Mighty Chalkdust . . . . . Hollis Liverpool
Mighty Duke . . . . Kelvin Pope
Mighty Sparrow . . . . . . Slinger Francisco
Preacher . . . . Barnett Henry
Ramrajee . . . . Ramrajee Prabhoo
Ras Shorty I . . . . Garfield Blackman
Rikki Jai . . . . Ricky Samraj Jaimungal

Roaring Lion . . . . Rafael de Leon
Scrunter. . . . . Irwin Reyes Johnson
Shadow . . . . Winston Bailey
Sonny Mann . . . . Ustad Sonny Mann
Sugar Aloes . . . . Michael Anthony Osouna
Sundar Popo. . . . . Sundar Popo Bahora
Super Blue . . . . Austin Lyons
Tambu . . . . Chris Herbert
Valentino . . . . Emrold Phillip
Watchman . . . . Wayne Hayde

references

🐾 Periodicals

The Nation: Organ of the People's National Movement. Port of Spain: PNM.
TnT Mirror. Barataria, Trinidad: T & T News Centre.

🐾 Official Periodicals

Legislative Council. *Debates (Hansard)*. Trinidad: Government Printing Office.
House of Representatives. *Parliamentary Debates (Hansard)*. Trinidad: Government Printery.

🐾 Recordings

Bally (Errol Ballantyne). [1991] 1992. "Calypso Coup." *The Best of Rootsman and Bally*, track 9. JW Records.
Black Stalin (Leroy Calliste). [1979] 1992. "Caribbean Unity." *Roots Rock Soca*, track 1. Rounder Records.
———. 1995. "Sundar." *Message to Sundar*, track 4. Ice Records.
Brother Marvin (Selwyn Demming). 1996. "Brotherhood of the Boat" [Jahaji Bhai]. *Carnival Soca Hit Compilation*, track 4. JMC Records.
Crazy (Edwin Ayong). [1989] 2000. "Nani Wine" *Soca Anthems*, track 8. Hot Vinyl.
Dempster, Sanell (and Blue Ventures). 1999. "River." *Soca Gold 1999*, track 3. VP Records.
Garcia, Chris. 1996. "Chutney Bacchanal." *Soca Carnival '96*, track 1. Tattoo Records.
Iwer George (Neil George). 1998. "Bottom in de Road." *Soca Gold 1998*, track 9. VP Records.

——. 2000. "Carnival Come Back Again." *Iwer and Family: Soca Compilation*, track 1. Crosby's.

Lewis, Nigel. [1995] 1996. "Movin'." *Caribbean Dream*, track 8. Crosby's.

The Lord Invader (Rupert Grant). [1950] 1993. "Rum and Coca-Cola." Live recording on *Calypso Calaloo*, CD accompanying Donald Hill, *Calypso Calaloo: Early Carnival Music in Trinidad*, track 12. Gainesville: University Press of Florida, 1993.

Lucas, Colin. [1991] 1995. "Dollar Wine." *De Trini Party*, track 7. Rituals Music.

Mann, Sonny. 1995. "Lota La" [Loota La]. *Chutney Party Mix*, track 1. M.C. Records.

——, with Denise Belfon, and General Grant. [1995] 1997. "Lootala." *Soca Gold 1997*, track 12. VP Records.

The Mighty Sparrow. [1956] 1992. "Jean and Dinah." *The Mighty Sparrow, Volume 1*, track 1. Ice Records.

Montano, Machel (and Xtatik). [1996] 1997. "Big Truck." *Carnival Soca Hit Compilation*, track 2. JMC Records.

Plummer, Denyse. 1990. "La Trinity." *Carnival Killer*, track 3. Dynamic.

Preacher (Barnett Henry). 1994. "Jump and Wave." *Soca Carnival '94*, track 1. Ice Records.

Ras Shorty I (Garfield Blackman). [1979] 1999. "Shanti Om." *Shorty: Greatest Hits*, track 7. Charlie's Records.

Rodriguez, Wayne (and Xtatik). 1998. "Footsteps." *Machel and Xtatik: Charge*, track 5. JW Productions.

Rudder, David. [1986] 1993. "Bahia Girl." *The Gilded Collection: 1986–1989*, track 2. Lypsoland.

——. [1987] 1993. "Calypso Music." *The Gilded Collection: 1986–1989*, track 3. Lypsoland.

Scrunter (Irwin Reyes Johnson). N.d. (1989). "Piece ah Pork." *A Decade of Scrunter: De Parang Now Start*, track 12. Crosby's.

——. N.d. (1990). "Anita." *A Decade of Scrunter: De Parang Now Start*, track 9. Crosby's.

——. N.d. (1995). "Chukaipan." *A Decade of Scrunter: De Parang Now Start*, track 8. Crosby's.

Shadow (Winston Bailey). 2001. "Stranger." *Just for You*, track 1. Cross Roads Records.

Super Blue (Austin Lyons). [1991] 1996. "Get Something and Wave." *King of the Road March: Greatest Hits*, track 1. Tattoo Records.

——. [1992] 1996. "Jab Jab." *King of the Road March: Greatest Hits*, track 5. Tattoo Records.

——. 1993. "Bacchanal Time." *Bacchanal Time*, track 1. Ice Records.

——. [1995] 1996. "Signal for Lara." *King of the Road March: Greatest Hits*, track 15. Tattoo Records.

——. 2000. "Pump Up." *Hot Caribbean Hits*, track 4. Rituals Music.

Tambu (Christopher Herbert). N.d. (1989). "Free Up." *Once Upon a Time*, track 4. JW Records.

——. N.d. (1990). "No No We Ent Going Home." *Once Upon a Time*, track 8. JW Records.

Voisin, Daisy. N.d. *Daisy Viosin: Memories of a Lifetime of Parang*. Crosby's.

Watchman (Wayne Hayde). N.d. (1991). "Attack with Full Force." *Plenty to be Sorry For*, track 6. Straker's Record World.

❧ Bibliography

Abrahams, Roger. 1983. *The Man of Words in the West Indies: Performance and the Emergence of Creole Culture*. Baltimore: Johns Hopkins University Press.

Alonso, Ana Maria. 1990. Men in "Rags" and the Devil on the Throne: A Study of Protest and Inversion in the Carnival of Post-Emancipation Trinidad. *Plantation Society in the Americas* 3:73–120.

American Psychiatric Association. 2000. *Diagnostic and Statistical Manual of Mental Disorders, Fourth Edition, Text Revision*. Washington, D.C.: American Psychiatric Association.

Anderson, Benedict. 1983. *Imagined Communities: Reflections on the Origin and Spread of Nationalism*. London: Verso.

Aschoff, Jürgen, ed. 1981. *Biological Rhythms*. New York: Plenum.

Averill, Gage. 1997. *Day for the Hunter a Day for the Prey: Popular Music and Power in Haiti*. Chicago: University of Chicago Press.

Baehr, Erin K., Charmane I. Eastman, William Revelle, Susan H. Losee Olson, Lisa F. Wolfe, and Phyllis C. Zee. 2003. Circadian Phase-shifting Effects of Nocturnal Exercise in Older Compared with Young Adults. *American Journal of Physiology: Regulatory, Integrative and Comparative Physiology* 284:R1542–R1550.

Bahadoorsingh, Krishna. 1968. *Trinidad Electoral Politics: The Persistence of the Race Factor*. London: Institute of Race Relations.

Bakhtin, Mikhail. 1981. *The Dialogic Imagination: Four Essays*. Austin: University of Texas Press.

——. [1968] 1984. *Rabelais and His World*. Translated by Helene Iswolsky. Bloomington: Indiana University Press.

Balliger, Robin. 1998. Popular Music and the Cultural Politics of Globalisation among the Post-Oil Boom Generation in Trinidad. In *Identity, Ethnicity and Culture in the Caribbean*, edited by Ralph R. Premdas, 54–79. St. Augustine, Trinidad: University of the West Indies School of Continuing Studies.

Barthes, Roland. 1974. *S/Z*. New York: Hill and Wang.

Basch, Linda, Nina Glick Schiller, and Christina Szanton Blanc. 1994. *Nations Unbound: Transnational Projects, Postcolonial Predicaments, and Deterritorialized Nation-States*. New York: Gordon and Breach.

Bateson, Gregory. 1972. *Steps to an Ecology of Mind*. New York: Ballantine.

Beetham, Edward Betham. 1958. *Address by His Excellency the Governor to the Legislative Council, Session 1957–1958.* Council paper no. 12. Trinidad: Government Printing Office.

Benítez-Rojo, Antonio. 1996. *The Repeating Island: The Caribbean and the Postmodern Perspective.* 2nd ed. Translated by James Maraniss. Durham, N.C.: Duke University Press.

Bhabha, Homi. 1994. *The Location of Culture.* New York: Routledge.

Birth, Kevin K. 1994. Bakrnal: Coup, Carnival, and Calypso in Trinidad. *Ethnology* 33:165–77.

———. 1995. The Ethnic Ambiguities of Getting Married: The Official Pronouncements, Local Interpretations, and Personal Experiences of Trinidadian Hindu Indians. *International Journal of Comparative Race and Ethnic Studies* 2, no. 2: 80–91.

———. 1996. Trinidadian Times: Temporal Dependency and Temporal Flexibility on the Margins of Industrial Capitalism. *Anthropological Quarterly* 69, no. 2: 79–89.

———. 1997. Most of Us Are Family Some of the Time: Interracial Marriage and Transracial Kinship in Eastern Trinidad. *American Ethnologist* 24, no. 3: 585–601.

———. 1999. *Any Time Is Trinidad Time.* Gainesville: University Press of Florida.

Black, Peter W. 1985. Ghosts, Gossip, and Suicide: Meaning and Action in Tobian Folk Psychology. In *Person, Self, and Experience: Exploring Pacific Ethnopsychologies,* edited by Geoffrey M. White and John Kirkpatrick, 245–300. Berkeley: University of California Press.

Bonnefond, Anne, Patricia Tassi, Joceline Roge, and Alain Muzet. 2004. A Critical Review of Techniques Aiming at Enhancing and Sustaining Workers' Alertness during the Night. *Industrial Health* 42, no. 1: 1–14.

Boomert, Arie. 1984. The Arawak Indians of Trinidad and coastal Guiana ca. 1500–1650. *Journal of Caribbean History* 19, no. 2: 123–88.

Bourguignon, Erika. 1973. Introduction: A Framework for the Comparative Study of Altered States of Consciousness. In *Religion, Altered States of Consciousness and Social Change,* edited by Erika Bourguignon, 3–35. Columbus: Ohio State University Press.

———. [1976] 1991. *Possession.* Prospect Heights, Ill.: Waveland.

Braithwaite, Lloyd. 1954. Cultural Integration in Trinidad. *Social and Economic Studies* 3, no. 1: 82–96.

———. 2001. *Colonial West Indian Students in Britain.* Mona, Jamaica: University of the West Indies Press.

Brathwaite, Edward. 1971. *The Development of Creole Society in Jamaica, 1770–1820.* London: Oxford University Press.

———. 1977. The Love Axe/1. *Bim* 16, no. 61: 53–65.

Brereton, Bridget. 1975. The Trinidad Carnival, 1870–1900. *Savacou* 11–12: 46–57.

———. 1979. *Race Relations in Colonial Trinidad, 1870–1900*. Cambridge: Cambridge University Press.

———. 1993. Social Organisation and Class, Racial and Cultural Conflict in Nineteenth-Century Trinidad. In *Trinidad Ethnicity*, edited by Kevin Yelvington, 33–55. Knoxville: University of Tennessee Press.

Brown, Wenzell. 1947. *Angry Men, Laughing Men: The Caribbean Caldron*. New York: Greenberg.

Burton, Richard D. E. 1997. *Afro-Creole: Power, Opposition and Play in the Caribbean*. Ithaca, N.Y.: Cornell University Press.

Buxton, Orfeu M., Calvin W. Lee, Mereille L'Hermite-Balériaux, Fred W. Turek, and Eve Van Cauter. 2003. Exercise elicits phase shifts and acute alterations of melatonin that vary with circadian phase. *American Journal of Physiology: Regulatory, Integrative, and Comparative Physiology* 284:R714–R724.

Carmichael, A. C. 1834. *Domestic Manners and Social Conditions of the Whites, Coloured, and Negro Population of the West Indies*. London: Whittaker.

Carrington, Edwin. 1971. The Post War Political Economy of Trinidad and Tobago. In *Readings in the Political Economy of the Caribbean*, edited by Norman Girvan and Owen Jefferson, 121–42. Kingston, Jamaica: New World Group.

Césaire, Aimé. 1983. Notebook of a Return to the Native Land. In *Aimé Césaire: The Collected Poetry*, translated by Clayton Eshleman and Annette Smith, 32–85. Berkeley: University of California Press.

———. [1944] 1996. Calling the Magician: A Few Words for a Caribbean Civilization. In *Refusal of the Shadow: Surrealism and the Caribbean*, edited by Michael Richardson and Krzysztof Fijałkowski, 119–22. London: Verso.

———. [1972] 2000. *Discourse on Colonialism*. New York: Monthly Review Press.

Chatterjee, Partha. 1993. *The Nation and Its Fragments: Colonial and Postcolonial Histories*. Princeton, N.J.: Princeton University Press.

Clark, Andy. 1997. *Being There: Putting Brain, Body, and World Together Again*. Cambridge, Mass.: MIT Press.

Collier, H. C. 1943. Carnival Capers in Calypso Land. *Canada–West Indies Magazine* 32, no. 1: 19–22.

Collins, John. N.d. Sound in Play in Salvador, Behia's *Gueto*: The Materiality of Inconclusion in a Brazilian Cultural Heritage Center. Unpublished manuscript.

Cowley, John. 1996. *Carnival, Canboulay and Calypso: Traditions in the Making*. Cambridge: Cambridge University Press.

Craig, Susan. 1985. Political Patronage and Community Resistance: Village Councils in Trinidad and Tobago. In *Rural Development in the Caribbean*, edited by P. I. Gomes, 173–93. Kingston, Jamaica: Heinemann Educational Books (Caribbean).

Crapanzano, Vincent. 1986. Hermes' Dilemma: The Masking of Subversion in Ethnographic Description. In *Writing Culture*, edited by James Clifford and George Marcus, 51–76. Berkeley: University of California Press.

Crowley, Daniel J. 1957. Plural and Differential Acculturation in Trinidad. *American Anthropologist* 59, no. 5: 817–24.

Csordas, Thomas. 1990. Embodiment as a Paradigm for Anthropology. *Ethos* 18, no. 1: 5–47.

———. 1994. *The Sacred Self: A Cultural Phenomenology of Charismatic Healing.* Berkeley: University of California Press.

Cudjoe, Selwyn. 1993. Introduction to *Eric E. Williams Speaks: Essays on Colonialism and Independence*, edited by Selwyn Cudjoe, 1–33. Wellesley, Mass.: Calaloux.

———. 2003. *Beyond Boundaries: The Intellectual Tradition of Trinidad and Tobago in the Nineteenth Century.* Wellesley, Mass.: Calaloux.

Czeisler, Charles A., Jeanne F. Duffy, Theresa L. Shanahan, Emery N. Brown, Jude F. Mitchell, David W. Rimmer, Joseph M. Ronda, Edward J. Silva, James S. Allan, Jonathan S. Emens, Derk-Jan Dijk, and Richard E. Kronauer. 1999. Stability, Precision, and Near-24-h Period of the Human Circadian Pacemaker. *Science* 284: 2177–81.

Damasio, Antonio. 1994. *Descartes' Error: Emotion, Reason, and the Human Brain.* New York: G. P. Putnam.

———. 1999. *The Feeling of What Happens: The Body and Emotion in the Making of Consciousness.* New York: Harcourt Brace.

D'Andrade, Roy. 1992. Schemas and Motivation. In *Human Motives and Cultural Models*, edited by Roy D'Andrade and Claudia Strauss, 23–44. Cambridge: Cambridge University Press.

———. 1995. *The Development of Cognitive Anthropology.* Cambridge: Cambridge University Press.

d'Anghiera, Pietro Martire. [1555] 1966. *The Decades of the Newe World or West India.* Translated by Rycharde Eden. Ann Arbor: Readex Microprint Corporation.

Dash, J. Michael. 1995. *Edouard Glissant.* Cambridge: Cambridge University Press.

Dávila, Arlene. 1997. *Sponsored Identities: Cultural Politics in Puerto Rico.* Philadelphia: Temple University Press.

Davis, Natalie Zemon. 1978. Women on Top: Inversion and Political Disorder in Early Modern Europe. In *The Reversible World: Symbolic Inversion in Art and Society*, edited by Barbara Babcock, 147–90. Ithaca, N.Y.: Cornell University Press.

Deosaran, Ramesh. 1987. The "Caribbean Man": A Study of the Psychology of Perception and the Media. In *India in the Caribbean*, edited by David Dabydeen and Brinsley Samaroo, 81–117. London: Hansib.

———. 1995. Voices of the Past, Visions of the Future. In *In Celebration of 150 Yrs of the Indian Contribution to Trinidad and Tobago*, edited by Diane Quentrall-Thomas, 175–90. Port of Spain: Historical Publications.

Desjarlais, Robert. 1992. *Body and Emotion: The Aesthetics of Illness and Healing in the Nepal Himalayas.* Philadelphia: University of Pennsylvania Press.

Dewey, John. [1934] 1980. *Art as Experience.* New York: Perigree.

Dirks, Robert. 1987. *The Black Saturnalia: Conflict and Its Ritual Expression on British West Indian Slave Plantations.* Gainesville: University Press of Florida.

Dookeran, Winston. [1974] 1985. East Indians and the Economy of Trinidad and Tobago. In *Calcutta to Caroni: The East Indians of Trinidad*, edited by John La Guerre, 63–73. St. Augustine: University of the West Indies, Extra-Mural Studies Unit.

Dudley, Shannon. 2004. *Carnival Music in Trinidad: Experiencing Music, Expressing Culture*. Oxford: Oxford University Press.

Durkheim, Emile. [1915] 1965. *The Elementary Forms of the Religious Life*. Translated by Joseph Ward Swain. New York: Free Press.

——. 1966. *The Rules of the Sociological Method*. Edited by George E. G. Catlin, translated by Sarah A. Solovay and John H. Mueller. New York: Free Press.

Edgewater, Iain. 1999. Music Hath Charms . . . : Fragments toward Constructionist Biocultural Theory, with Attention to the Relationship of Music and Emotion. In *Biocultural Approaches to the Emotions*, edited by Alexander Hinton, 153–81. Cambridge: Cambridge University Press.

Elder, J. D. 1966. *Kalinda*—Song of the Battling Troubadours of Trinidad. *Journal of the Folklore Institute* 3, no. 2: 192–203.

——. 1967. *Evolution of the Traditional Calypso of Trinidad and Tobago: A Socio-Historical Analysis of Song-Change*. PhD diss., University of Pennsylvania.

——. 1998. Cannes Brûlées. *Drama Review* 42, no. 3: 38–43.

Eriksen, Thomas Hylland. 1992. *Us and Them in Modern Societies: Ethnicity and Nationalism in Mauritius, Trinidad and Beyond*. Oslo: Scandinavian University Press.

Falassi, Alessandro. 1987. Festival: Definition and Morphology. In *Time out of Time: Essays on the Festival*, edited by Alessandro Falassi, 1–10. Albuquerque: University of New Mexico Press.

Fanon, Frantz. 1963. *The Wretched of the Earth*. Translated by Constance Farrington. New York: Grove.

——. 1967. *Black Skin, White Masks*. Translated by Charles Lam Markmann. New York: Grove.

——. [1956] 1967. Letter to the Resident Minister. In *Toward the African Revolution*, translated by Haakon Chavalier, 52–54. New York: Grove.

Feld, Steven. 1982. *Sound and Sentiment: Birds, Weeping, Poetics and Song in Kaluli Expression*. 2nd ed. Philadelphia: University of Pennsylvania Press.

Figueredo, Alfredo E., and Stephen Glazier. 1982. Spatial Behavior, Social Organization, and Ethnicity in the Prehistory of Trinidad. *Journal de la Société des Américanistes* 68:33–39.

Findlay, Ronald. 1982. On W. Arthur Lewis's Contributions to Economics. In *The Theory and Experience of Economic Development*, edited by Mark Gersovitz, Carlos F. Diaz-Alejandro, Gustav Ranis, and Mark R. Rosenzweig, 1–14. London: George Allen and Unwin.

Fish, Stanley. 1980. *Is There a Text in this Class? The Authority of Interpretive Communities*. Cambridge, Mass.: Harvard University Press.

Flinn, M. V. 1999. Family Environment, Stress, and Health during Childhood. In

Hormones, Health, and Behavior: A Socio-ecological and Lifespan Perspective, edited by C. Panter-Brick and C. M. Worthman, 105–38. Cambridge: Cambridge University Press.

Folkard, Simon. 1997. Black Times: Temporal Determinants of Transport Safety. *Accident Analysis and Prevention* 4:417–30.

Foner, Nancy. 2001. Introduction. West Indian Migration to New York: An Overview. In *Islands in the City: West Indian Migration to New York*, edited by Nancy Foner, 1–22. Berkeley: University of California Press.

Forte, Maximilian C. 2005. *Ruins of Absence, Presence of Caribs: (Post)Colonial Representations of Aboriginality in Trinidad and Tobago*. Gainesville: University Press of Florida.

Foucault, Michel. 1979. *Discipline and Punish: The Birth of the Prison*. Translated by Alan Sheridan. New York: Vintage.

——. [1971] 1994. *The Order of Things: An Archaeology of the Human Sciences*. New York: Vintage.

Frake, Charles O. 1997. Plying Frames Can Be Dangerous: Some Reflections on Methodology in Cognitive Anthropology. In *Mind, Culture, and Activity: Seminal Papers from the Laboratory of Human Cognition*, edited by Michael Cole, Yrjö Engeström, and Olga Vasquez, 32–46. Cambridge: Cambridge University Press.

Freilich, Morris. 1960. *Cultural Diversity among Trinidadian Peasants*. PhD diss., Columbia University.

Fux, Johann Joseph. [1725] 1965. *Study of Counterpoint*. Edited and translated by Alfred Mann. New York: W. W. Norton.

Geurts, Kathryn Linn. 2001. *Culture and the Senses: Bodily Ways of Knowing in an African Community*. Berkeley: University of California Press.

Gilroy, Paul. 1993. *The Black Atlantic: Modernity and Double Consciousness*. Cambridge, Mass.: Harvard University Press.

Glazier, Stephen D. 1980. Aboriginal Trinidad and the Guianas: An Historical Overview. *Archaeology and Anthropology* 3, no. 2: 119–24.

——. 1983. *Marchin' the Pilgrims Home: Leadership and Decision-making in an Afro-Caribbean Faith*. Westport, Conn.: Greenwood.

Glissant, Édouard. 1989 *Caribbean Discourse: Selected Essays*. Translated by J. Michael Dash. Charlottesville: University Press of Virginia.

——. 1997. *Poetics of Relation*. Translated by Betsy Wing. Ann Arbor: University of Michigan Press.

Gluckman, Max. 1969. *Custom and Conflict in Africa*. New York: Barnes and Noble.

Godelier, Maurice. 1999. *The Enigma of the Gift*. Translated by Nora Scott. Chicago: University of Chicago Press.

Gomes, Albert. 1974. *Through a Maze of Colour*. Port of Spain: Key Caribbean.

Goodman, Felicitas. 1972. *Speaking in Tongues: A Cross-cultural study of Glossolalia*. Chicago: University of Chicago Press.

Government of Trinidad and Tobago. 1969. *Draft of Third Five-Year Plan, 1969–1973*. Trinidad: Government Printery.

Green, Garth L. 2002. Marketing the Nation: Carnival and Tourism in Trinidad and Tobago. *Critique of Anthropology* 22:283–304.

Guss, David M. 2000. *The Festive State: Race, Ethnicity, and Nationalism as Cultural Performance*. Berkeley: University of California Press.

Hall, Stuart. 1997. The Work of Representation. In *Representation: Cultural Representations and Signifying Practices*, edited by Stuart Hall. London: Sage.

Halliburton, Murphy. 2004. Gandhi or Gramsci? The Use of Authoritative Sources in Anthropology. *Anthropological Quarterly* 77, no. 4: 793–817.

Handler, Richard. 1988. *Nationalism and the Politics of Culture in Quebec*. Madison: University of Wisconsin Press.

——. 1994. Is "Identity" a Useful Cross-Cultural Concept? In *Commemorations: The Politics of National Identity*, edited by John R. Gillis, 27–40. Princeton, N.J.: Princeton University Press.

Harney, Stefano. 1999. Soca and Social Formations: Avoiding the Romance of Culture in Trinidad. In *Caribbean Romances: The Politics of Regional Representation*, edited by Belinda J. Edmondson, 39–55. Charlottesville: University Press of Virginia.

Harris, Wilson. 1967. The Question of Form and Realism in the West Indian Artist. In *Tradition, the Writer and Society: Critical Essays*. London: New Beacon.

——. 1999. *Selected Essays of Wilson Harris: The Unfinished Genesis of the Imagination*. Edited by Andrew Bundy. New York: Routledge.

Hebdige, Dick. 1987. *Cut-n-Mix: Culture, Identity and Caribbean Music*. London: Methuen.

Henke, Holger. 2004. Ariel's Ethos: On the Moral Economy of Caribbean Experience. *Cultural Critique* 56:33–63.

Henry, Paget. 2000. *Caliban's Reason: Introducing Afro-Caribbean Philosophy*. New York: Routledge.

Herskovits, Melville J. 1966. Trinidad Shouters: Protestant African Synthesis. In *The New World Negro: Selected Papers in Afro-American Studies*, edited by Frances Herskovits, 229–53. Bloomington: Indiana University Press.

Herskovits, Melville J., and Frances Herskovits. 1947. *Trinidad Village*. New York: Knopf.

Hill, Donald R. 1993. *Calypso Calaloo: Early Carnival Music in Trinidad*. Gainesville: University Press of Florida.

Hill, Errol. 1972. *The Trinidad Carnival: Mandate for a National Theatre*. Austin: University of Texas Press.

Hintzen, Percy C. 1989. *The Costs of Regime Survival: Racial Mobilization, Elite Domination, and Control of the State in Guyana and Trinidad*. Cambridge: Cambridge University Press.

Holland, Dorothy, William Lachicotte Jr., Debra Skinner; and Carole Cain. 1998. *Identity and Agency in Cultural Worlds*. Cambridge, Mass.: Harvard University Press.

Holquist, Michael. 1990. *Dialogism: Bakhtin and His World*. New York: Routledge.

Hutchins, Edwin. 1995. *Cognition in the Wild*. Cambridge, Mass.: MIT Press.

Iser, Wolfgang. 1978. *The Act of Reading: A Theory of Aesthetic Response*. Baltimore: Johns Hopkins University Press.

James, C. L. R. 1959. Independence, Energy and Creative Talent of Carnival Can Do Other Wonders. *Nation*, February 21, 1959.

——. [1938] 1963. *The Black Jacobins*. New York: Vintage.

——. [1962] 1977. *Nkrumah and the Ghana Revolution*. London: Allison and Busby.

——. [1948] 1980. *Notes on Dialectics: Hegel, Marx, Lenin*. Westport, Conn.: L. Hill.

——. [1962] 1984. *Party Politics in the West Indies*. Port of Spain: Inprint.

——. 1986. *Cricket*. Edited by Anna Grimshaw. London: Allison and Busby.

——. [1950] 1986. *State Capitalism and World Revolution*. Chicago: Kerr.

——. [1963] 1993. *Beyond a Boundary*. Durham, N.C.: Duke University Press.

Jameson, Fredric. 1988. Cognitive Mapping. In *Marxism and the Interpretation of Culture*, edited by Cary Nelson and Lawrence Grossberg, 347–57. Urbana: University of Illinois Press.

Jankowiak, William, and C. Todd White. 1999. Carnival on the Clipboard: An Ethnological Study of New Orleans Mardi Gras. *Ethnology* 38, no. 4: 335–49.

Janssen, Daniela, and Friedhelm Nachreiner. 2004. Health and Psychosocial Effects of Flexible Working Hours. *Revista de Saúde Pública* 38 (supplement): 11–18.

Jha, J. C. [1974] 1985. The Indian Heritage in Trinidad. In *Calcutta to Caroni: The East Indians of Trinidad*, edited by John La Guerre, 21–30. St. Augustine: University of the West Indies, Extra-mural Unit.

John, A. Meredith. 1988. *The Plantation Slaves of Trinidad, 1783–1816: A Mathematical and Demographic Enquiry*. Cambridge: Cambridge University Press.

Johnson, Kim. 2002. *Renegades: The History of the Renegades Steel Orchestra of Trinidad and Tobago*. Oxford: MacMillan.

Jones, James M.; and Liverpool, Hollis. 1976. Calypso Humour in Trinidad. In *Humour and Laughter: Theory, Research and Applications*, edited by Anthony J. Chapman and Hugh C. Foot, 259–86. London: John Wiley and Sons.

Joseph, E. L. 1838. *History of Trinidad: A Descriptive Account of the History and Geography of Trinidad*. London: A. K. Newman and Company.

Juneja, Renu. 1989. We Kind of Music. *Popular Music and Society* 13:37–51.

Keil, Charles, and Steven Feld. 1994. *Music Grooves: Essays and Dialogues*. Chicago: University of Chicago Press.

Khan, Aisha. 1993. What Is "a Spanish"? Ambiguity and "Mixed" Ethnicity in Trinidad. In *Trinidad Ethnicity*, edited by Kevin Yelvington, 180–207. Knoxville: University of Tennessee Press.

——. 2001. Journey to the Center of the Earth: The Caribbean as Master Symbol. *Cultural Anthropology* 16, no. 3: 271–302.

——. 2004. *Callaloo Nation: Metaphors of Race and Religious Identity among South Asians in Trinidad*. Durham, N.C.: Duke University Press.

Koningsbruggen, Petrus Hendrikus van. 1997. *Trinidad Carnival: A Quest for National Identity*. London: Macmillan Education.

Korom, Frank J. 2003. *Hosay Trinidad: Muharram Performances in an Indo-Caribbean Diaspora*. Philadelphia: University of Pennsylvania Press.

La Guerre, John Gaffar. 1972. The General Elections of 1946 in Trinidad and Tobago. *Social and Economic Studies* 21:184–204.

———, ed. 1997. *The General Elections of 1995 in Trinidad and Tobago*. St. Augustine, Trinidad: University of the West Indies, School of Continuing Studies.

Lakoff, George, and Mark Johnson. 1980. *Metaphors We Live By*. Chicago: University of Chicago Press.

———. 1999. *Philosophy in the Flesh: The Embodied Mind and Its Challenge to Western Thought*. New York: Basic.

Langer, Susanne. 1953. *Feeling and Form: A Theory of Art Developed from Philosophy in a New Key*. New York: Charles Scribner's Sons.

———. 1979. *Philosophy in a New Key: A Study in the Symbolism of Reason, Rite, and Art*. 3rd ed. Cambridge, Mass.: Harvard University Press.

Lave, Jean, and Etienne Wenger. 1991. *Situated Learning: Legitimate Peripheral Participation*. Cambridge: Cambridge University Press.

Lavie, P. 2001. Sleep-wake as a Biological Rhythm. *Annual Review of Psychology*, 52:277–303.

Le Roy Ladurie, Emmanuel. 1979. *Carnival in Romans*. New York: G. Braziller.

Ledgister, Fragano. 1998. *Class Alliances and the Liberal-Authoritarian State: The Roots of Postcolonial Democracy in Jamaica, Trinidad and Tobago, and Surinam*. Trenton, N.J.: Africa World Press.

Leon, Raphael de. N.d. *Calypso: From France to Trinidad, 800 Years of History*. San Juan, Trinidad: General Printers.

Lewis, Gordon K. 1968. *The Growth of the Modern West Indies*. New York: Monthly Review Press.

Lewis, W. Arthur. 1950. The Industrialization of the British West Indies. *Caribbean Economic Review* 1:1–61.

———. 1954. Economic Development with Unlimited Supplies of Labour. *Manchester School* 22, no. 2: 139–91.

———. 1955. *The Theory of Economic Growth*. Homewood, Ill.: Richard D. Irwin.

———. [1965] 1973. On Being Different. In *The Aftermath of Sovereignty: West Indian Perspectives*, edited by David Lowenthal and Lambros Comitas, 293–302. Garden City: Anchor.

Linger, Daniel. 1992. *Dangerous Encounters: Meanings of Violence in a Brazilian City*. Stanford, Calif.: Stanford University Press.

Littlewood, Roland. 1988. From Vice to Madness: The Semantics of Naturalistic and Personalistic Understandings in Trinidadian Local Medicine. *Social Science and Medicine* 7, no. 2: 129–48.

———. 1993. *Pathology and Identity*. Cambridge: Cambridge University Press.

Liverpool, Hollis. 1990. *Kaiso and Society*. Diego Martin, Trinidad: Juba.

———. 1994. Researching Steelband and Calypso Music in the British Caribbean and the U.S. Virgin Islands. *Black Music Research Journal* 14, no. 2: 179–201.

——. 2001. *Rituals of Power and Rebellion: The Carnival Tradition in Trinidad and Tobago, 1763–1962*. Chicago: Research Associates School Times.

Lobdell, Richard. 1972. Patterns of Investment and Credit in the British West Indian Sugar Industry, 1838–1918. *Journal of Caribbean History* 4:31–53.

Lomax, Alan. 1962. Song Structure and Social Structure. *Ethnology* 1, no. 4: 425–51.

London, Clement B. G. 1991. Forging a Cultural Identity: Leadership and Development in Mass Education in a Developing Caribbean Country. *Journal of Black Studies* 21, no. 3: 251–67.

Lukes, Steven. 1985. *Emile Durkheim, His Life and Work: A Historical and Critical Study*. Stanford, Calif.: Stanford University Press.

Lutz, Catherine. 1986. Emotion, Thought, and Estrangement: Emotion as a Cultural Category. *Cultural Anthropology* 1, no. 3: 287–309.

MacAloon, John J. 1984. Olympic Games and the Theory of Spectacle in Modern Societies. In *Rite, Drama, Festival, Spectacle: Rehearsals toward a Theory of Cultural Performance*, edited by John J. MacAloon, 241–80. Philadelphia: Institute for the Study of Human Issues.

Manuel, Peter. 1995. *Caribbean Currents: Caribbean Music from Rumba to Reggae*. Philadelphia: Temple University Press.

——. 2000. *East Indian Music in the West Indies: Tan-singing, Chutney and the Making of Indo-Caribbean Culture*. Philadelphia: Temple University Press.

Marriott, McKim. 1966. The Feast of Love. In *Krishna: Myths, Rites, and Attitudes*, edited by Milton Singer, 201–12. Chicago: University of Chicago Press.

Mason, Peter. 1998. *Bacchanal: The Carnival Culture of Trinidad*. Philadelphia: Temple University Press.

Mauss, Marcel. 1967. *The Gift: Forms and Functions of Exchange in Archaic Societies*. Translated by Ian Cunnison. New York: Norton.

McEachron, Donald L., and Jonathan Schull. 1993. Hormones, Rhythms, and the Blues. In *Hormonally Induced Changes in Mind and Brain*, edited by Jay Schulkin, 287–355. San Diego: Academic Press.

Merleau-Ponty, Maurice. 1962. *Phenomenology of Perception*. New York: Humanities.

Miller, Daniel. 1990. Fashion and Ontology in Trinidad. *Culture and History* 7:49–77.

——. 1991. Absolute Freedom in Trinidad. *Man* 26, no. 2: 323–41.

——. 1993. Christmas against Materialism in Trinidad. In *Unwrapping Christmas*, edited by Daniel Miller, 134–53. Oxford: Clarendon.

——. 1994. *Modernity: An Ethnographic Approach—Dualism and Mass Consumption in Trinidad*. Oxford: Berg.

——. 1997. *Capitalism: An Ethnographic Approach*. Oxford: Berg.

Mistlberger, Ralph E., and Debra J. Skene. 2005. Nonphotic Entrainment in Humans? *Journal of Biological Rhythms* 20:339–52.

Mohammed, Patricia. 2002. Taking Possession: Symbols of Empire and Nationhood. *Small Axe* 11:31–58.

Monk, Timothy H. 2000. What Can the Chronobiologist Do to Help the Shift Worker? *Journal of Biological Rhythms* 15: 86–94.

Monteleone, Palmiero, Antonio Fuschino, Giovanni Nolfe, and Mario Maj. 1992. Temporal Relationship between Melatonin and Cortisol Responses to Nighttime Physical Stress in Humans. *Psychoneuroendocrinology* 17:81–86.

Moodie-Kublalsingh, Sylvia. 1994. *The Cocoa Panyols of Trinidad: An Oral Record.* London: British Academic Press.

Moore-Ede, Martin C. 1993. *The 24-Hour Society: Understanding Human Limits in a World That Never Stops.* Reading, Mass.: Addison-Wesley.

Moore-Ede, Martin C., Frank M. Sulzman, and Charles Fuller. 1982. *The Clocks That Time Us: Physiology of the Circadian Timing System.* Harvard, Mass.: Harvard University Press.

Mordecai, John. 1968. *Federation of the West Indies.* Evanston, Ill.: Northwestern University Press.

Mrosovsky, N. 1996. Locomotor Activity and Non-photic Influences on Circadian Clocks. *Biological Reviews of the Cambridge Philosophical Society* 71:343–72.

Mrosovsky, N., S. G. Reebs, G. I. Honrado, and P. A. Salmon. 1989. Behavioral Entrainment of Circadian Rhythms. *Experientia* 45:696–702.

Munasinghe, Viranjini. 2001. *Callaloo or Tossed Salad? East Indians and the Cultural Politics of Identity in Trinidad.* Ithaca, N.Y.: Cornell University Press.

Myers, Helen. 1998. *Music of Hindu Trinidad: Songs from the Indian Diaspora.* Chicago: University of Chicago Press.

Naipaul, V. S. [1962] 1981. *The Middle Passage: Impressions of Five Societies—British, French, and Dutch—in the West Indies and South America.* New York: Vintage.

National Planning Commission. 1963. *Draft: Second Five-Year Plan, 1964–1968.* Trinidad: Government Printery.

Ong, Walter J. 1982. *Orality and Literacy: The Technologizing of the Word.* New York: Methuen.

Ortiz, Fernando. [1947] 1995. *Cuban Counterpoint: Tobacco and Sugar.* Durham, N.C.: Duke University Press.

Oxaal, Ivar. 1982. *Black Intellectuals and the Dilemmas of Race and Class in Trinidad.* Cambridge, Mass.: Schenkman.

Pastor, Robert. 1992. *Whirlpool: U.S. Policy toward Latin America and the Caribbean.* Princeton, N.J.: Princeton University Press.

Premdas, Ralph R. 1998. The Ascendance of an Indian Prime Minister in Trinidad and Tobago: The 1995 Elections. In *Identity, Ethnicity and Culture in the Caribbean,* edited by Ralph R. Premdas, 323–58. St. Augustine, Trinidad: University of the West Indies School of Continuing Studies.

Prendas, Ralph R., and Bishnu Ragoonath. 1998. Ethnicity, Elections and Democracy in Trinidad and Tobago: Analysing the 1995 and 1996 Elections. *Commonwealth and Comparative Politics* 36, no. 3: 30–53.

Prime Minister's Best Village Trophy. 1967. *The Prime Minister's Best Village Trophy.* Port of Spain.

Puri, Shalini. 2004. *The Caribbean Postcolonial: Social Equality, Post-Nationalism, and Cultural Hybridity*. New York: Palgrave MacMillan.

Quera-Salva, Maria Antonia; Christian Guilleminault, Bruno Claustrat, Remy Defrance, Philippe Gajdos, Catherine Crowe McCann, and Jacques De Lattre. 1997. Rapid Shift in Peak Melatonin Secretion Associated with Improved Performance in Short Shift Work Schedule. *Sleep* 20, no. 12: 1145–50.

Quevedo, Raymond. 1983. *Atilla's Kaiso: A Short History of Trinidad Calypso*. St. Augustine: University of the West Indies, Department of Extra-mural Studies.

Quinn, Naomi. 1982. "Commitment" in American Marriage: A Cultural Analysis. *American Ethnologist* 9, no. 4: 775–98.

——. 1996. Culture and Contradiction: The Case of Americans Reasoning about Marriage. *Ethos* 24, no. 3: 391–425.

Rajaratnam, Shantha M. W., and Josephine Arendt. 2001. Health in a 24-h Society. *Lancet* 358: 999–1005.

Ramnarine, Tina K. 2001. *Creating Their Own Space: The Development of an Indian-Caribbean Musical Tradition*. Kingston, Jamaica: University of the West Indies Press.

Ramsaran, Ramesh F. 1994. The Theory and Practice of Structural Adjustment with Special Reference to the Commonwealth Caribbean. In *Structural Adjustment, Public Policy and Administration in the Caribbean*, edited by John La Guerre, 9–37. St. Augustine, Trinidad: University of the West Indies, School of Continuing Studies.

Reddock, Rhoda. 1999. Jahaji Bhai: The Emergence of a Dougla Poetics in Trinidad and Tobago. *Identities* 5, no. 4: 569–601.

Regis, Louis. 1999. *Political Calypso: True Opposition in Trinidad and Tobago*. Gainesville: University Press of Florida.

Richardson, Michael, and Krzysztof Fijałkowski. 1996. Introduction to *Refusal of the Shadow: Surrealism and the Caribbean*, edited by Michael Richardson and Krzysztof Fijałkowski, 1–33. London: Verso.

Roberts, John Storm. 1972. *Black Music of Two Worlds*. Tivoli, N.Y.: Original Music.

Rodney, Walter. 1981. *A History of the Guyanese Working People, 1881–1905*. Baltimore: Johns Hopkins University Press.

——. [1969] 1990. *The Groundings with My Brothers*. London: Bogle-L'Ouverture Publications.

——. 1990. *Walter Rodney Speaks*. Trenton, N.J.: Africa World Press.

Rohlehr, Gordon. 1990. *Calypso and Society in Pre-Independence Trinidad*. Port of Spain.

——. 1992a. Articulating a Caribbean Aesthetic: The Revolution of Self-Perception. In *My Strangled City and Other Essays*, 1–16. Port of Spain: Longman Trinidad.

——. 1992b. The Shape of That Hurt: An Introduction to *Voiceprint*. In *The Shape of That Hurt and Other Essays*, 164–90. Port of Spain: Longman Trinidad.

——. 1992c. Apocalypso and the Soca Fires of 1990. In *The Shape of That Hurt and Other Essays*, 305–71. Port of Spain: Longman Trinidad.

———. 1997. The Culture of Williams: Context, Performance, Legacy. *Callaloo* 20, no. 4: 849–88.

———. 1998. "We Getting the Kaiso That We Deserve": Calypso and the World Music Market. *Drama Review* 42, no. 3: 82–95.

———. 2004a. Change and Prophecy in the Trinidad and Tobago Calypso towards the Twenty-first Century. In *A Scuffling of Islands: Essays on Calypso*, 335–73. San Juan, Trinidad: Lexicon Trinidad.

———. 2004b. Calypso Reinvents Itself. In *A Scuffling of Islands: Essays on Calypso*, 374–449. San Juan, Trinidad: Lexicon Trinidad.

———. 2004c. A Scuffling of Islands: The Dream and Reality of Caribbean Unity in Poetry and Song. In *A Scuffling of Islands: Essays on Calypso*, 22–101. San Juan, Trinidad: Lexicon Trinidad.

———. 2004d. The Calypsonian as Artist: Freedom and Responsibility. In *A Scuffling of Islands: Essays on Calypso*, 164–97. San Juan, Trinidad: Lexicon Trinidad.

Rouget, Gilbert. 1984. *Music and Trance: A Theory of the Relationship of Music and Possession.* Chicago: University of Chicago Press.

Rubin, David C. 1995. *Memory in Oral Traditions: The Cognitive Psychology of Epic, Ballads, and Counting-out Rhymes.* Oxford: Oxford University Press.

Rubin, Vera. 1962. Culture, Politics and Race Relations. *Social and Economic Studies* 11:433–56.

Ryan, Selwyn. 1972. *Race and Nationalism in Trinidad and Tobago.* Toronto: University of Toronto Press.

———. 1989. *Revolution and Reaction: A Study of Parties and Politics in Trinidad and Tobago, 1970–1981.* St. Augustine, Trinidad: Institute of Social and Economic Research, University of the West Indies.

———. 1990a. *The Pursuit of Honour: The Life and Times of H. O. B. Wooding.* St. Augustine, Trinidad: Institute of Social and Economic Research.

———. 1990b. *The Disillusioned Electorate: The Politics of Succession in Trinidad and Tobago.* Port of Spain: Inprint.

———. 1991. *The Muslimeen Grab for Power: Race, Religion and Revolution in Trinidad and Tobago.* Port of Spain: Inprint.

———, ed. 1991. *Social and Occupational Stratification in Contemporary Trinidad and Tobago.* St. Augustine: Institute of Social and Economic Research, University of the West Indies.

———. 1996. *Pathways to Power: Indians and the Politics of National Unity in Trinidad and Tobago.* St. Augustine, Trinidad: Institute for Social and Economic Research.

———. 1999. *The Jhandi and the Cross: The Clash of Cultures in Post-Creole Trinidad and Tobago.* St. Augustine, Trinidad: Sir Arthur Lewis Institute of Social and Economic Studies.

———. 2003. *Deadlock: Ethnicity and Electoral Competition in Trinidad and Tobago, 1995–2002.* St. Augustine, Trinidad: Sir Arthur Lewis Institute of Social and Economic Studies.

Scher, Philip W. 2002. Copyright Heritage: Preservation, Carnival and the State in Trinidad. *Anthropological Quarterly* 75, no. 3: 453–84.

——. 2003. *Carnival and the Formation of a Caribbean Transnation.* Gainesville: University Press of Florida.

Segal, Daniel. 1989. *Nationalism in a Colonial State: A Study of Trinidad and Tobago.* PhD diss., University of Chicago.

——. 1993. "Race" and "Colour" in Pre-independence Trinidad and Tobago. In *Trinidad Ethnicity*, edited by Kevin Yelvington, 82–115. Knoxville: University of Tennessee Press.

——. 1994. Living Ancestors: Nationalism and the Past in Postcolonial Trinidad and Tobago. In *Remapping Memory: The Politics of TimeSpace*, edited by Jonathan Boyarin, 221–39. Minneapolis: University of Minnesota Press.

Selvon, Samuel. 1987. Three into One Can't Go—East Indian, Trinidadian, West-indian. In *India in the Caribbean*, edited by David Dabydeen and Brinsley Samaroo, 13–24. London: Hansib.

Shephard, C. Y. 1935. Agricultural Labour in Trinidad. *Tropical Agriculture* 12:3–9, 43–47, 56–64, 84–88, 126–31, 153–57, 187–92.

Simpson, George Eaton. 1966. Baptismal "Mourning" and "Building" Ceremonies of the Shouters in Trinidad. *Journal of American Folklore* 79, no. 314:537–50.

Singh, Kelvin. 1985. Indians and the Larger Society. In *Calcutta to Caroni: The East Indians of Trinidad*, edited by John La Guerre, 33–60. St. Augustine, Trinidad: University of the West Indies, Extra-mural Studies Unit.

Smith, M. G. 1965. *The Plural Society in the British West Indies.* Berkeley: University of California Press.

Smith, Raymond T. 1996. *The Matrifocal Family: Power, Pluralism, and Politics.* New York: Routledge.

Sobo, Elisa. 1993. *One Blood: The Jamaican Body.* Albany: SUNY Press.

Spivak, Gayatri Chakravorty. 1988. Subaltern Studies: Deconstructing Historiography. In *Selected Subaltern Studies*, edited by Ranajit Guha and Gayatri Chakravorty Spivak, 3–32. New York: Oxford University Press.

Stewart, John O. 1986. Patronage and Control in the Trinidad Carnival. In *The Anthropology of Experience*, edited by Victor Turner and Edward Bruner, 289–315. Urbana: University of Illinois Press.

Stoler, Ann Laura. 1997. On Political and Psychological Essentialisms. *Ethos* 25:101–06.

Stoller, Paul. 1997. *The Taste of Ethnographic Things: The Senses in Anthropology.* Philadelphia: University of Pennsylvania Press.

Strauss, Claudia. 1992. Models and Motives. In *Human Motives and Cultural Models*, edited by Roy D'Andrade and Claudia Strauss, 1–20. Cambridge: Cambridge University Press.

Strauss, Claudia, and Naomi Quinn. 1997. *A Cognitive Theory of Cultural Meaning.* Cambridge: Cambridge University Press.

Stuempfle, Stephen. 1995. *The Steelband Movement: The Forging of a National Art in Trinidad and Tobago*. Philadelphia: University of Pennsylvania Press.

Taylor, Daphne Pawan. 1977. *Parang of Trinidad*. Trinidad and Tobago: National Cultural Council.

Thomas, Clive. 1988. *The Poor and the Powerless: Economic Policy and Change in the Caribbean*. New York: Monthly Review.

Turner, Victor. 1967. *The Forest of Symbols: Aspects of Ndembu Ritual*. Ithaca, N.Y.: Cornell University Press.

———. 1974. *Dramas, Fields, and Metaphors: Symbolic Action in Human Society*. Ithaca, N.Y.: Cornell University Press.

———. 1977. *The Ritual Process: Structure and Anti-Structure*. Ithaca, N.Y.: Cornell University Press.

———. 1987. *The Anthropology of Performance*. New York: PAJ.

United States Congress, Office of Technology Assessment. 1991. *Biological Rhythms: Implications for the Worker*. Washington, D.C.: United States Government Printing Office.

Van Dongen, Hans P. A., Greg Maislin, Janet M. Mullington, and David F. Dinges. 2003. The Cumulative Cost of Additional Wakefulness: Dose-Response Effects on Neurobehavioral Functions and Sleep Physiology from Chronic Sleep Restriction and Total Sleep Deprivation. *Sleep* 26:117–26.

Van Reeth, Olivier, Jeppe Sturis, Maria M. Byrne, John D. Blackman, Mireille L'Hermite-Balériaux, Rachel Leproult, Craig Oliner, Samuel Refetoff, Fred W. Turek, and Eve Van Cauter. 1994. Nocturnal Exercise Phase Delays Circadian Rhythms of Melatonin and Thyrotropin Secretion in Normal Men. *American Journal of Physiology: Endocrinology and Metabolism* 266:E964–E974.

Vertovec, Steven. 1992. *Hindu Trinidad: Religion, Ethnicity, and Socio-Economic Change*. London: MacMillan.

Vygotsky, L. S. 1978. *Mind in Society: The Development of Higher Psychological Processes*. Cambridge, Mass.: Harvard University Press.

Wade, Peter. 2000. *Music, Race, and Nation: Música Tropical in Colombia*. Chicago: University of Chicago Press.

Walcott, Derek. 1986. The Spoiler's Return. In *Collected Poems, 1948–1984*, 432–38. New York: Farrar, Straus and Giroux.

———. [1992] 1993. The Antilles, Fragments of Epic Memory: The 1992 Nobel Lecture. *World Literature Today* 67, no. 2: 260–67.

Wardle, Huon. 2002. Ambiguation, Disjuncture, Commitment: A Social Analysis of Caribbean Cultural Creativity. *Journal of the Royal Anthropological Institute* 8, no. 3: 493–508.

Warner, Keith. 1982. *Kaiso! The Trinidad Calypso*. Washington, D.C.: Three Continents Press.

———. 1993. Ethnicity and the Contemporary Calypso. In *Trinidad Ethnicity*, edited by Kevin Yelvington, 275–91. Knoxville: University of Tennessee Press.

Waters, Anita. 1985. *Race, Class, and Political Symbols: Rastafari and Reggae in Jamaican Politics.* New Brunswick, N.J.: Transaction Books.

Wedenoja, William. 1990. Ritual Trance and Catharsis: A Psychobiological and Evolutionary Perspective. In *Personality and the Cultural Construction of Society,* edited by David K. Jordan and Marc J. Swartz, 275–307. Tuscaloosa: University of Alabama Press.

Weibel, L., and G. Brandenberger. 1998. Disturbances in Hormonal Profiles of Night Workers during Their Usual Sleep and Work Times. *Journal of Biological Rhythms* 13, no. 3: 202–8.

Weibel, L., M. Follénius, and G. Brandenberger. 1999. Les rythmes biologiques: leur altération chez les travailleurs de nuit. *La Presse Médicale* 28:252–58.

Weiner, Annette. 1992. *Inalienable Possessions: The Paradox of Keeping While Giving.* Berkeley: University of California Press.

Wells, Diana E. 1999. Re-dyeing the Cloth: The Women's Political Platform and Trinidad and Tobago's General Election of 1995. *Identities* 5, no. 4: 543–68.

Wenger, Etienne. 1998. *Communities of Practice: Learning, Meaning and Identity.* Cambridge: Cambridge University Press.

Wertsch, James V. 1985. *Vygotsky and the Social Formation of Mind.* Cambridge, Mass.: Harvard University Press.

West India Royal Commission. 1945. *Report.* London: His Majesty's Stationery Office.

Wever, Rütger A. 1979. The Circadian System of Man: Results of Experiments under Temporal Isolation. New York: Springer-Verlag.

Whitehead, Neil. 1997. Introduction to Sir Walter Ralegh's *The Discoverie of the Large, Rich and Bewtiful Empyre of Guiana,* 3–116. Norman: University of Oklahoma Press.

Williams, Eric. [1962] 1964. *History of the People of Trinidad and Tobago.* New York: Praeger.

——. 1969. *Inward Hunger: The Education of a Prime Minister.* London: Deutsch.

——. [1964] 1981. Report to the People on the "Meeting of the People" Tour. In *Forged from the Love of Liberty,* edited by Paul Sutton, 217–21. Trinidad: Longman Caribbean.

——. [1962] 1993. Massa Day Done. In *Eric Williams Speaks,* edited by Selwyn Cudjoe, 237–64. Wellesley, Mass.: Calaloux.

——. [1970] 1993. The Chaguaramas Declaration. In *Eric Williams Speaks,* edited by Selwyn Cudjoe, 272–316. Wellesley, Mass.: Calaloux.

Williams, Leroy "Flathead." 1991. *1991 Carnival and Calypsos.* Santa Cruz: Leroy "Flathead" Williams.

Williams, Raymond. 1977. *Marxism and Literature.* Oxford: Oxford University Press.

Williams-Connell, Erica. [1991] 1993. Bournes Road Address. In *Eric Williams Speaks,* edited by Selwyn Cudjoe, 369–96. Wellesley, Mass.: Calaloux.

Willis, Paul. 2000. *The Ethnographic Imagination.* Cambridge: Polity.

Wood, Donald. 1968. *Trinidad in Transition: The Years after Slavery*. London: Institute of Race Relations.

Worthman, Carol. 1999. Emotions: You Can Feel the Difference. In *Biocultural Approaches to Emotions*, edited by Alexander Laban Hinton, 41–74. Cambridge: Cambridge University Press.

Wynter, Sylvia. 1981. In Quest of Matthew Bondsman: Some Cultural Notes on the Jamesian Journey. *Urgent Tasks* 12: 54–68.

Yelvington, Kevin. 1993. Ethnicity at Work in Trinidad. In *The Enigma of Ethnicity: An Analysis of Race in the Caribbean and the World*, edited by Ralph R. Premdas, 99–122. St. Augustine: University of the West Indies, School of Continuing Studies.

———. 1995a. *Producing Power: Ethnicity, Gender, and Class in a Caribbean Workplace*. Philadelphia: Temple University Press.

———. 1995b. Ethnicity 'Not Out': The Indian Cricket Tour of the West Indies and the 1976 Elections in Trinidad and Tobago. In *Liberation Cricket*, edited by Hilary Beckles and Brian Stoddart, 205–21. Manchester: Manchester University Press.

———. 2001. The Anthropology of Afro-Latin America and the Caribbean: Diasporic Dimensions. *Annual Review of Anthropology* 30:227–60.

index

Kevin K. Birth is an associate professor of anthropology at Queens College, CUNY. He is the author of *Any Time Is Trinidad Time: Social Meanings and Temporal Consciousness*.

Library of Congress Cataloging-in-Publication Data

Birth, Kevin K., 1963-
Bacchanalian sentiments: musical experiences and
political counterpoints in Trinidad / Kevin K. Birth.
p. cm.
Includes bibliographical references and index.
ISBN 978-0-8223-4141-3 (cloth : alk. paper)
ISBN 978-0-8223-4165-9 (pbk. : alk. paper)
1. Folk music—Trinidad and Tobago—History and criticism.
2. Trinidad and Tobago—Social life and customs.
3. Music—Social aspects—Trinidad and Tobago. I. Title.
ML3565.B57 2008
780.972983—dc22
2007032557